AF378654

Small Acts

*Performance,
the Millennium and the
Marking of Time*

edited by Adrian Heathfield

Contents

Small Acts: Performance, the Millennium and the Marking of Time

The *Small Acts* **project** – comprising a series of commissioned performances from diverse British artists and a linked-yet-independent publication containing essays, art works for the page and performance documents – raises a series of questions about the way that experiences of art, time and society are framed and understood in a contemporary context. Contrasting with the epic, populist and homogenising nature of many Millennial events, *Small Acts* concerns itself with forgotten, private and ephemeral orders of experience, or else with the possibilities of minor, marginalised or subversive approaches to the public sphere.

Perhaps Castro had the right idea. Certainly the footage of indifferent chess-playing Cubans 'denied' the chance to celebrate the Millennium until the end of 2000, beamed across the world in news items as an icon of the dictator's humourless intransigence, looked like a welcome respite from the endless claptrap and fireworks the rest of us had to endure. Throughout the media-space of the Western world the Millennium proved a convenient time for official and orthodox culture (national, corporate, transnational) to assert its naive futurism and its tired but comforting stories about human achievement and social progress. Erasing difference, denying conflict and assuming ludicrous levels of (actual or aspired to) consensus and homogeneity in our populations, these stories continue to form a part of the way in which the contemporary world is shaped and defined in the image and interests of the few at the expense of the many. There were certainly those who felt the Millennium (and the stories above) might better deserve an ambivalent marking rather than a celebration. There were certainly

others who wished to focus on different aspects of social and community histories in order to produce something that might more fully be respected. There were certainly artists, writers and thinkers who were thinking about time, about newness, about history in the sense of individual lived-experience and about the re-drawing of boundaries and possibilities in the social sphere, in ways that were significantly more dynamic and challenging. *Small Acts* became a way to bring some of these people together, touching on such themes as personal and community histories, memory, anonymity, mental health, public space, disability, rumour-making and itineracy, to create a project which uses the occasion of the Millennium to swim against the cultural tide.

Whilst diversity and contradiction are key to the works collected here as part of *Small Acts* there are a number of concerns to which both artists and essayists return in different registers. The performance works repeatedly test the nature of social or public space not via grand gestures or dramatic interventions (tactics which are already suspicious or problematic) but rather by means of infiltration, private task, public ritual or subtle intervention in the shared space of a street, a city, or a landscape. In this vein Daniel Gosling's *10.01.00 > > 30.01.00 > > > <* involved a three week, more or less unplanned hitch-hike across the UK, and encounters with numerous strangers and performances at dusk in the car parks of motorway service stations, whilst Kira O'Reilly, operating as "An Anonymous Artist", planned and held a birthday party for herself and a group which mixed strangers and casual acquaintances in a city which she did not know. Scanner sampled images from news coverage of the Millennium celebrations, extracting individual figures and then isolating them on cryptic and inexplicable postcards left all over the UK, whilst Robert Pacitti worked on rumours, leaving a series of tantalising parcels containing fragmentary texts and scrambled stories in public places, playing back the language of the media with a web of half-truths, distortions and misleading phone-numbers. Meanwhile, Brian Catling summoned a film from a series of wanders through the streets of Cambridge and the City of London in the after-hours. Here, in alleys, gutters and doorways, he placed half-human constructions, semblances of discarded lives; these were silent rituals which sanctified the existences eked out in these places. Even where projects did have a strongly public and interventionist form there was, as a matter of course, a twist in the approach. Ronald Fraser-Munro's unlikely and idiosyncratic Black Pope was a walking, talking and irreverent contradiction, Ann Whitehurst's invitations to celebrate her conception, and with it a Millennium of disability, were sent to celebrities and media figures but without addresses, spilling into the postal system and trickling slowly to their destinations (or not at all), whilst Bobby Baker's nine hour public performance held during Mental Health Action Week in the environs of Trafalgar Square, broadcast the unfathomable slogan "PULL YOURSELF TOGETHER" through the streets of the capital, assailing the public with something between a protest, an ironic order and an elusive, unanswerable demand.

Other works were resolute attempts to chart personal history in spite, or in the gaps of, official Millennial culture in public space. Chris Dorley-Brown's work documented the Millennium night from the area immediately around his house – a series of 'sampled' conversations, internet chats, tv images and sound recordings (the latter taken from his bedroom window) – an almost solitary and sedentary form of witnessing of an overly mediated 'historical' moment. Both Alex Kelly of Third Angel and Mike Pearson chose to excavate their childhoods, their places of origin, in the form of a single school photograph (Kelly) and through the traces and stories associated with a particular geographical location (Pearson). Kirsten Lavers and cris cheek made an interactive work in which a broad sample of people were asked to propose "things not worth keeping" to form a special Millennium Collection of late twentieth century disposables, associated in the words of their donors with once-personal

memories. Each of these projects, as well as the colliery installation of Meloni Poole and Graeme Miller's star maps re-named by specific individuals, sought to emphasise and to some degree champion the everyday and the personal, the value of real, complex and transient communities and forgotten or discarded biographies. Few of the Millennial experiences and stories arising here will be present in the manufactured and mythological alternatives available at a shopping mall near you.

Continuing in a rich tradition of time-based art work, many of the artists deployed transient and ephemeral forms. Two new artists' works for the page are also presented here, each in their own way dealing with issues of time. Emma Kay has created a series of drawings of the world from memory, an unaided act of recollection of a deliberately preposterous scope that plays with the relation between time, knowledge and imagination. Hugo Glendinning, who has documented much of the work of the *Small Acts* series, has created a parallel photographic essay, a set of portraits in snow taken with a flashgun at night, a visual elegy for now lost moments of looking, relation and intimacy. For this publication these artists are joined by essayists from a broad range of disciplines who approach the themes of the Millennium, the experience of time, and the relation between lived experience and its shadows in various spaces of cultural representation. The selection of essays combines cultural commentary with fiction, art criticism, and philosophy in the firm belief that complex and contradictory times require multiple approaches to open out their meaning. If there is one realisation drawing the distinct works of these writers together, it is that time is not a given or neutral category, not something necessarily unified, linear or progressive, but something that is produced by societies, shaped and narrated by cultures. Whether discussing personal experiences, Millennial anxiety, the drive towards a mythological purity in British culture, short-term mind sets and arts practice, the cultural value of the new, or the relation between art and capitalism, these essays, like the art works they complement, question and contest the stories that culture tells itself about time. The correspondences and clashes between these various essays, images and documents, their multiplicity, challenges any singular understanding of the time we are living through. It really is true to say that there is no time like the present.

Tim Etchells, Adrian Heathfield, Lois Keidan

things not worth keeping

The Millennium Collection

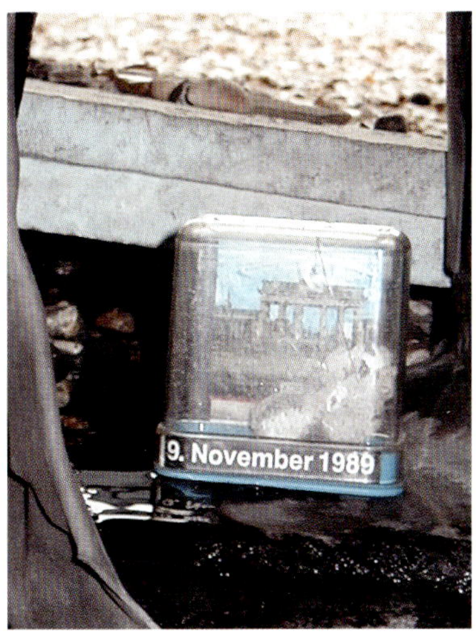

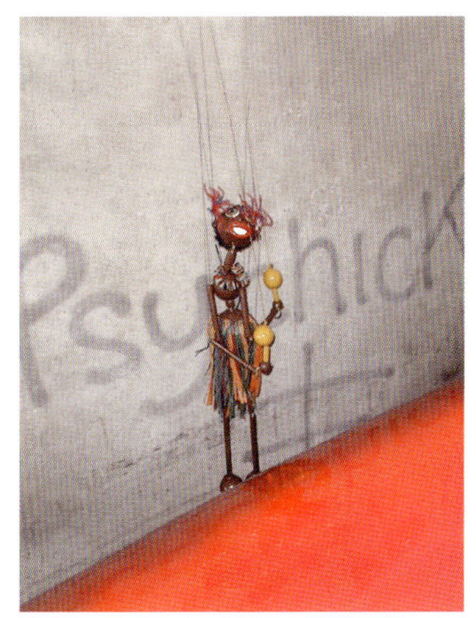

Description of thing Small portion of the Berlin Wall in a clear plastic case labelled 9 November 1989.
Reason not worth keeping I want to keep it as a romantic relic of the twentieth century and, as it's probably fake anyway, as a symbol of how the great events of our times are replicated and packaged into bite-sized commodities. However I believe it's not worth keeping because it will always remind me of the great wasted opportunity of the Millennium.
Nominated by a collector (and now discarder) of cultural icons and curios

Description of thing Lullabelle puppet made by Pelham Puppets, still in its original box. Given to me by my father on my fifth birthday.
Reason not worth keeping I don't have much of a memory of being given it, except that I have a sense of its strings becoming tangled almost immediately. I think I was too small to be able to hold it up high enough.

Trying hard to think of something for this collection I remembered that this 'thing' was still lurking at the bottom of a drawer in my parents' house, where it's been for the past forty-odd years, like a special preserve, an heirloom. At first I thought it had been given to me by my dad's shop assistant, a Miss Pinkney (or Pink Knee), but my dad has since corrected me. It's certainly a 'class', even a 'classic' toy. Beautifully made and all the more disturbing and fetishistic for that. As with most toys it carries a strong gendering and aspirational ideology. In this case of course, from my point of view, hideous colonial stereotypes of sexual control and cultural power. The thought of

giving this to a five year old white boy is pretty tough to chew on, let alone the impact that it might have made and that I might still be grappling with. Despite the fact that I know that in his own way my dad had all of the best intentions to give me a really 'good' toy, its full gruesomeness has now blotted out any affection.

The 'game', as I remember it dimly lit (I haven't played or toyed with it since I tangled its ropes, probably on the first or second day), was to make 'her' dance. To make her shake her maracas. To make her walk. To animate her. I have no clear idea whether I took genuine delight in doing any of these things, or in the prospect of doing so. I can only project onto it and that act of projection strikes me as the purpose of any toy. I want to make me shake my bones. To make me walk. To animate me. Outcomes pending ...
Nominated by driver

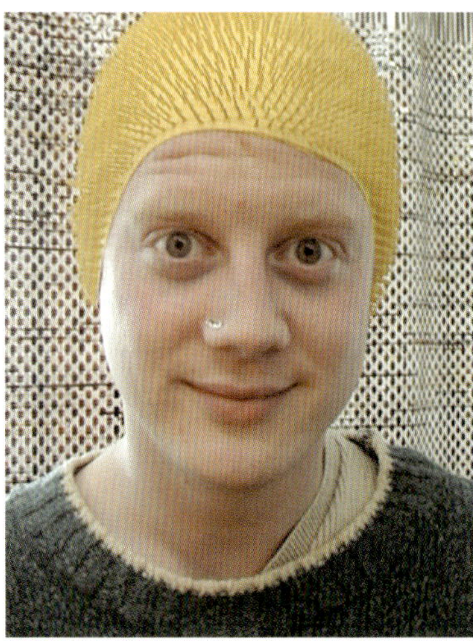

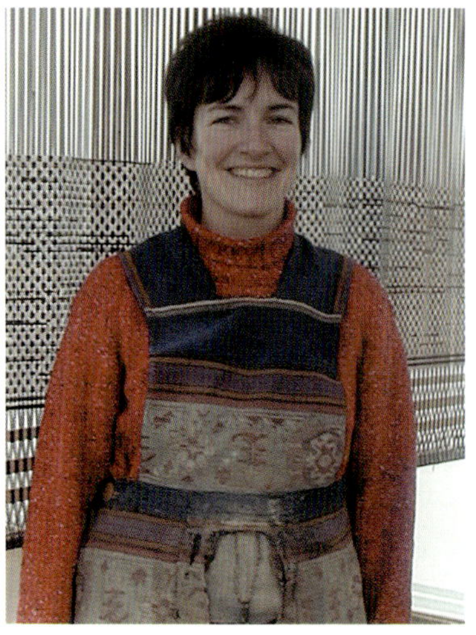

Description of thing Yellow rubber woman's swimming hat, close-fitting and covered with hundreds of spiky fronds like a sea anemone or such like (made by Canon Rubber Manufacturers, Ashley Road, Tottenham, London, N4) contained in original plastic string draw bag with what seems to be a prizewinning tombola number still attached.

Reason not worth keeping It is over thirty years old and hasn't been worn for twenty years. It will not be worn by me again and I don't want to keep it any longer.

Nominated by retired physiotherapist

(Modelled by visitor to opening exhibition of The Millennium Collection.)

Description of thing Threadbare cotton apron, dark blue with buff, yellow and red markings; unusual design of garment suggests constructed out of fabric left over from another project, possibly soft furnishings; hand and machine-sewn probably between 1950 and 1965; repeatedly mended and patched; new button and buttonhole c. 1988. Acquired at an auction in Cambridge in 1969 – included in 'dressing up box' belonging to a long-established nursery school which was closing down. Assiduously used first by children for games of make believe and later for about twenty years as a work apron by a potter, many times discarded and resuscitated.

Reason not worth keeping I keep forgetting (the reason). (Worn Out. Exhausted. Tried beyond endurance. Represents a culture of handsewing, mending and recycling at an end. I need a new fetish.)

Nominated by potter and spontaneous combuster

(Modelled by visitor to opening exhibition of The Millennium Collection.)

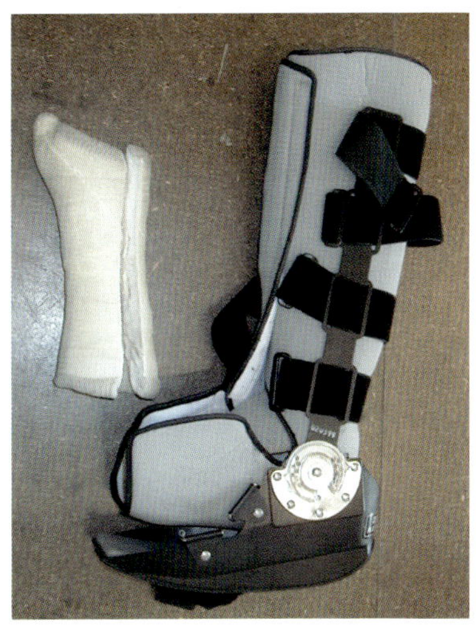

Description of thing Metal, plastic & material leg brace, with an angled foot piece and mechanical setting device. A series of straps up to the knee, to restrict movement of the ankle. I had a long overdue operation to repair/replace ligaments in my right ankle in the spring of 1999. It was an intricate and painful operation, but absolutely necessary as the severe ligament erosion had been preventing me from walking properly. The origins of this damage probably took place in my early teens and for many years the ankle had been so weak and unsupported that I would stumble and fall over on it. An awareness of my ankle and its movements developed over this twenty-year period and towards the end I had to consciously keep an eye on each of my steps, in the hope of preventing a further fall.

Reason not worth keeping After the operation I had to re-teach the ankle how to function. The muscles and ligaments needed to be strengthened, but the interesting part was re-developing the relationship between my mind and my ankle. I had to teach my mind to send messages to my ankle, telling it when it needed to support itself. As the 'message' relationship between these parts of the body had been so disturbed for all these years the reunification process was always going to take time. A year later, although far less conscious of my ankle and what it is doing next, I still have moments when I do not fully trust it to support my body and I feel the anxiety return ...

As the operation was a success and my abilities to walk properly on the ankle increase, the leg brace, having served its purpose is no longer needed or wanted.

Nominated by student

Description of thing Cotton + resin thumb spica cast for immobilising my scaphoid bone, broken in a car accident.

Reason not worth keeping The cast is coming off at the end of January 2000 having served its function. In the cocoon of this temporary exoskeleton my bones have re-grown. Now I don't need it anymore.

Nominated by tabla player

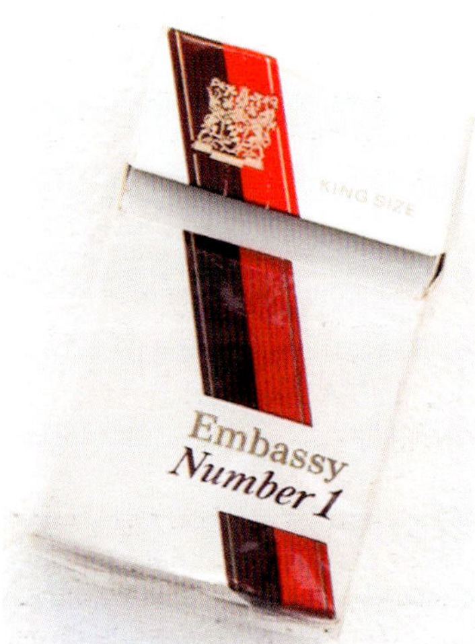

Description of thing Open box of love letters and postcards, cards, poems and related givings c. 1969-1999.
Reason not worth keeping LOVE's an abstract, not a thing. It cannot be pinned down. Yet here is love's solid shadow in the past, though it was 'lost'. Or not?. Were those loves LOVE at all? Or, in now frozen words, was LOVE its opposite, hate? And if this was LOVE then memory should be enough – though enough there was of hurt. On N.Y. DAY 2000, at forty-six, I found love – enough to still those old snapshot words into dust. Now, for me, thinking back I want rid of them, but burning flames might find me crying into ashes. Though NOW THIS, SHE HAS ALL MY WISHES.
Nominated by bearded, of middle age, a sometime poet

Description of thing Empty packet of Embassy cigarettes. I have been 'keeping' this empty packet for nearly twelve years now. I found it in the glove compartment of my brother's car when I collected it from the police compound after he had committed suicide in it by carbon monoxide poisoning. There were no cigarettes left in the packet – I also kept the cassette tape that was in the tape deck – the soundtrack from the film of the book *Christine.* by Stephen King about an evil car. The last song that had played before the engine was turned off by the security guard who found him was called *Bad to the Bone* by George Thorogood and The Destroyers. His favourite song was *American Pie* sung by Don McLean. He was a lorry driver, a great cook, a generous, troubled soul, he chain smoked, took five sugars in his tea, six foot seven inches tall and twenty-five years, one month and sixteen days old when he died.
Reason not worth keeping He left very few objects behind him in the world and at first I was reluctant to let go of those that there were – especially things that had been close to him when he died. Eventually I sold the car to a Mr Fox who ran the local Hunt Saboteurs group. I still have all his music tapes including the ninety-minute cassette of *American Pie* recorded over and over again. The cigarette box kept hanging around – like my grief – and until now I've not been able to just toss it into the bin.
Nominated by older sister

Description of thing My first high-tech vibrator. 'Jessica Rabbit' model (transparent shocking pink colour with tickler rabbit and rotative coloured balls for extra massage). Now it has been taken apart, cut with a scalpel for being able to study better how it once worked before old age death – living life approximately two years.
Reason not worth keeping It is too frustrating to keep object – it reminds me of all the good time(s) without being able to access it/them again.
Nominated by circus performer

Description of thing Old key.
Reason not worth keeping No idea what it opens.
Nominated by psychotherapist

Description of thing Roofing slate painted with an Irish prayer. In the spirit of the Millennial Boxing Day, I would like to nominate a representative Gift. This sort of Gift is purchased at a Gift show or in a Gift shop. They cannot be described except as a Gift, and the only purpose of these objects is to be a Gift. Generally, they have some sort of innocuous ethnic or holiday theme, which represents the one thing you might know about the interests of someone to whom you are giving the Gift. I am nominating a roofing slate painted with an 'Irish' prayer made in New England given to me by my perhaps future mother-in-law.
Reason not worth keeping These items, perpetually Gifts, exist in a world of Guilt. They are not allowed to appear in rummage, tag, yard, or garage sales, flea markets, or car boot sales. The larger and more expensive Gifts must be on display when the giver visits. They cannot be merely thrown away, and in America, they cannot be given away, as there is no Boxing Day. Gifts cannot be recycled. Even if you would wish to give the Gift to someone, anyone, else, good taste, concern for others, and guilt prevent you from presenting it as new. Ironically, then, Gifts occur, yet cannot be passed on or run forwards.
Nominated by Irish poet

Description of thing My Thunderbird pyjamas.
Reason not worth keeping They don't stay up.
Nominated by seven year old boy

Description of thing Ringo Starr LP called
Ringo's Rotogravure. It has been beautifully
preserved in a special plastic cover to protect
the cover which protects the vinyl. There are
lots of photos on the inside of Ringo's mates
eating burgers etc. John Lennon looks a bit thin.
Reason not worth keeping Cos it's shit. I
was obsessed with John Lennon after he got
shot and wanted to buy everything that had
even the faintest connection. Bit sick really,
seeing as Mark Chapman probably did
something similar. He may even be the only
other owner of *Ringo's Rotogravure* for all I
know. Anyway, now he's being released it seems
a good time to part company with this
unadulterated pile of cock. (Sorry Ringo, but
it's John I love.)
**Nominated by prematurely nostalgic
dog-owner from Cleator Moor**

Description of thing No-thing. I've tried to
lead an austere life and not to accumulate, or
covet, possessions. Those objects I do have,
I tend to invest with memory, as aides-memoire,
as the material locale of absence. As I am now
fifty this memory becomes important:
replaying, reliving become essential functions
of imagination.
Reason not worth keeping But as I become
more and more a matrix of nostalgia, regret,
aches, frustrated hopes, perhaps I should
nominate myself – living exhibit of sixties 'man',
man – to be left behind. Sorry to be obtuse.
Your question was deeply stimulating and
provocative – thanks!
Nominated by Sixties man

Description of thing Used wedding ring.
Reason not worth keeping Of doubtful
value or efficacy. Unlikely to be re-used (by self
or others) in short, always already redundant.
Nominated by sinologist

Description of thing Out-of-date car tax disc.
Reason not worth keeping I thought I
might start a collection of them but I only ever
got this one as we don't have a car in my family
and anyway I think the government shouldn't
get money from cars or cigarettes because they
cause pollution and damage the atmosphere.
**Nominated by fifteen year old
sk8board activist**

Description of thing Canister of St. Michael
Spray from South America, 'Instructions: Shake
Well. Hold can upright and point nozzle away
from you. Press button down and spray. Let Us
Pray. Make the sign of the cross. Air freshener
deodorizer'.
Reason not worth keeping
1 It stinks to high heaven (no pun intended).
2 It's probably chock-a-block full of CFCs – yes
it is, I checked.
3 It has a tacky image of St. Michael fighting
the devil on the front.
4 I gave it to a friend for their birthday, they
sent it to someone else for their birthday and it
was finally given back to me for my birthday.
**Nominated by a domestic sanitary
engineer from Staines**

Description of thing Epilady – for take off
the hair legs.
Reason not worth keeping For a long time
I would like to try this. My friend in Brazil she
told me hurt a little bit but it is efficient (*eficaz*).
I saw three years ago in a school May Fair and I
have for £1.00 ponds. I was thinking would be a
bargain. It was, but I never used because I worry
about the little pain and also about hygiene.
Fortunately, I don't have much hair on my legs.
**Nominated by Assistant Librarian and
bookmark collector**

Description of thing Little skliff of
unperfumed clear soap, it was bought while
having an illicit affair in order for the illicit lover
to wash after our liaisons and return to his
legitimate partner, smelling of nothing.
Reason not worth keeping It lasted longer
than the affair.
**Nominated by diligent diva moving on
in life**

Description of thing Five pence piece. All
our money will eventually go electronic, so let's
start with THE FIVE PENCE PIECE which is no longer
worth keeping.
Reason not worth keeping You can make a
telephone call with a 10p piece, but the 5p buys
nothing; notice that people who see them lying
on the pavement rarely stop to pick them up.
Unlike the 7bn 1p and 4bn 2p coins – which are
used by retailers to make attractive prices, the
99p and 98p price points – the 3bn 5p pieces
no longer serve a useful function. So let's
make a start towards the new Millennium
money and banish the 5p piece. It is no longer
worth keeping.
**Nominated by screenwriter and
stained-glass artist**

Description of thing Small plastic whistle
in the shape of a bird.
Reason not worth keeping
1 I don't think it can whistle.
2 I can't hear it anyway.
3 I tried to make a photo about 'Augury' with it
but it just isn't photogenic in that way.
4 CONTRADICTION 'To the poet nothing is useless'
(Ancient Greek saying?). Hence donation to you.
Nominated by deaf poet

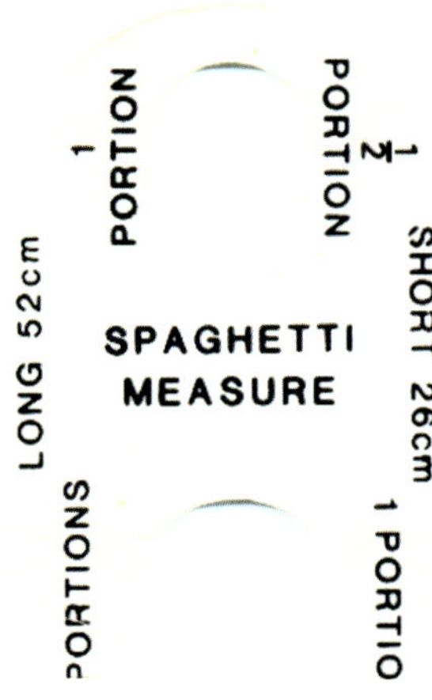

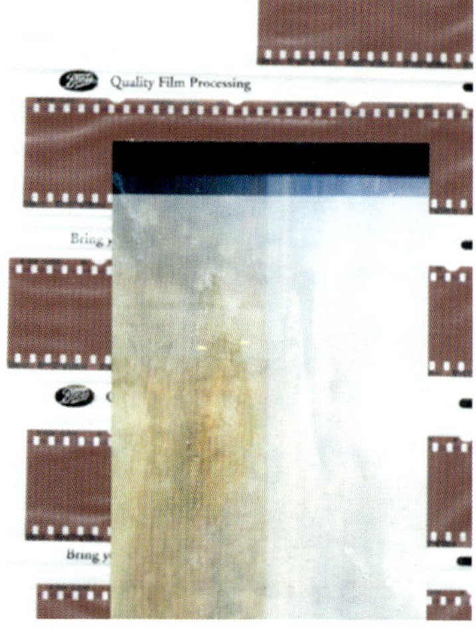

Description of thing Countdown to 2000 wristwatch.
Reason not worth keeping I don't need reminding of what a huge anti-climax the whole Millennium thing is (as well as being a piece of state propaganda) I want to celebrate something that really does change my everyday life. (How about a watch that can count the number of hours you play with children, go dancing, run around, have sex ...)
Nominated by autonomous astronaut

Description of thing Millennium Dome opening night invitation (declined) + accompanying security forms.
Reason not worth keeping. Past its sell-by date.
Nominated by party pooper

Description of thing Spaghetti measure – a piece of plastic with several holes to pass dry spaghetti through to signify ½ 1 2 3 ... portions.
Reason not worth keeping It is not worth the time to find it, use it and put it away after use. Once you use your eye as a measure the object is superfluous.
Nominated by eclipse witness

Description of thing Strip of 34 negatives + one print –-our holiday souvenir of the last total solar eclipse of the Millennium (taken in the path of totality on August 11th 1999).
Reason not worth keeping The camera jammed resulting in a totally blank film apart from one print containing 34 superimposed images. What a way to capture this once-in-a-lifetime experience! We won't be needing this for our family album.
Nominated by eclipse witnesses

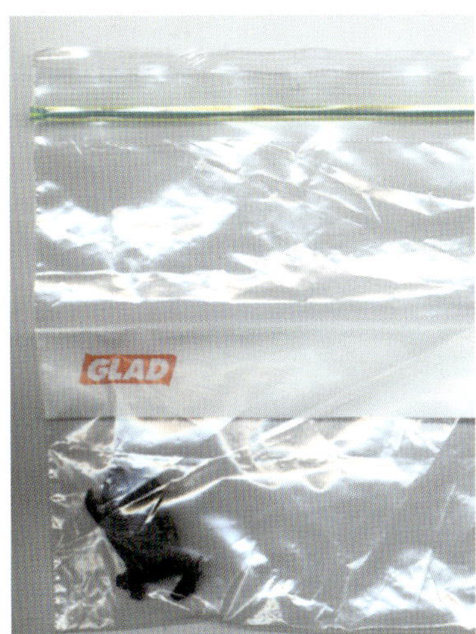

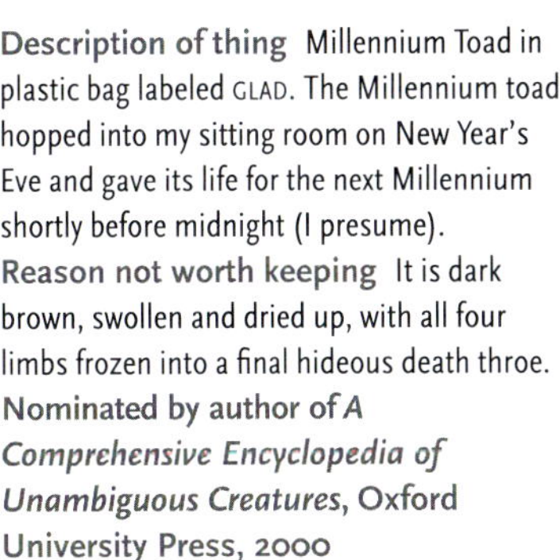

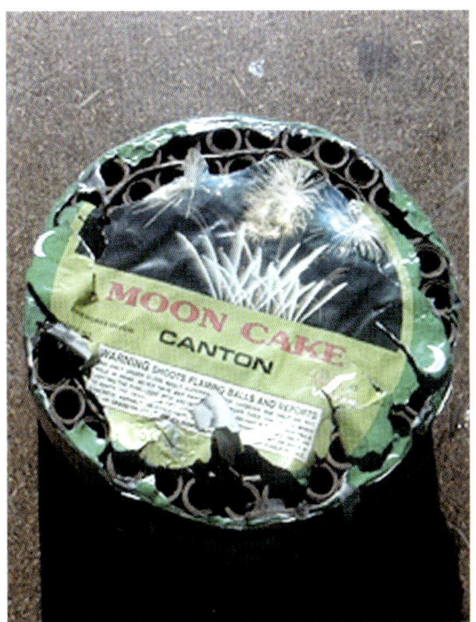

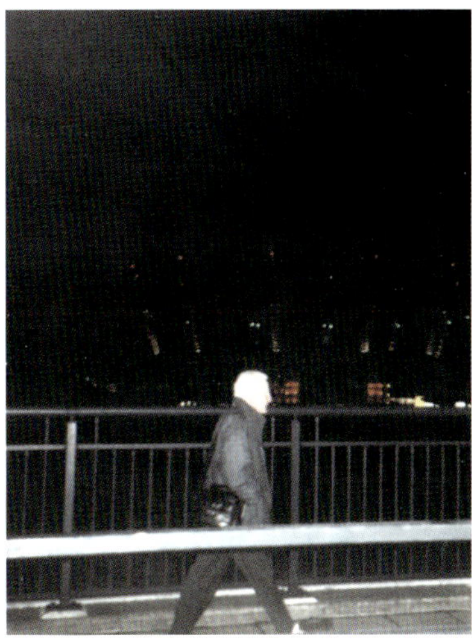

Description of thing Millennium Toad in plastic bag labeled GLAD. The Millennium toad hopped into my sitting room on New Year's Eve and gave its life for the next Millennium shortly before midnight (I presume).
Reason not worth keeping It is dark brown, swollen and dried up, with all four limbs frozen into a final hideous death throe.
Nominated by author of *A Comprehensive Encyclopedia of Unambiguous Creatures*, Oxford University Press, 2000

Description of thing Moon cake container.
Reason not worth keeping Becos' it's a spent firework let off on New Year's Eve 1999.
Nominated by cabinet maker

Description of thing Photograph of the Dome taken on New Year's Eve at approx. 7.30pm from a fly-over in the Canning Town area. The occasion was a champagne picnic with about fifteen other people including a fold-out table and a fairy.
Reason not worth keeping It is poorly exposed and would not be readable to anyone else. I don't know the passer-by and have other better pictures of the event. I should have known that with the camera and film it wouldn't have come out, also, I guess it's a comment on the Dome which strikes me as a fairly hollow exercise.
Nominated by friend of the artists

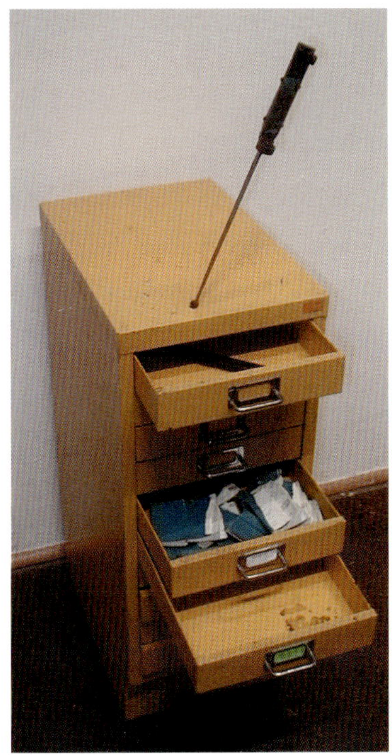

Description of thing I nominate a small yellow filing cabinet, with thin drawers for papers. The filing cabinet has a bayonet blade sticking in to it. Its sheath is in the top drawer. In one drawer there is the remains of a photograph which stuck to the drawer and left the reversed image when I peeled it off. In another drawer marked 'finance' are the cheque stubs from my current account. I haven't checked the dates but they are probably from the 80s, part of a hoard I have of cheque stubs and other financial documents, which I can't throw away in case I have to justify some expenditure at some point. I think I bought the cabinet in 1979 on moving to a new flat, hoping to use it to become organised in a new flat and a new job. But, it suddenly occurs to me that since one of the labels on the drawers says 'piano' it might have been bought early in the 1970s when I was living with a musician. The musician and I broke up in 1976 or so. I met my new lover in 1980. We did not live together at that time – my new lover lived in Scotland. I remember going downstairs with my bags to take the coach to Glasgow for a big Poll Tax demo (I think it was

Poll Tax) at which I was going to meet my new lover. I switched off the lights in my flat, opened the door and reached out in the darkness for the passage light switch. Instead of wall or switch, I touched something that felt like a pelt (but was a woolly jumper on my ex-lover's chest). Surprised, I switched on the flat light beside me to find my ex-lover standing there with the blade in his hand. He forced me upstairs to my kitchen, and after some talk or shouting, punched me on the jaw. He then forced me up to the bedroom where he forced me into the bed. At this point he thrust the bayonet blade into the cabinet. I think this was the point at which I decided to stop resisting, but it also seemed to be the point at which he had discharged some of the energy. He attempted to make me make love to him, but we were now talking and some time later, with him calmer, I said I could still catch my bus to Glasgow, so he drove me to the bus stop. When I moved out of London ten years later, I cleared out the filing cabinet and found the photograph of him stuck in the drawer. One of my last experiences in London was a threatening phone call.

Reason not worth keeping I suppose my reason is a reverse reason. It is not that this object is not worth keeping but that I have found no way to get rid of it (indeed, no way to contemplate its disposal), until now. It has been sitting in my flat, unusable because of the memories it evokes, and unavoidable. Originally I kept the bayonet blade in case it was needed as evidence later on. I had got an injunction to prevent him coming near my flat (he had taken to throwing bricks through the windows). The cabinet and blade were unprocessable material. I couldn't just throw them away. When I first thought of what I might nominate for things not worth keeping, I thought I could get rid of the bags of financial material I can't throw away (just in case). But then I suddenly realised, what a startling opportunity to rid myself of the cabinet in a way that was neither surreptitious, nor personally spectacular. The object itself could have been exhibited by anyone except me. To me, it is unprocessed and unprocessable.

Since nominating it and its acceptance, I have been finding two separate strands of response in myself: first, I have found that I am remembering the years he and I spent together and remembering for the first time in twenty years the good parts. I found photographs of him, including a copy of the one in the drawer, and have started showing them to friends as 'one of my ex-lovers, isn't he handsome'; something I couldn't have done last year. I have been falling back in love with my memory of him at the time we were together. I was 19 (and therefore illegal) when I met him. The decision to deal with this material now, prompted by the request for things not worth keeping, has been as much to decide that the trauma itself, the way it has dominated me for twenty years, is not worth keeping. Secondly, I have great difficulty in confronting the piece in its new setting, with all the other stuff not worth keeping. Each time I see it I rerun that night, the next six months, the next ten years. In my own flat, it had this potential but did not usually trigger this recycling. Now, extracted and exposed, it is at last possible for me to talk about the trauma (all of it) to myself without the self-deceptions, the euphemisms.

My claim to be a Gay Activist is pertinent here. Prior to the attack I had been in the core of the Gay Liberation Front, had been one of the key workers in Gay Rights At Work. After the attack, clinging to my new lover, I withdrew from gay political activity. I am reclaiming my activism here.

I cannot imagine how I could have got rid of this monstrous albatross without your help. You have provided me with a method of disposal that meets my needs.

P.S. As I was typing this document, I received an email message from the ex-lover just before this one, after twenty-eight years without contact, asking if I would want to re-connect:

>>why would you want to contact me again? Who knows? But maybe you also are curious – and maybe also still have fond memories.<<

All this healing and processing stuff is really getting beyond a joke. Take the bloody thing, get it out of my sight.
Nominated by gay activist

Suzanne Moore

Nothing Happened

It didn't happen. Nothing happened. The news that circuited around the globe as the Millennium dawned was non-news. All systems were go. Nothing was failing. Life would go on pretty much as before. Disappointment was tangible. The cult of the Millennium bug which had overtaken even the most sensible minds in the land was shown to be based on zero. Or strings of zeros, all of which were perfectly capable of adjusting themselves for the next thousand years. Now it all seems like a blip, an embarrassing interlude, PMT. Pre-millennial tension. Oh no, that's for wimps. We knew that everything would be just fine didn't we? Yet only a few months ago our media were filled with warnings of what we must not do on Millennium night and what we must stock up on. Cans of food, bottled water and flash-lights were recommended. A friend of mine in Melbourne, a former government advisor no less, was buying cans of tuna as if it were going out of fashion. She told me quite seriously that I must do the same but I reassured her that the Turkish shop at the end of my road would be open even if there was a nuclear holocaust. "You want cheap cigarettes darling?"

Still I was uneasy, for I could see that she had succumbed to the burgeoning cult. I tried to book a flight between San Francisco and New York for around New Year's Eve as I sat reading headlines that told me that no-one should fly for at least a five week period over the Millennium. The young guy at the other end of the phone found me a flight. He was, we both knew, working on commission but even that didn't stop him. "I wouldn't fly then myself", he told me chirpily. "Nothing is really going to happen is it?" I asked. "Well, put it this way love", he cheerfully informed me, "Just try getting travel insurance." Those last few weeks of 1999 were like that. On the one hand there was a 'business as usual' ethos, on the other murmurs, whispers, quiet unease about what form the end of the world would take. In the popular imagination, it seemed, not much would have to go wrong for civilisation to collapse. If microwave ovens suddenly ceased to function and car park barriers no longer worked properly and cash machines were emptied then obviously anarchy would prevail. In a very short time there would be all sorts of rioting and mayhem. Peter Agar, a deputy director of the CBI, warned of the ultimate signal that Armageddon was upon us. Tills might no longer operate correctly leading to problems "that could bring down the government". One could but hope.

All of this, we loosely understood, was due to possible computer failure. As everything in our lives was now computerised, if these machines were unable to cope with the very concept of the year 2000 then presumably everything in our lives would unravel. The veneer of culture, of civic society, of community and responsibility and rights and duties, the New Labour mantras, suddenly all seemed to be remarkably fragile. Everything could be disrupted forever by mechanised binary codes – everything that makes us a cohesive society could disappear. We would soon all be survivalists, living in remote dark places scavenging for food. Each day some new catastrophe would bring us further away from our old lives. Planes would fall from the sky and we would survive that perhaps. But how could we cope with the failure of lifts, with our bank accounts being wiped clean, with nuclear missiles going off at random, with ships unable to dock, floating forever abandoned in wild seas? How would we deal with the inevitable cyber-terrorism that would ensue? The anarchists and vigilantes whose day had now come?

We would take to the hills and horde, just as those strange men in Montana have been doing since the 80s. Yet unlike other doomsday cults it was not clear who were to be the chosen ones, those lucky and devout enough to be whisked straight to the non-digital paradise. And even in survivalist mode, when our lives might be falling apart, it was clear that some of us were still desperate to maintain our lifestyles. As Kelly Hoppen, interior designer, told *You* magazine on Boxing Day 1999, "I'm making sure I definitely have reserves of tequila, candles and matches, lots of sexy underwear and deodorant. Also large supplies of Star Flower Essences *Angel Spray* to clear my aura, and *Crystal Clear* to clear any negative energies from my home." Novelist Jilly Cooper confided meanwhile, "I cannot live without tranquillisers for my dog Hero, who is a very nervy lurcher and goes into complete hysterics if ever there is thunder and lightning."

Others took the whole thing much more seriously. Angela and Jeremy Perron abandoned their Wiltshire home and headed for a hillside cottage near Forres to escape the chaos of Y2K. She was a PR executive and he a computer programmer. She was soon to be seen on our screens urging us to buy up supplies of food and fuel. The couple began to hunt rabbits and learnt how to chop wood. At the beginning of the year they announced it was still too soon to issue an all-clear. But by May 2000 the end had arrived in a more banal way for the couple. They were to divorce. Angela Perron said that she regretted spending so much time on the Millennium bug issue when she should have been repairing the problems in her relationship. Yet others did not admit defeat so easily, Briony Williams of the Y2K Community Action Network, a Millennium bug pressure group, still wanted to blame someone else: "I'm angry that the focus is on the Perrons and not the government's failure to provide us with adequate information."

So did the government provide us with adequate information? It certainly created a Millennium bug logo – a ten-legged beast. It sent every household unhelpful and confusing pamphlets, but mostly it spent a hell of a lot of money. We are given to understand that this was money well spent, that because of our 'massive preparedness' we escaped the fantasised disruption. Yet countries who are less fixated on computers, such as Italy spent hardly anything and suffered no more disruption than we did. Was the estimated £400 billion spent world-wide actually necessary? Or was this simply just more empire building by computer corporations? A vast conspiracy to extort frightened governments out of money? Why has there been no public outcry over the bug that never was? How come professional alarmists such as Robin Guenier, who invested an awful lot in telling us how terrible it would all be, are now allowed simply to say in their defence, "It all seems a long time ago. I think it's a boring subject." We fret publicly and endlessly about the amount of money wasted on that franchised vision of the future – the Dome – when we need schools and hospitals, but the billions spent on the bug seems to have been written off. Where did all that cash go? Why is no one complaining about it?

There was at the time a sense of embarrassment, as the *Daily Telegraph* pointed out, it was not just that the promised disruption failed to materialise, "but that nothing happened anywhere." It made no difference whether money had been pumped into combating the bug or not. Perhaps though, we are embarrassed about more than just money. What did materialise was an atmosphere, for a few weeks anyway, that owed little to the silicon age and everything to a much earlier time of Nostradamus and *Revelation*, of plague and pestilence, of ancient fears that revealed a huge distrust of the technology that most of us use every day of our lives. In a wired world it is easy enough to forget that three-quarters of women aged over 60 are still afraid of cash machines and will never use them. The confidence and cockiness of the Internet generation masks another more uncomfortable reality – of the information-poor, the dispossessed of the shiny new world, the many for whom cyberspace remains another planet. Yet even those of us who use computers on a daily basis were easily drawn into the doomsday scenarios. We kid ourselves that we are connected but we are still strangely afraid and distanced from the machines that we use every day of our lives. We do not know how they work, only that they could go wrong, and so we believed that should they go wrong, life as we knew it would be over.

The bug was a peculiar collective delusion, an hysterical over-reaction dressed up as ultra-rationalism. The bug gave us a focus for our fears of the future, our fear that the present was morphing too quickly into the future for our liking. It became a problem that could at least be fixed. Its actions could be calculated and controlled and if only you had the right experts, comprehended. It was the mask we needed to disguise our deeper, more primal, more unconscious panic. For what does it say about us that we were so taken in? That the doomsday scenarios so vividly imagined did not happen, means we are left alone to recognise our immaturity around technology, that quite possibly in the year 2000 we are not so modern after all. Disaster, we have been persuaded, was averted by shadowy figures who have now come and gone. Baudrillard has claimed with his customary grumpiness that the Millennium never happened. In a sense he is right, and as we watched the fireworks – the light and the noise that frightens away the evil spirits – we were reminded that in every beginning the traces of the past make themselves felt.

In the end the digits took care of themselves. Microwaves still pinged and cash machines were still overflowing with money. The ten-legged beast, the life-threatening virus, did not appear. We were still in control of our own destinies and that thought, for a split-second, terrified us more than the prophesied failure of technology. Collectively we had survived the newness of a world that is changing too fast for most of us to know what to be properly afraid of anymore. Our oldest fears clustered around our newest machines and tools as if everything were out of our hands. A crisis was imagined and then heroically and expensively prevented but the crisis was always about human error and not technological failure. No wonder no-one wants to talk about it anymore. For underneath, part of us must know, that delusions on this scale belong to another Millennium, not this one.

Scanner

Flood

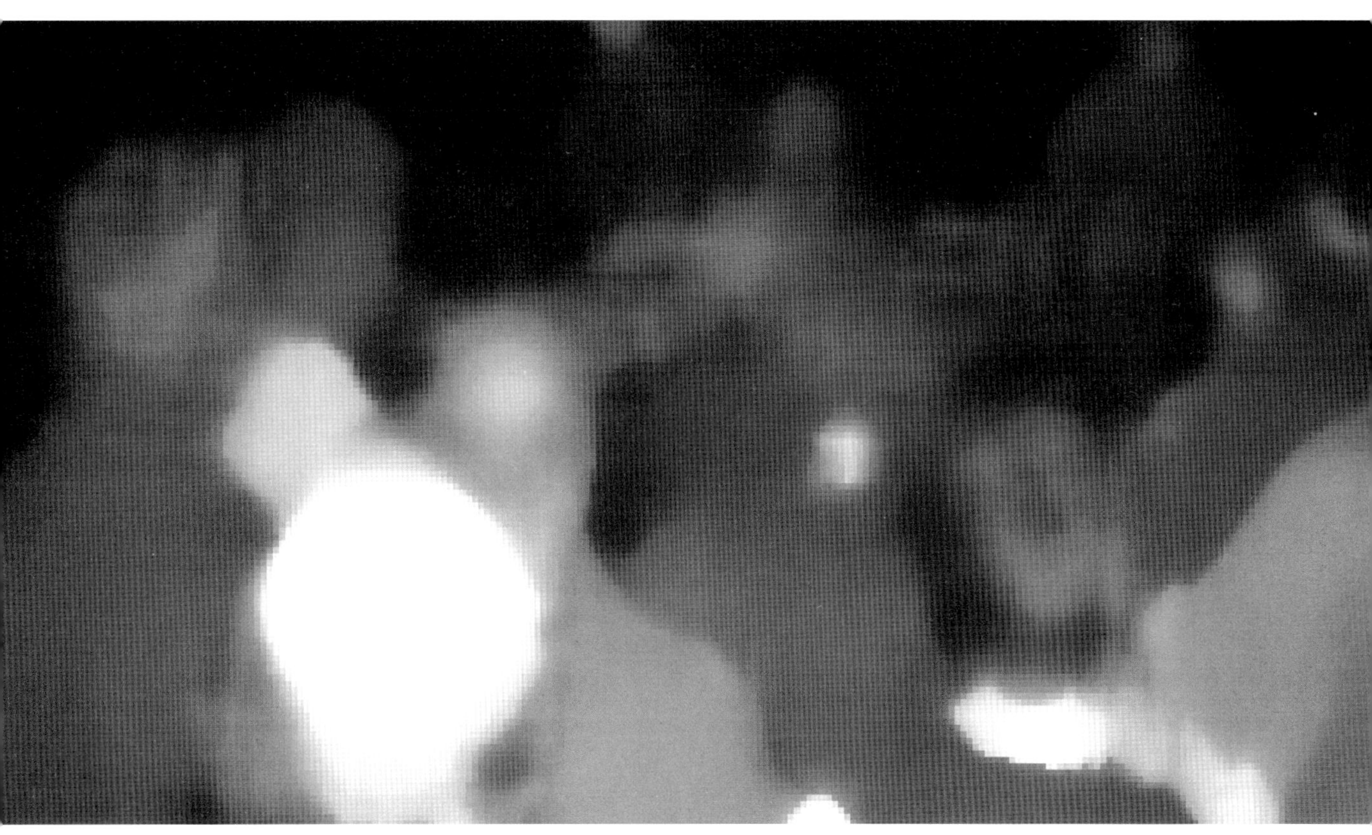

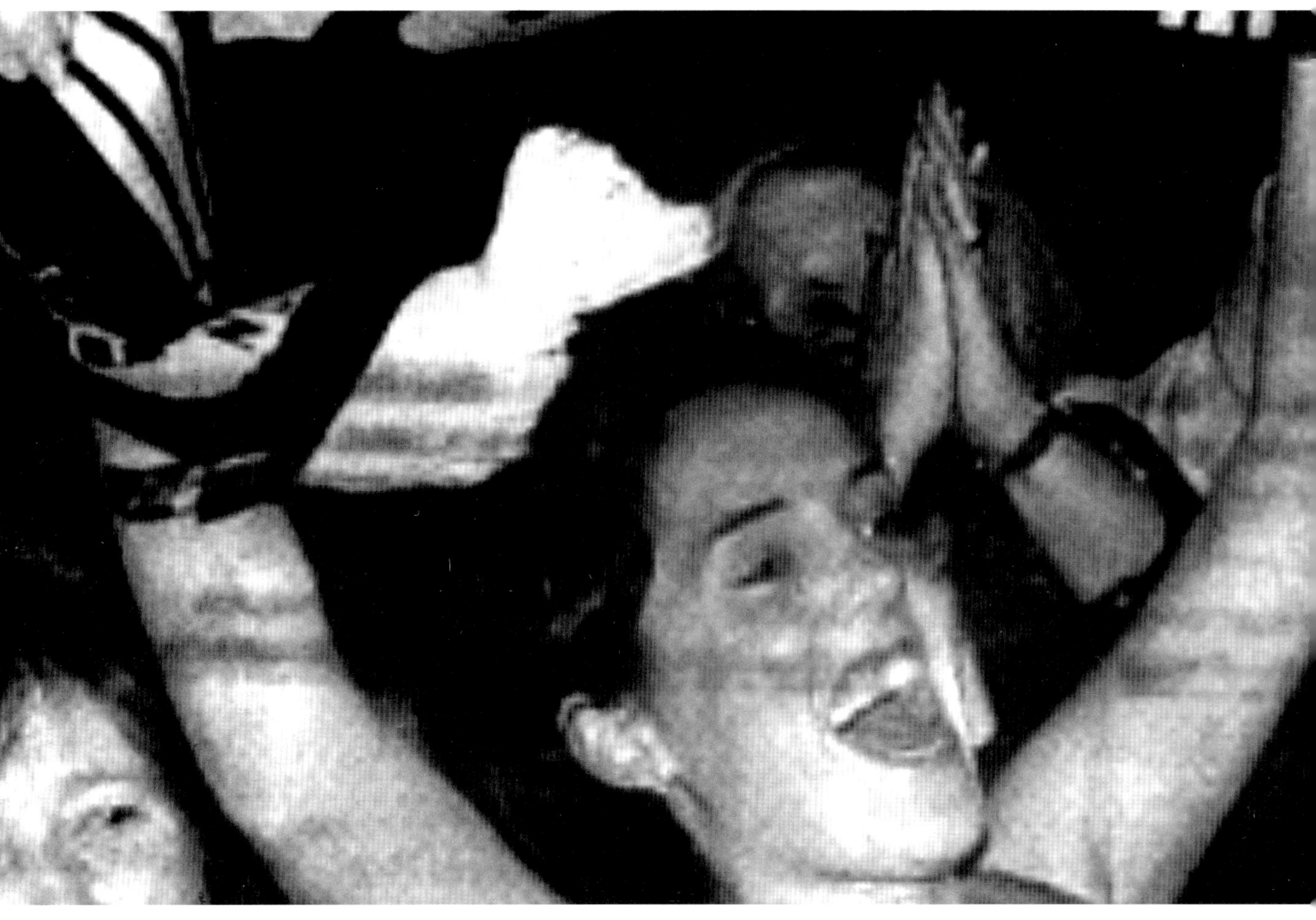

*Me and me mates went out for a quick pint it was crazy.
I don't remember how I got home. Me bleeding phone didn't
work so I couldn't ring. I couldn't believe how much everything
cost. Janice was sick all over my jacket. It took forever to get a
cab. Dad was still up when I got in nursing a hangover. I lost
my purse in the crowd. We argued for hours before I could
leave. I cried in the morning.*

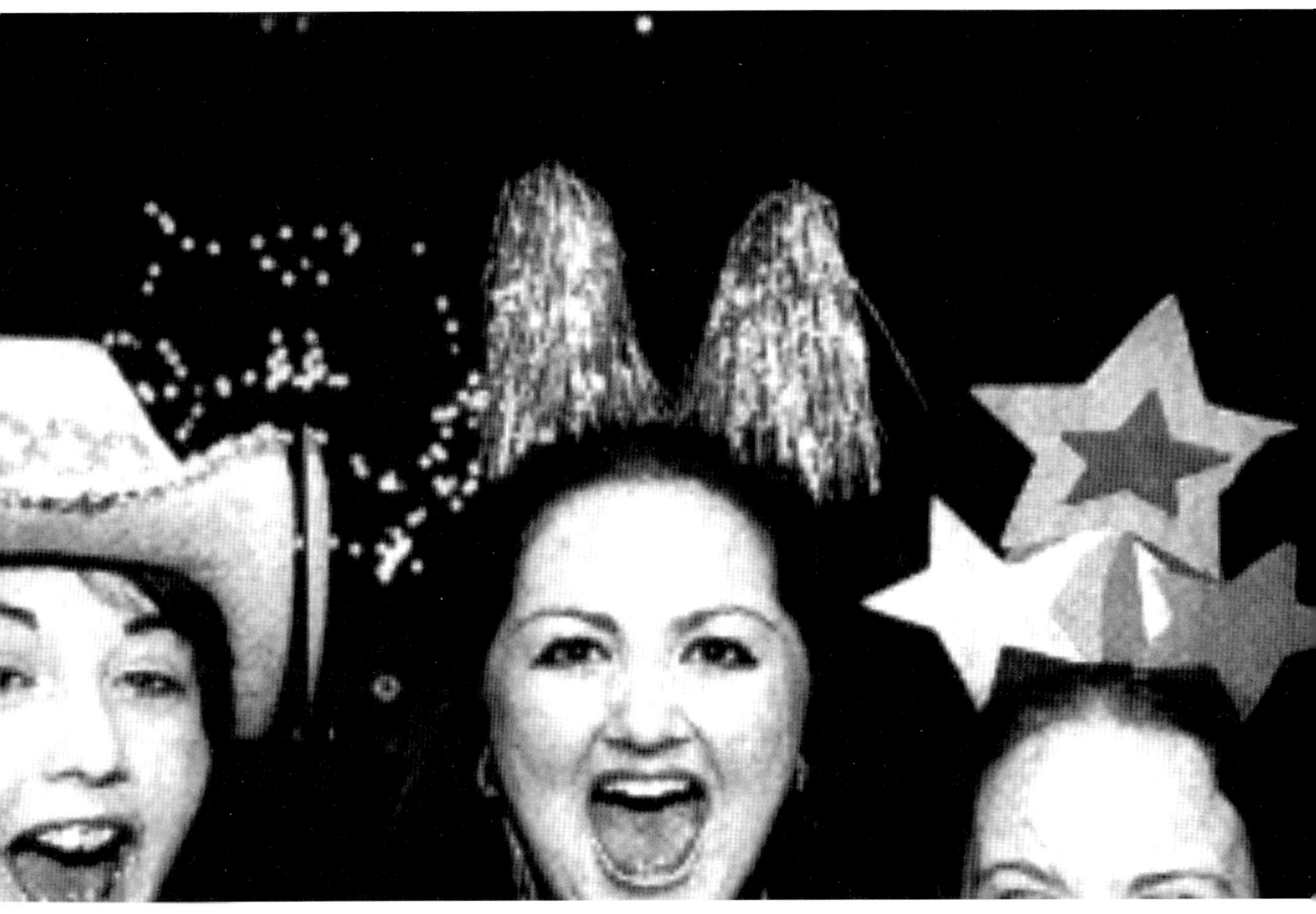

Everyone was out that night. We had such a laugh.
Dave kissed me. I laughed 'til my tummy hurt. It was
just like a movie. The fireworks were so pretty. I felt
like a princess in my tiara. I broke one of my heels.
I wish every year was like this.

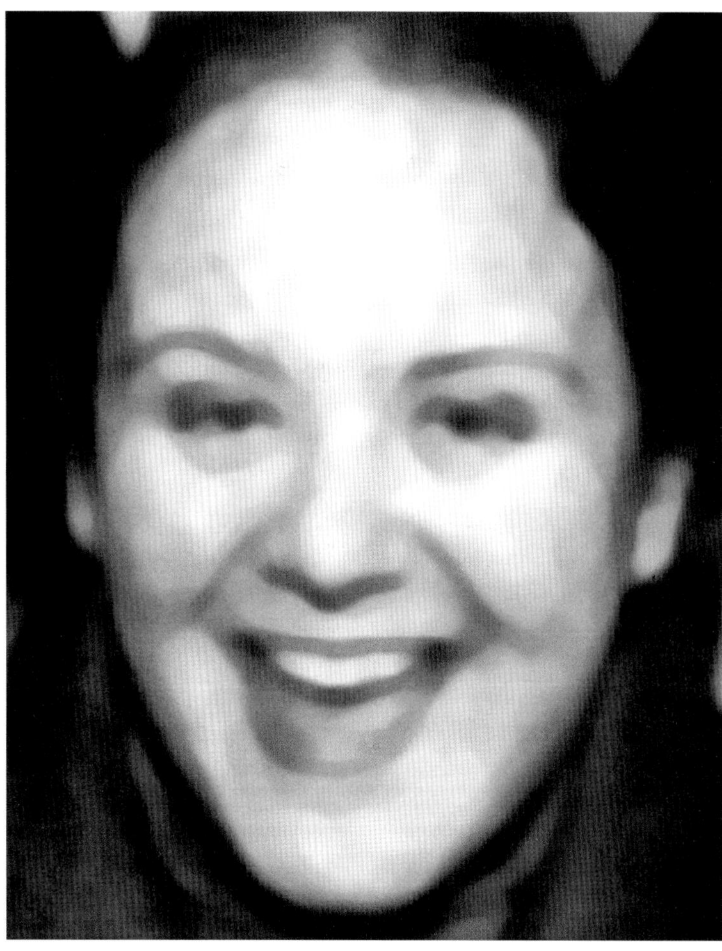

*I wasn't sure what I felt. I had expected so much more.
It was darker than we were told and less people. Julie and
Stephanie never arrived until really late by which time we were
all so upset. All the free drinks had gone and the bar was
closed. I had a small flask in my bag which helped to raise
our spirits. All our watches seemed to have different times so
we tuned in the TV. We couldn't get a good picture inside,
but heard the cheers from outside so recognised it was time.
I went to bed around 01.00.*

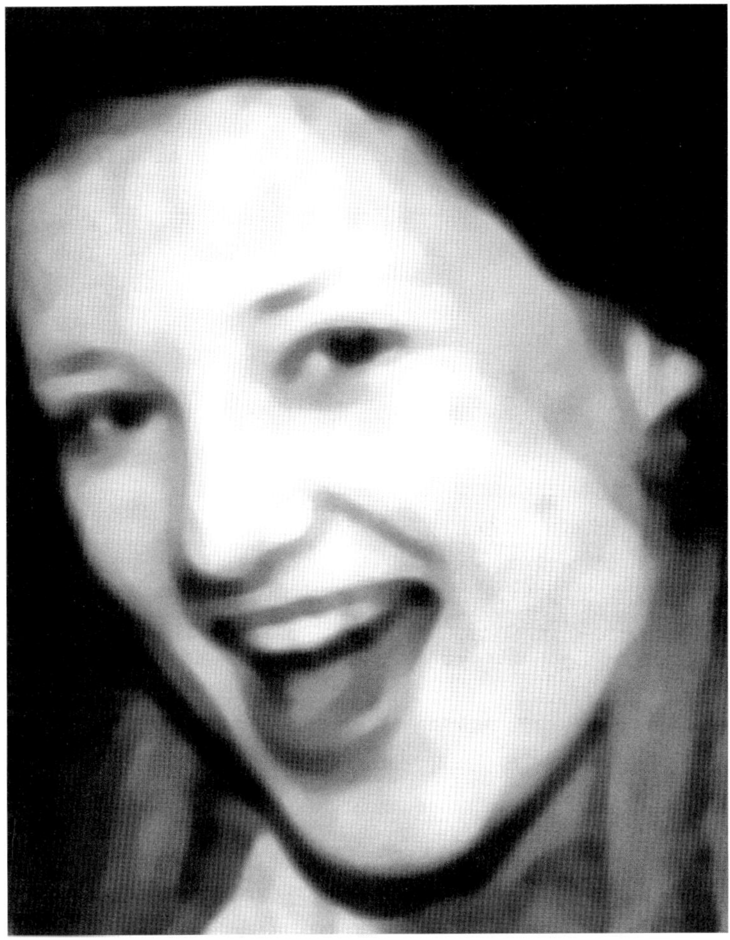

*Stewart and I spent the evening together and it was so incredible.
He is a lovely man. We had booked a fancy restaurant some
time ago and it was worth it as everyone looked really posh in
there and Stewart looked so handsome in his new suit.
The food was yummy and the waiters really friendly and when
we told them we were getting engaged today they brought out
a rose and boldly handed it to me and I couldn't hold the tears
back. Stewart wrapped his arms around me and told me he
loved me and for that moment it felt as everything in the world
was colourful, promising and perfect. The taxi driver took us
back to the flat at around 23.00 and we had a few drinks at
home on the sofa, kissed and made love, and I wanted to freeze
frame this moment forever and to seal it in a glass case and
treasure it. The world was alive and so was I.*

Tim Etchells

Permanent Midnight

The hole worlde switches from Gregorian/Augustian to Bullshit Nintendo Calendar and in midst of all conversion/confusion Time itself (*sic*) is decimalised. You and many other unfortunate bastards lose your birthday(s) – the rest of the worlde gets olde and you stay 'young'. You 'can't get no kicks anymore'© and give up to deep melancholia/an all new kind of AIDS. Picture this. You, sat like a sweat-stained vampire, exhausted at prospect of *Self For Eternity* by Calvin Klein.

There's some kind of vaguely arty/retro cinema effect like a wipe or a dissolve. The cops are after you. You shoot up this drug that makes time run faster only the cops have shot up the same stuff and they are chasing you only the stuff they have shot up is stronger than the stuff you have shot up and they are waiting in the future, ready to catch you.

Another dissolve.

You lie in bed and make up different kinds of time, like counting sheep. There's black time when you're feeling sad, no, that's blue time, and there's red time when you're angry or cold. There's soft time, and long time and thin time too …

Something makes it impossible to sleep.

The performance by Franko B is only two minutes long.

Franko lies on the floor. Naked. Body smeared in white. He wears a large flea collar of dirty coloured plastic. He lies prone. A beaten animal. A smear of white foot-prints around him. A snake of blood from the wound in his stomach. Face to the ground. His fingers are moving. His eyes are at the floor.

From the moment you are ushered into the room there are perhaps only 100 seconds remaining. You see. White room: a few wood panels, some seemingly ancient electrical wires rising vertical, dead and redundant,

from a conduit at the wall. These, in particular, with their strange almost sculptural form and their suggestion of impromptu torture seem to resonate, burn bright on the retina. And the footprints again. A white room. A few wood panels. A window (?) that gives onto rooftops and other windows in the middle distance. You wonder, once, very briefly, about the lives behind those windows. About what those lives might make of this one. About the kind of pain over there, compared to the one happening in here. But that thought only flickers. And sky. It's a sunny day but somehow you confuse/ remember it as grey. Perhaps it is getting to dusk. It doesn't matter. Yes. All that. But in the end there's only Franko, and in particular his eyes, to look into.

The context of the Millennium with its trumpets, its thousand flying flags, bogus universalism, corporate fireworks, and its earth swathed in sponsor's logos. All talk of the long haul. A thousand years of this and that. Parties in the street. The long long list of human achievements. As if all of history were nothing but crowds, progress, schools and parliaments. Fuck the lot of it.

You start to think about the private. About time and the private. About the spaces in a life where time is felt differently. About the solitary. The territory is not singular. Not easy to grasp. Perhaps not even a territory at all. A conglomeration of things. Facts. Stories. Dreams. Slow time. Altered time.

Time waiting.

Time in the beds of hospitals.

Time hungover.

Time in the beds of lovers.

On the motorway/driving at night.

Drugged time.

Sex and illness = time spent locked in the body of a self

or another with all of the silence, beauty, terror and
uncertainty this implies.
Time alone or in unspeakable intimacy with another.
Time that somehow breaks or slips under the clock.
Time as it is felt.
Long time and short time.

Beginning at midnight and passing from night to
morning and back again to midnight, our twenty-four
hour long performance *Who Can Sing a Song to Unfrighten
Me?* (Forced Entertainment, 1999) is somewhere
between a journey and a vigil, an act of staying up all
night as protection from the demons hidden in darkness,
and a way of marking and sharing time.

Through the night and into the day there are sleazy
disappearing routines, lists of fears, deaths and
resurrections involving pantomime animals, skeletons
dancing and long long never-to-be-completed bedtime
stories from a line of fourteen kings.

You watch, slumped in the torn seat of a theatre,
struggling with sleep.

Back to Franko.

You step forwards, tilt your head to be in the same
plane, as he lies on the floor. Make eye contact and
measure the moment. Of the two minutes, there are
perhaps only 80 seconds remaining.

His fingers are moving. Time goes by in fractions,
very slow. The exhausted state of his body and the
troubled motion of his breathing cast a spell upon time,
the room and all who enter it. In amongst the acres of
apparent nothingness you wonder if he will 'do' something.
You wonder – about touching him. About lying down
beside him. But in this version of events at least there is
no action of this sort. Instead you look at him and try to
make him smile.

Your eyes exchange the incomprehensible. Or the
untranslatable. Breathing. Eyes. He knows that you are
there. Watching him. And you know that he is there.
Prone. Self-wounded. In pain. And it's always a
performance. And he knows that you know. And you know
that he knows that you know. An endlessness. A loop.
An endlessness.

His lips move. Fractionally. It's so black in his mouth
you think perhaps he'll let go a little blood. But he
doesn't. No. Instead he smiles, a weak smile that's

shared with the eyes. And the arrhythmic rise and fall of
his breathing. Troubled breathing. Like someone
exhausted from running. Though clearly (?) he hasn't
moved in hours.

You watch and then step forwards.

Only a 'psychotic govt. of fools'© could have thought up
that idea of a Big Celebrity Stripathon televised live for
the Millennium. But it needed to be done. Who would
have thought that the dick of Bruce Forsyth and the
sagging breasts of Anna Ford would have graced our
screens that night in the early hours, Cher flown in nude
on Concorde, the chorus line of Michael Parkinson,
Jimmy Tarbuck, Jim Davidson, Cleo Laine, etc., etc., all
stark naked and stumbling about under the floods in
Pinewood Studios (or whatever), all delirious with shame
and fame, and the hosts B. Elton, Melinda Messenger,
King Charles and G. Halliwell all working (nude and
goose fleshed) in shifts. Keith Chegwin fills a lime green
bucket with puke, measured with the dipstick of that
bloke from Five while Jo Wiley and M. Lammar disrobe in
the background, feigning sexuality. You are drunk.
You will not remember this properly tomorrow and the
papers will not report it. Static bursts the screen. You die.

You are in a scene where all movement originates from
the body right next to yours, or from your own. There is
nothing but the close-up. You are both beneath a
sheet. You have been in this bed for the best part of three
days. Talking. Fucking. Touching. Your eyes locked into
each other. The burden of the close-up. The minute detail
of skin surface, open lips, dilated pupils, freckles in
shattered patterns beneath the lover's eye. Around the
bed an accumulation of coffee cups, bottles, an ashtray,
a knife, a plate which once held fruit. Time is slowed.
Contained and distorted by the spell in your bodies.
The one clock in this place is invisible from where you lie.
The telephones are unplugged. You can tell if it is day or
night by the way the light through the skylights is
changing. But that's all.

When you leave this space you will be shocked by the
outside. By the widescreen of it, by the invention of
cinemascope. The crowd makes you jumpy. The width of
the street is an explosion. Your eyes struggle to digest the
light. And time changes, shifting back to its well known
register. You last half an hour in the streets of any stupid

day and then retreat to the apartment, bed and private time.

You know (now, clearly) that time is a function of bodies and space. That it bends with the proximity to another that love, sex and intimacy bring.

Making theatre we've most often engaged with the architecture of an hour-and-a-half, the shifting but predictable demand of dramatic structures, the tyranny of rise and fall. For project after project we've found some way to upset or reset these expectations: slowing things down, speeding things up, smashing everything to shards. But in the end an hour-and-a-half was always a certain shape; an economy with expectations, a pattern tied to forms and biorhythms. We began to yearn for something more.

Beginning in 1991 we made a number of projects which spilled out of theatre's temporal economy towards something else; struggling to deal with lengths of time and performance tasks that, in some ways, were deliberately beyond our control. A six-hour piece, a twelve-hour piece, a nine-hour piece. At twenty-four hours perhaps *Who Can Sing a Song to Unfrighten Me?* is what lies down the end of this particular road. What is so strange about this piece is that one cannot know what it is, even having done it several times. The duration itself removes the work from the realm of the knowable. The night of fear it tries to discuss – fear at the unknowableness of the world, the unknowableness of stories, the unknowableness of language, the unknowableness of power, the unknowableness of one's own death – is mirrored by an unknowableness in the work itself.

Even the brave souls who stay with us through the whole performance in London, Munich or Vienna surrender to coffee breaks, a nice walk by the river or at the very least sleep – dreaming the show's continuation as they recline in their seats, but missing it, losing it, letting their hold on it slip. Indeed, even the performers don't manage to be in the whole thing or see all of the performance. There are times when they too must sleep in the concrete bunkers downstairs, times when they sleep on the stage. The show, as they say in some forgotten genre of movies 'is bigger than us, bigger than all of us'. I like this fact, that it is impossible to see all of the work.

November 18th 1999. At midnight in Brussels S

completes a performance with her own company, does the get-out, goes to the bar and drinks with friends. All through that, in another time and space, we are performing. She drives home. Sleeps. Wakes, showers and has breakfast. Through all of that we are performing. She takes a train to the airport, checks in and waits at the gate. She flies one hour and a half, arrives Munich and takes the S-Bahn into town. Through all of that we are performing. And when she arrives in the theatre to see the piece there are still nine hours left for her to see. Time has gone strange. The theatre is a raft in the dark. As if everyone in the building, or near it, is under a spell. And the spell multiplies, corrupting the world, enveloping everything.

London. June 19th, 1999. At three in the afternoon I leave my sons with D in the daylight of the foyer and go back underground. I sleep in a dressing room, a blanket on the floor. The performance continues above me, unseen, reaching me only in dreams, through the tannoy.

Your memory of London is full of absences: bits you missed whilst sleeping, bits you missed but saw in silence on the monitors backstage, blurred shapes, as much noise as signal. Rumours circulating in the coffee bar. As if the whole performance were as much invented or forgotten as remembered, as much an addition to the unknowable as it is to the known.

Franko again. You step forwards. Squat. To be closer. In the same plane. You smile. Try to be here, now and open. His lips move. Again the feeling that he might produce blood. But instead he speaks. He says.
Looking up from the floor he says.
"Are you OK?"
A voice. Tired. With a bit of a smile to it.
"Are you OK?"
And the full irony/reversal strikes you at once: that, in *this* situation, he should be asking *you* that question. All wrong. It's the question which you might, after all, have decided to ask him.
Him: Are you OK?
You: Yeah. I'm fine. *(Nodding. Smiling.)* You?
Him: Yeah. I'm OK. *(Soft voice.)*
You: Tired?
Him: Yeah. A little bit. Coming to the end. I know it's near the end.
You: Yeah.

I think, then, that there is an acre of silence. More looking. Passing time. An acre. But it must be only seconds later that the door swings open and you are ushered out. Back to the real world, where the woman you love is already smoking a cigarette on the stairs.

People in the past get addicted to drugs that are only available in the future. It mainly starts as a problem for just a few 'elite type' people (*sic*), but soon there is apparently a huge explosion of drug trafficking across the borders of time. The whole of the eighteenth century gets addicted to crack. Ancient Rome in reefer madness. Twelfth century Japan gets turned onto LSD and the culture changes overnight; the Seven Samurai daub their hands and faces dayglo and that Hokusai bloke makes vast (very big) psychedelic landscapes using cans of Humbrol spray paint which have also been stolen from the future.

T. Blair cuts the ribbon on a huge Bankside mural made of pigmented human excrement – a lively scene what celebrates the ascension to 'heaven' © of Diana, that bloke off Eastenders and Bobby Sands. It is the fucking (fcuking) Goode Olde Days. A vaudeville chorus of slithering liars. It is one nation under a groove. It's free milk and all pull together for a flat earth. Death itself is digitised, cast out. Starbuck Coffee is free on each purchase. Kids shit in an abandoned flat.

Something means you cannot sleep.

And Franko again. Remembered.

The two minutes of the performance function as this sliver of time which one must replay; a holographic shard which contains more than its surface and duration suggest.

Franko. The room.

We talk about it endlessly, trying to uncover the burden of what took place, in all its delicacy, banality, simplicity, fakery, nothingness.

And one approaches the burden of what did happen through the lens of what did not. The things one thought of doing or saying but did not. Story. Speculation. The things that each or any of us could have done/said. The risk he takes, alone in a room like that with a procession of strangers. The possibilities. Some stories circulate of encounters, or actions and reactions from others, not present, rumours, myths already, fictitious histories.

And S says to me that she keeps wishing that she could go back in, and I think that this is perfect, because somehow I've been thinking the same thing. This desire to revisit is a part of performance, its performative legacy.

The meeting with Franko, locked tight in the two minute frame, becomes a superheated fraction in which the possibilities of an encounter with a stranger are made manifest. A situation. An invitation: to stay, act, stay mute or speak. The ethical burden of every blink, word, and step you might take.

I keep wishing I could go back in.

But those minutes, like all others, are gone.

Gone in their specialness. In their ordinariness. And in their out-of-the-ordinariness.

Two minutes. Two minutes. And what that can contain.

Darling. You cannot go back in. That's all you can be sure of.

You pause. You think about the meaning of the time you spent in there. Of what happens between two people in the real unreal.

The first time I visited X I stayed four days and we only left the house once, to buy alcohol and cigarettes. The rest of the time it was nothing but touch, little talk and sex, sleep, drink and eye contact. We were strangers, almost, and existed solely in the present.

Touch. The strangeness of each other's skin. How it touches, how it tastes. A constant measuring of the distance between you that is performed by eye contact. You in each other. Fingers. Hands. Tongues. Cock. Arses. Cunt. Or whatever. In any case a delirium of touching. Sex and sleeping. The phone unplugged for several days, the door unanswered. Mobiles off. You learn to please each other but have no language (yet) to speak of it. So you fuck and you laugh and you sleep and then do it again. Eyes checking the situation, your edges, the other's edges. Surfaces and orifices – eyes, mouth, nose, ears, arse, cunt – all open. Something between disappearing into each other, probing and falling, and at the same time knowing that these holes are the borders which cannot ever be crossed, proximity and the impossibility of union. Time transformed by the spell of your bodies.

You can tell it is probably warm outside. And the light changes through the window down below the bed. Once there is rain. It can be heard against the roof and

Permanent Midnight makes reference
to the perfomance *Aktion 398* by
Franko B presented at Toynbee Studios,
London, in February 2000. It also concerns
the twenty-four hour performance
Who Can Sing a Song to Unfrighten Me?
by Forced Entertainment, co-produced
by LIFT, The Royal Festival Hall and
Spiel Art (Munich) and performed in
London, June 1999, Munich, November
1999 and Vienna, June 2000.

there are buckets which need to be moved to catch the
drips. The fridge gets emptier and emptier.

A thousand years of this?

Who Can Sing a Song to Unfrighten Me?
At times during rehearsals we talk about somehow
marking the passage of time as a part of the
performance: seeing clocks onstage, or breakfast, lunch
and dinner breaks as reminders of 'what might be going
on outside'. But in the end we resist this and begin to
speak instead about a frozen time for the performance,
a night mood and an atmosphere: a concentration that
will be maintained irrespective of the time outside. To
come to the piece, to enter its world, will be, somehow,
to surrender to this time, this temporary kingdom, a time
we start to think of as a permanent midnight.

Brian Catling

The Disciples

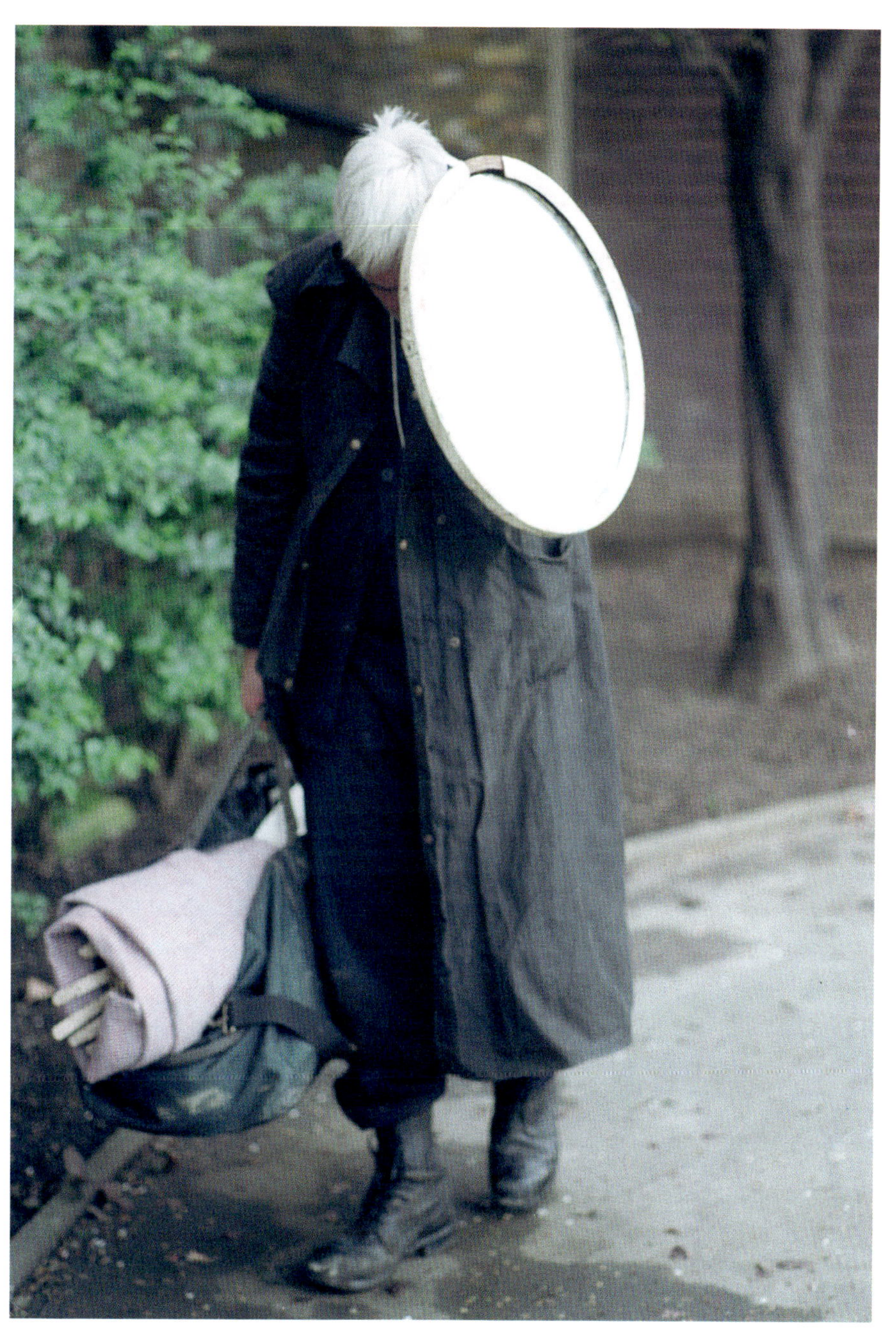

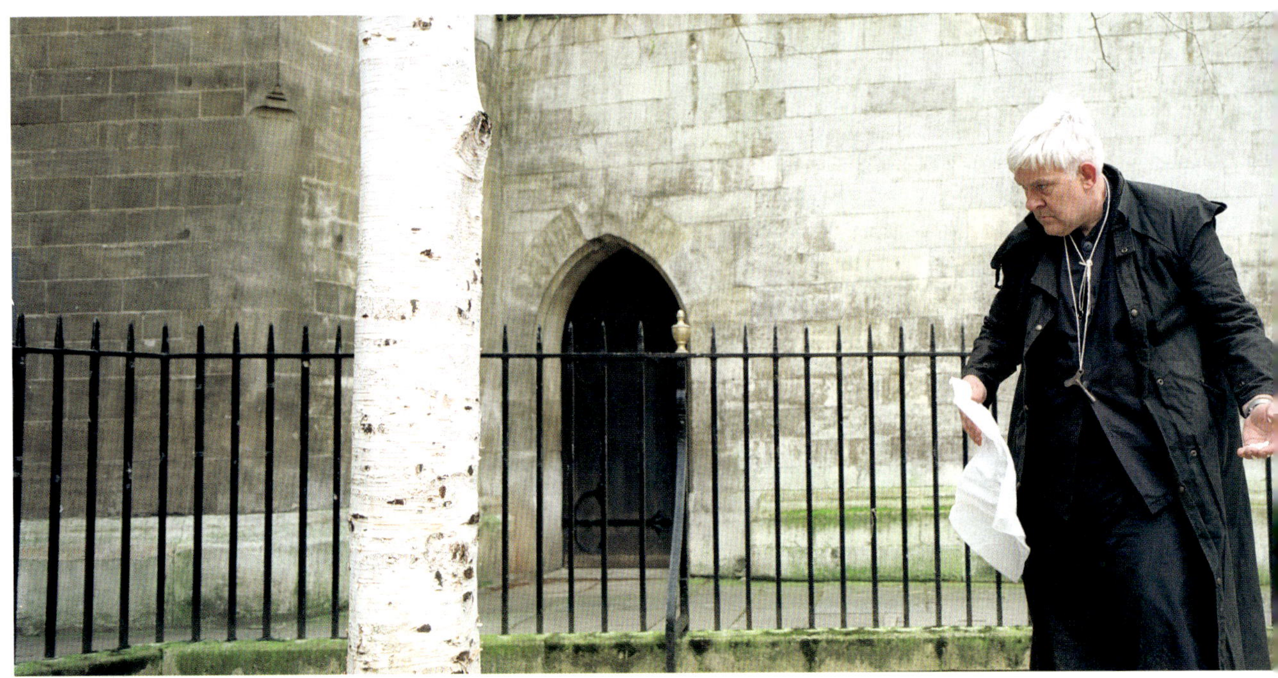

Small Acts

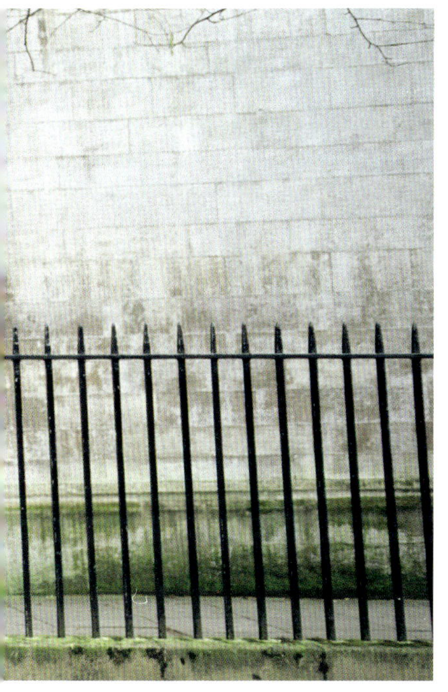

The rolling of the year has its central movement, the one watched by the many, the focus of celebration, anticipation and fear, the personal attachment to fictional time.
The inevitable conclusion of that moment is the outcome of a mass of smaller details and incidents; the cogs spinning and crawling together deep inside. These intimate concealments are ferociously tenacious and work both sides of the crudity of any bronze chiming. These moments, these small acts, are normally hidden, kept in the warm oiled dark where they are constantly attended by the slavery of the subconscious. Once seen and exposed their true nature is revealed. The fragment displaced from the secure monolith of machine is irrational and frail, overwrought and compulsive. These are the butterflies of a distant forest, a swarm being continually crushed to establish the pulse and quiver of cause and effect; the echo in the ligaments of stiff history and obvious awareness.
The same events and moments sign themselves in human terms as crimes, follies, accidents and distortions. Categories which attempt again and again to make and hide their function and necessary purpose.

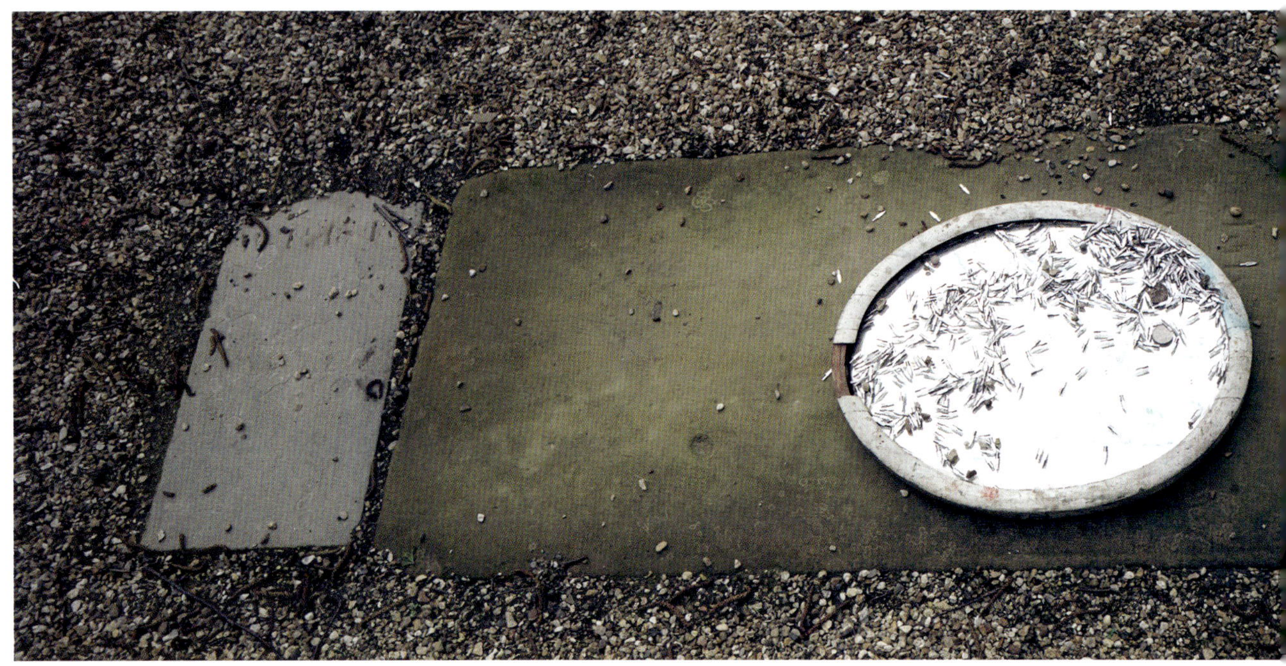

Of the days

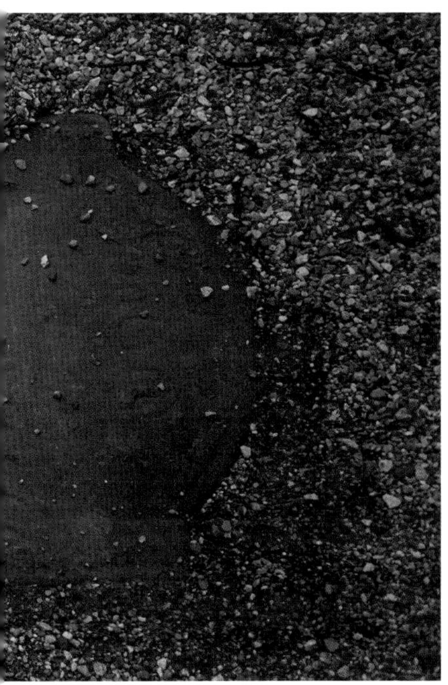

1   *Seen at dawn in a place where the ancient dead are rested. The gates still locked.*
Some here are living. Sleeping secretly in the park's shelter. The light is beginning to
believe in itself as it crawls into the sky. The sound is an infinity of invisible birds.
The metal is silver. The attendant animal is a fox. Elder and ash trees grow amongst
the stones.

The blanket on the paving stones is unoccupied. A bent and buckled metal
dinner plate is under a small and stained pillow. A wooden arm lies alongside,
partially covered by the blanket. It is larger than a normal human arm, it would
be heroic if its material was not so shabby. Splintered wood is braided and glued
together to form the muscle fibres. The overall surface is irregular and unsubtle.
It could be the packing case for another more delicate arm, an exoskeleton
designed for portage. It could be a bungled imitation.

The owner, or at least operator, of these contrivances appears with an oval
mirror, which he places beneath the articulated fingers of the arm. He pours a
brown liquid onto the early morning reflection in the mirror. The hand begins to
move as the owner walks away. Trees, wind and sky are tapped between the
glass, the wooden fingers and the fluid. Its scent vigorously clings to the pale
air. Vinegar.

In the Pitt Rivers Museum in Oxford, in the glorious jumble of the collection
not on display, is an object that looks like a guitar. It is a pidgin guitar, a
reformed artefact built on similarity but not an imitation. So thick is its wood
that no resonance could ever be made. Its proportion is inflated and graceless.
Its strings sinewy vines. The maker of this most strange and enigmatic
instrument did not understand the purpose or the mechanical function of the
guitar he once saw and so admired. Or perhaps they were irrelevant to his
passionate understanding of the sacred device. His version is another thing, a
cargo cult ghost, made to sing where the flesh should be. Only he could be the
virtuoso of its imagined music.

2   *Seen in the bright morning in a place near the river. The sound is water.*
The metal is steel. The attendant animal is a snail, nearby grows moss.

There is something distasteful in the old man's hand. He stares
uncomprehendingly at a white sticky paste. Something may have just occurred;
there is a muddled array of rags and wires strewn among the pebbles and drift
wood on the foreshore. How much belongs to this operator is unknown. He
smears the slime onto a gold circle, which has been finger painted on a sheet of
paper. This Copydex halo is signing an incident or action. Pressed against a wall,

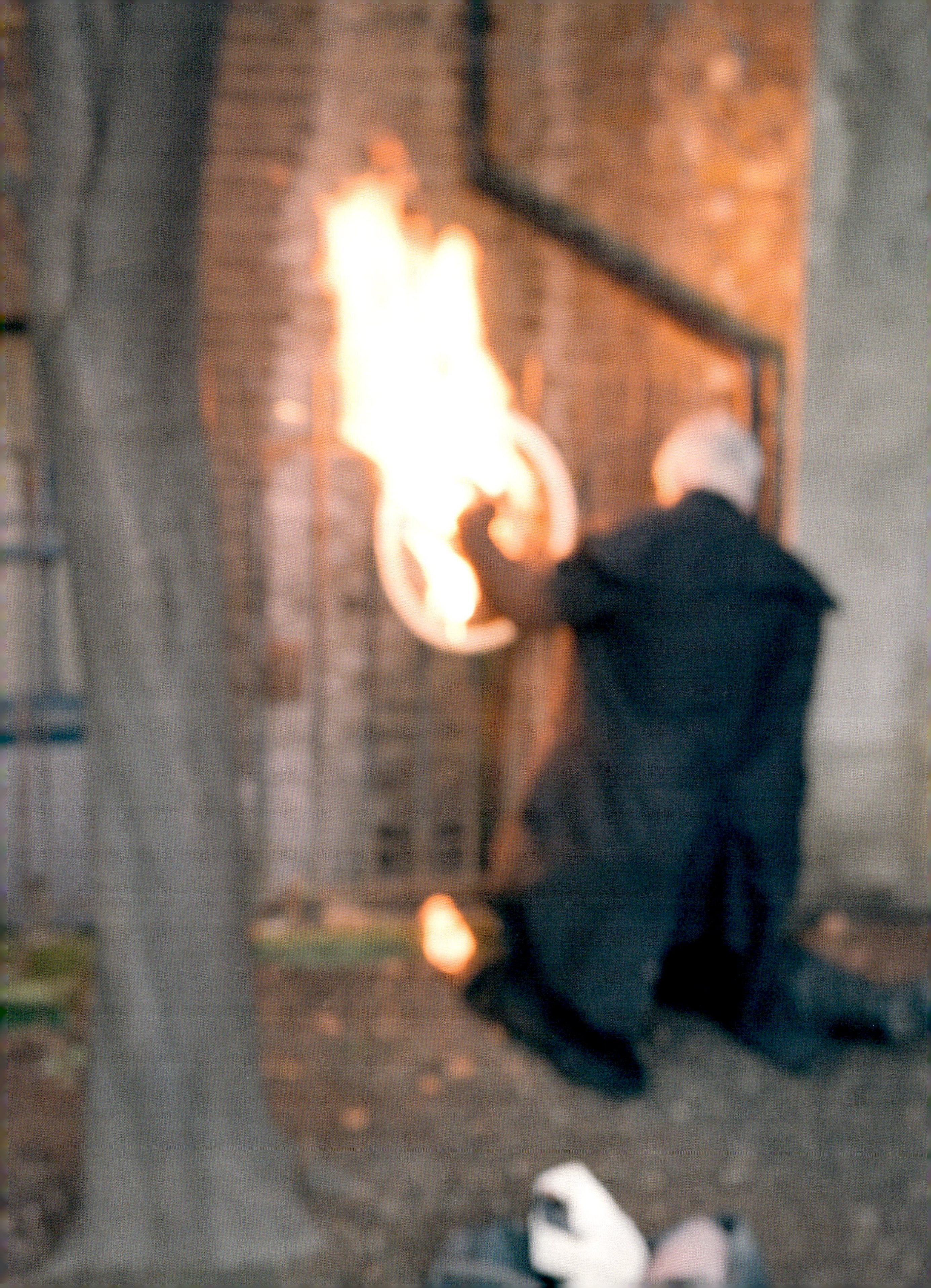

the thin paper will disappear with the rising tide. Leaving the rubbery gilded stigmata. He leaves a halo after his crimes, each colour-coded against the greys. Iridescent whites, pale golds, strident coppers, pearls and exotic insects ground to perpetual fixed illumination.

The river strips and layers time. Last week's gangster's chopped spine is equally polished with fossil remains and ox bones. The plastic coloured string gives unexpected but constant bright notes to the knuckled fugue. Sweet Thames flow softly.

3   *Seen at noon in a place where the light worries at the new stone while ignoring the crumbling weight of older buildings. The sounds are the white grey of traffic. The metal is tin. The attendant animal is the linnet. Nearby grows wild chamomile.*

He stands by the crossroads pointing in a direction where there is no road, in the shadow of a tall church. He seems indifferent to the question that he picks open in the minds of passing travellers.

An abnormal act seen in periphery flushes impetuously through the mind. Experience and memory offer quick shouts at its meaning before it is gone. The cut of its flow leaves troubled banks where other thoughts cannot glide or flourish without discoloration and taint.

4   *Seen in the afternoon in a place where the light is constant but wet. The sounds have muffled in the rain, a broken purr in the hiss. The metal is pewter. The attendant animal is a black beetle, sheltering beneath a cardboard box. Nearby grows privet.*

On his knees he is polishing the kerb. The task pleases him, for he wears the joyful expression of disengagement, beatific and smooth; a cross between martyrdom and parenthood. Black lead is scrubbed into the concrete and then buffed hard to shine. Red lead is rubbed over it and polished. A gentle gleaming bruise is made. The proud act, its energy and its artefact, separate themselves from the rain and translucent passer-by.

It is remembered from Ian Breakwell's wonderful diaries, that a dispossessed woman was often seen below his eyrie near St. John's Gate. She polished the brass plaque of a corner bank, every morning in her passing. Unpaid and unknown, in an hour when only the meat market was open, bringing her own cleaning materials and dusters, torn from her clothing.

5   *Seen in the tired part of the afternoon when light and sound are stationary, forgetting their animation in the drying breeze. The metal is lead. The attendant animal is a dog unaware of cars. Nearby grows a rampant thicket of nettles.*

After so many outward gestures, the figure divides, leaving one part to play with blunt coins. While the other bandages his grubby left hand with black shiny ribbon. The hand is escorted to the dripping mirror, which is now hanging on a fence in an earthy corner. The black thing is examined in the safety of its reflection. It bursts into a bush of flames. Soot and heat roasting the glass. The smoking shredded sleeve is hidden quickly in his coat, the mirror lifted onto his shoulders to make a new and compulsive head.

Like a memory, the disjointed clip of image is added to the puzzle. The vast empty doss house in Fieldgate Street, east London. Here five hundred damaged

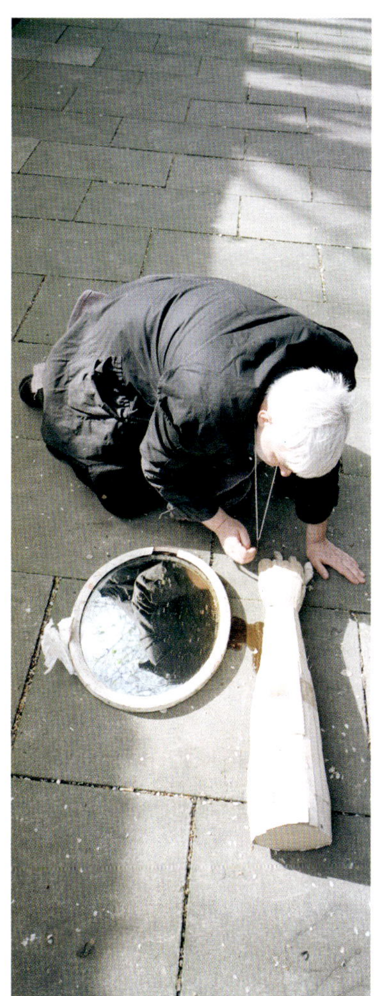

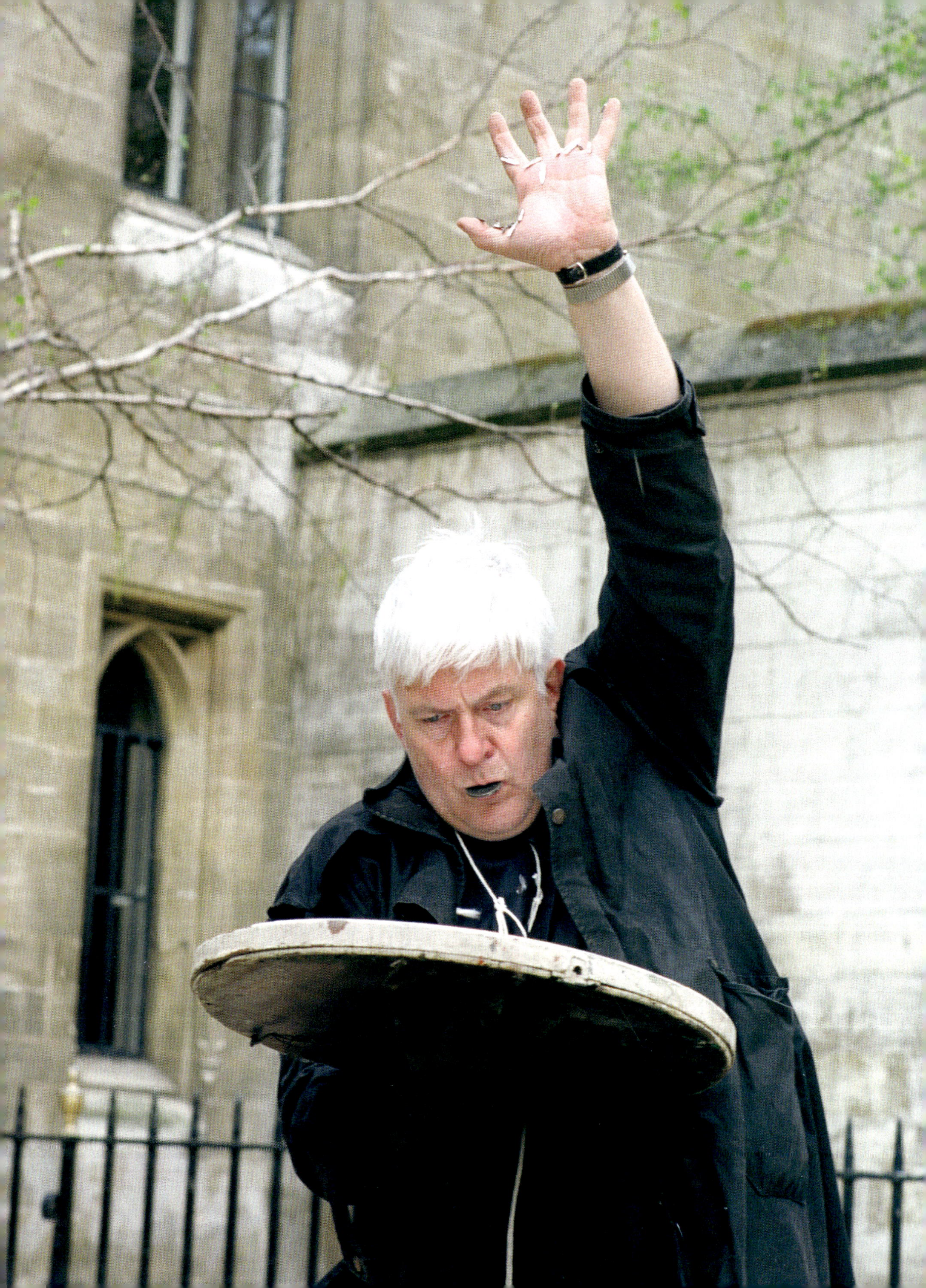

souls were once stored. Their dreams rotted into the cream walls and piss echoed corridors. They have gone, turned onto the vacant streets to quickly disappear. A lost tribe. Disciples of neglect. In the empty communal dinner hall a huge circle of salt has been made. At its centre are two men. One kneeling, holding the head of the lying other in his lap. The kneeling man looks upward towards the light, giving a pietà-like composition to the tableau. He is making a small movement with one hand. Rubbing the dark stain off the surface of large heavy coins in the eyes of the other man. Water, tears, polish and grit run down the man's impassive face.

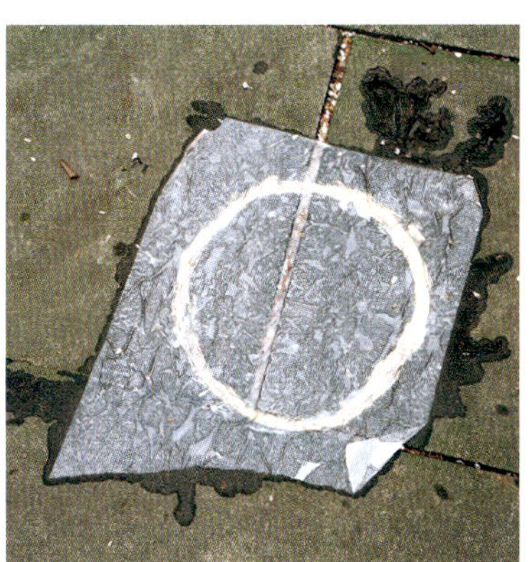

6   *Seen in the dusk. In a place where sound is swallowing itself. The metal is mercury. The attendant animal is the bat. Nearby overgrows mistletoe.*

In a shelf made by one wall crossing another he has jammed a wooden head under the wisteria which writes dry gothic evening shadows on the rough brick. The head is also like the arm made of slatted wood. Gaps in its structure suggest possible expressions and different faces. He takes a brass key on a string from around his neck and carefully winds the clockwork machine in the head. This is made difficult by the height of the head and blistering burns on his hand, but it is achieved. The motor is set in motion, a loud whirring cracking beneath the wood. Nothing moves on the surface. Blankly it winds down to stillness. No sign of purpose, change or achievement has appeared. The thinking is blind and totally self-possessed.

In other countries clocks are given faces that lie, to confuse the devil and counterfeit the East.

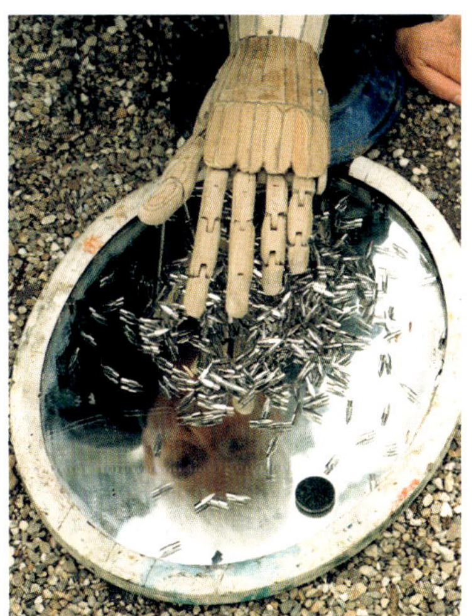

7   *Seen at night near a locked library. With the wind rising to explain silence. The metal is iron. The attendant animal is a cat. Silver birch gleams nearby.*

All shapes merge, the sun was a boundary, only a white dinner plate can be seen hovering like another halo, drunk with china's smoothness in the city's gravel of dark. Poor gin is washed against the wounds, party flares dance the rigged scarlet fires, blood halos jumping the cranial ridge. The old man is only a knotted smirk on the plate. Teeth gnawing the porcelain in the dark.

The smile is the most complex of automatic anatomical reactions. The subtle tugs and gentle adjustments give minute inflections of meaning. Any attempt at conscious control of the mouth instantly leads to terrible and embarrassing social misunderstandings. Better to snarl and dribble with intoxication than tweak the lips badly with the politics of necessity and acted response. Better to snap the jaw loose and use it to dig through into another fictional time.

8   *Not seen at all, but there, in the depth of night, where the wind holds its ribs against dream. The metal is gold. The attendant animal is the worm. And nearby grows hawthorn.*

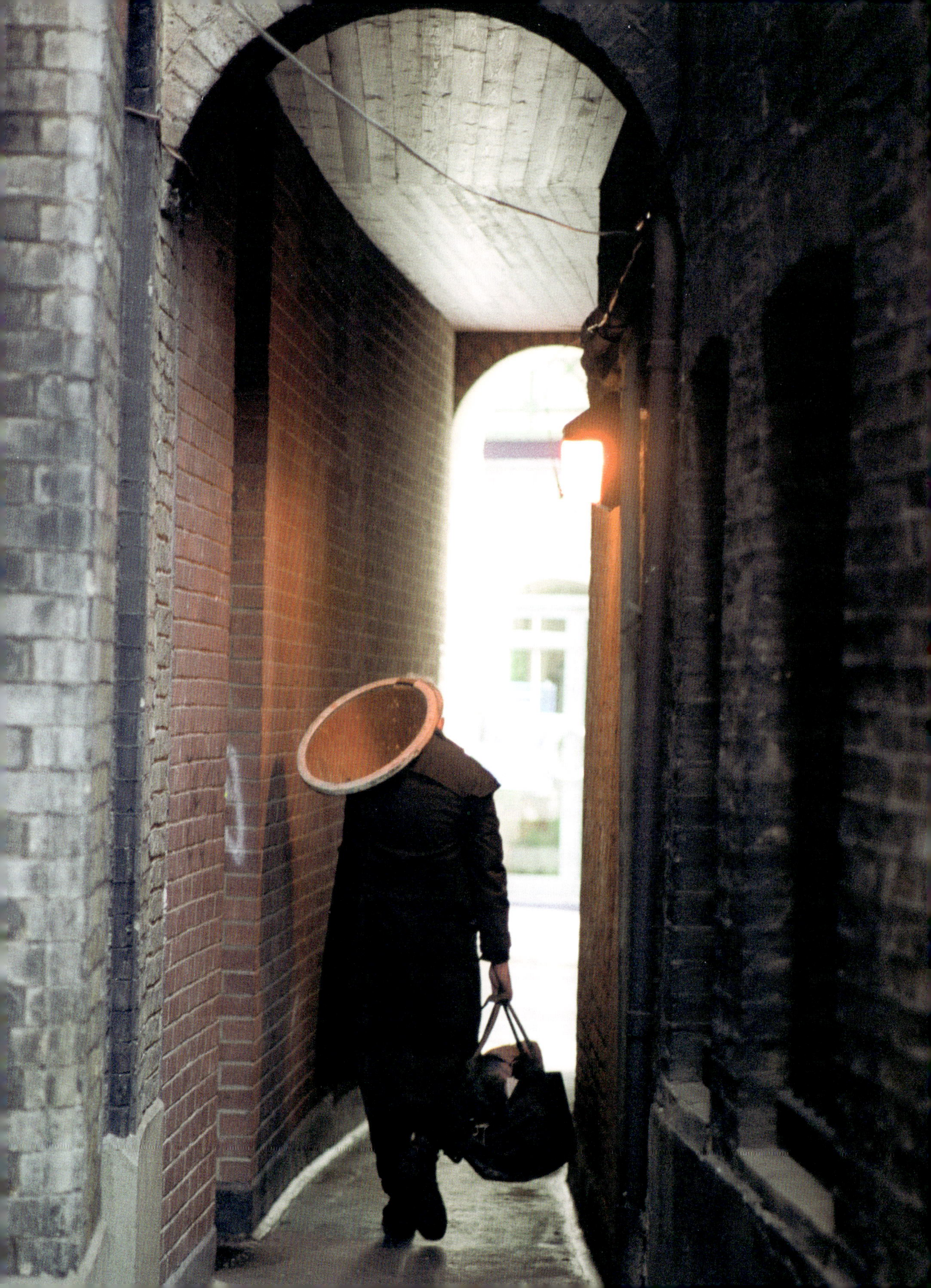

Third Angel

Class of '76

text by Alex Kelly

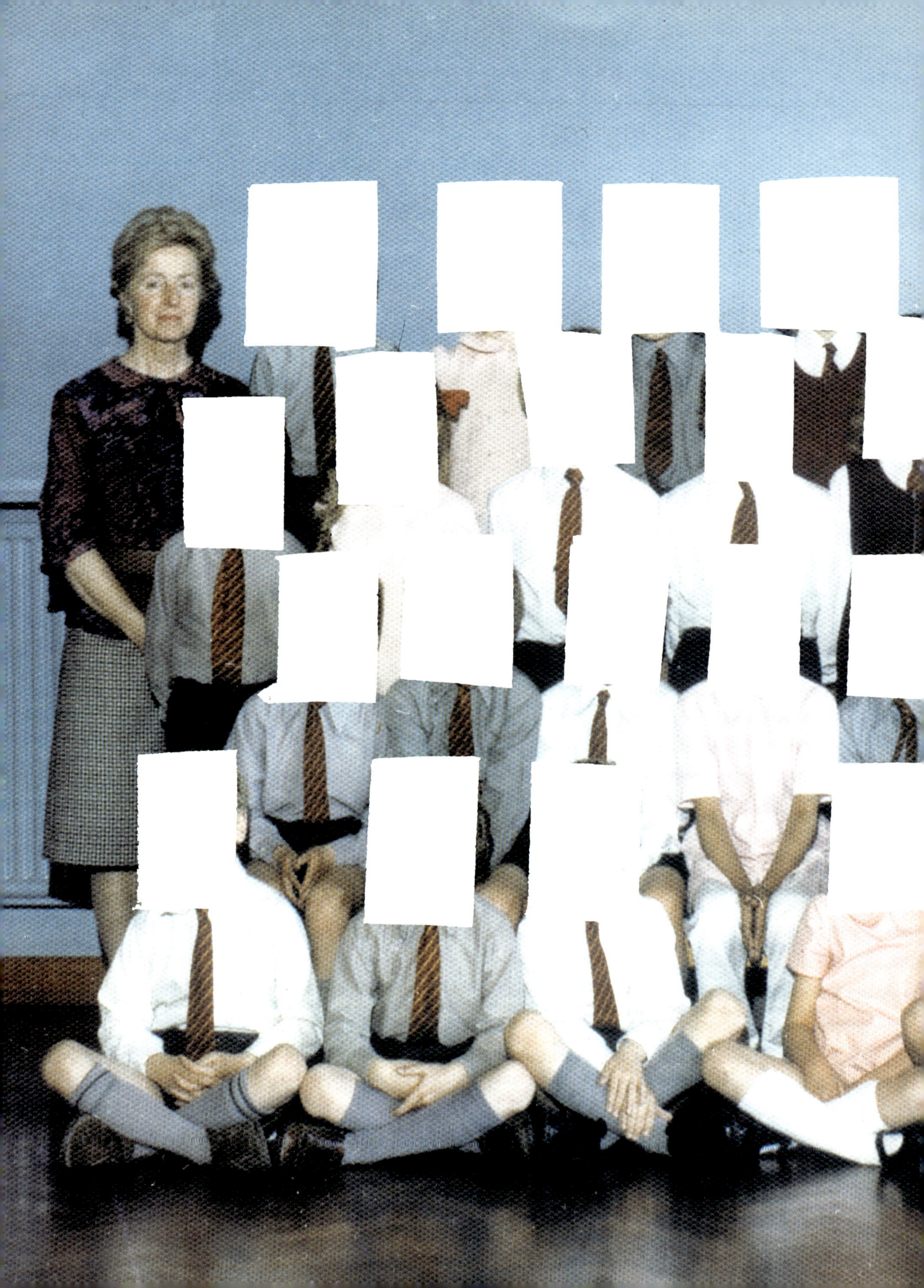

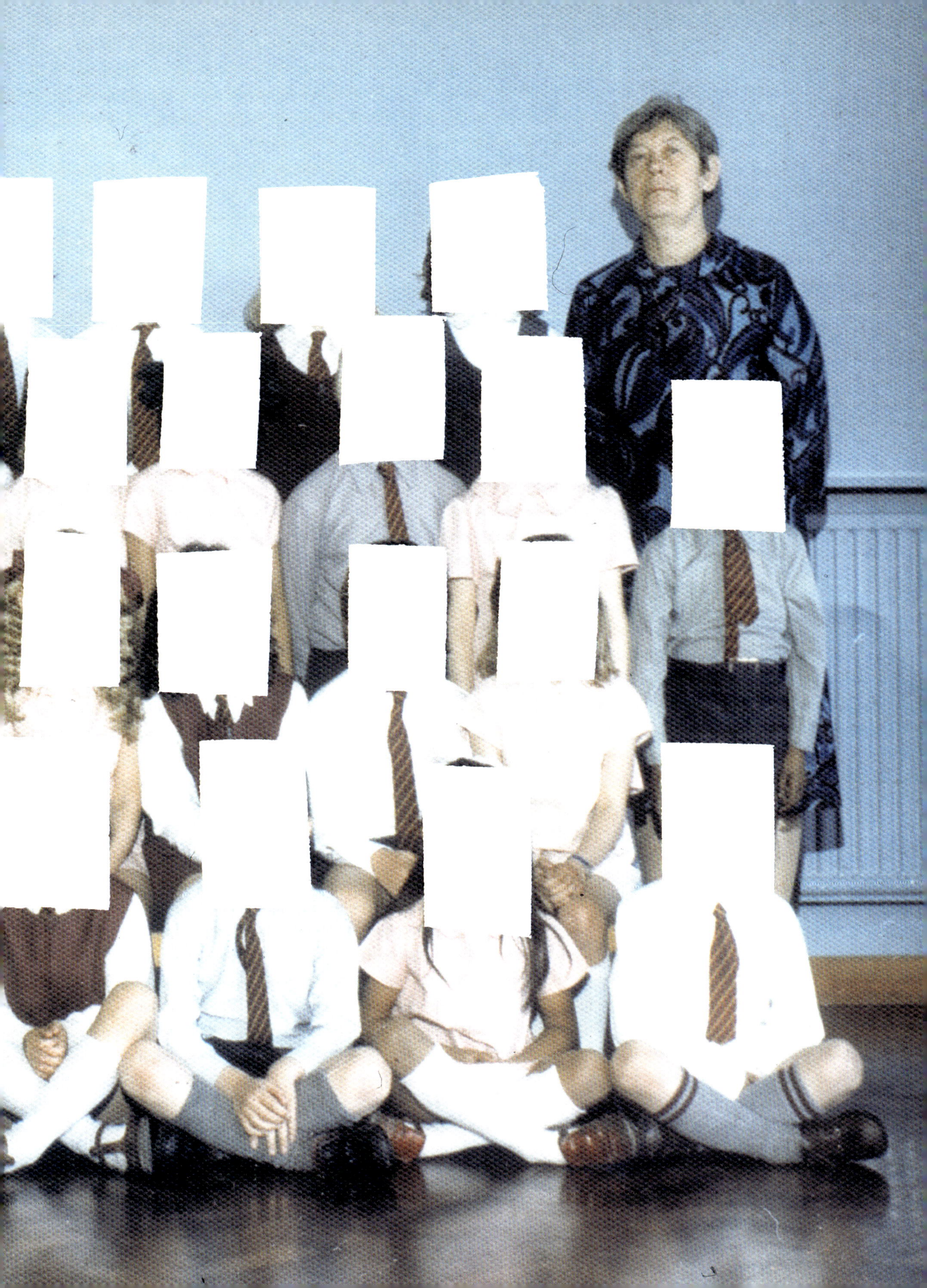

What Can I Tell You?

In January 1999, Third Angel made a fifteen-minute performance piece called *Class of '76* for a cabaret night in Coventry called *Successophobia*. We used my class photo from Chuckery Infants School in 1976, and told lies and fibs about those innocent faces staring out at the audience. What they were like at school, what they were doing now. The mundane and the fantastic side by side. We said that Lahkvir Singh played football for the world. We said that Paul Groombridge was bumped off by a cartel of car manufacturers. We made stuff up. I couldn't even remember everyone's name, so we made some of those up too.

Unfinished business. I was still in touch with a couple of my classmates from that photograph. Back in Walsall I would hear rumours of what people were doing, who got married, who moved away ... I'm the sort of person who sees an old name in the address book, someone I haven't seen in years, and wonders, "What are they doing now? What if I just dialled that number?" And this show seemed to be that urge writ large. And for once why not satisfy that urge? Find all the other thirty-four kids from that class photo, and ask them what they've been doing for the last twenty-four years. Then perform *Class of '76* again, but tell the truth.

I got a year register list from Chuckery Infants School. I'd hoped that the register would quickly fill in the blanks for me, but there were 128 kids listed: too much information. I couldn't tell which names were from my class, and which were from the other classes in our year. So I started with the easy ones: Iain Daniels with whom I'm still friends. Jason Frost, Richard Sadler, and Gillian Shakespeare: I was in touch with them in my early/mid twenties and still had their parents' numbers. I filled in the rest of the names with Gillian's help. Thought about where people's parents had lived. I got out the phone book. Cold calling. "Hi, my name's Alex and I was at school with Alison ..." Some of the class had clues to other people, and slowly the network spread. Some of them would talk for ages on the phone, wanting to know what everyone else was doing; some just weren't interested. I could understand that. I hadn't set out to make a reunion, but it was soon obvious that it would become one by default, or a partial one at least.

That class photo has been in my Mum's photo album since I brought it home in 1976. I have looked at it I don't know how many times. It is part of my history. Those faces, those children. The names I could remember. The names I couldn't. Some of those children I found I had clear memories of, particularly those I ended up at Aldridge Comprehensive with. I remember them more as teenagers or adults. Others I remember as children in infants and juniors. With about a third of them, however, the third whose names I couldn't remember, I found that this class photo, (along, perhaps, with the photo from the previous year) is my memory of them. The tilt of their head, their facial expression, their body language. This is how I remember them. A small two-dimensional image, recorded on that day in 1976.

My classmates were myths from my childhood. The memories I have of them probably bear little relation to what they were really like. My perception of them as children is defined completely by memories of one or two incidents. Talking to my old classmates on the phone, this project became about what we remembered of each other (and why?), and whether people had turned out as we expected. Iain Daniels a barrister in London – we expected that. We always knew he was

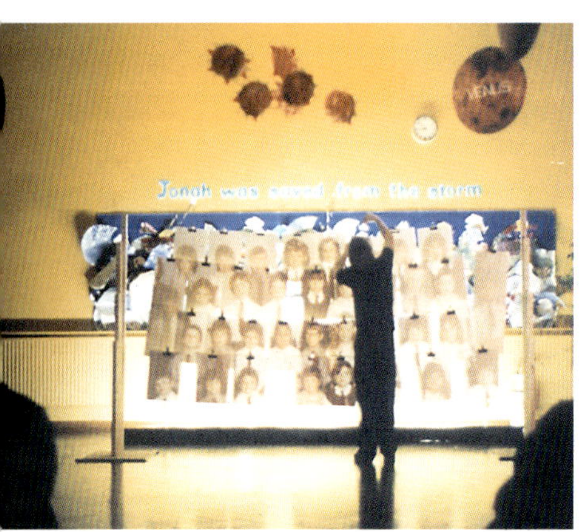

London-bound. Alison Cooper in a band, yes. Paul Groombridge: I don't really know what a Processing Geo-Physicist is (and he's explained it), but it's no surprise that Paul's one. This wasn't just about catching up on what people had done for the last twenty four years, it was about finding out who those children were back then, and why they became what they did: tracing a line from the past to the present.

More clues. More phone calls. More conversations. I'm running out of time. We have to start making the show, so rehearsals begin with a few conversations still outstanding. The actual performance is built around a simple visual trick. By projecting a slide of our class photo, I am able to recreate it (just larger than) life-size, on the spot that the photo was taken. I build the image one face at a time. School hall magic, summoning ghosts of the living. This is the visual peg to hang the stories on. There's way too much information in my notebook, and in the recorded telephone conversations. And other memories are still being recovered and caught each day.

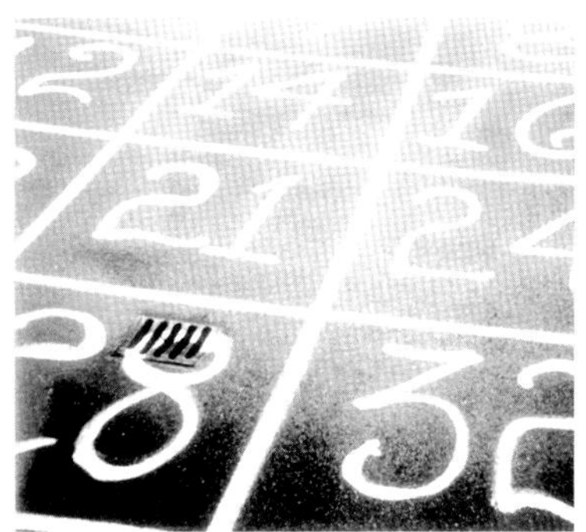

We are used to making work that borrows stories from our own lives and other people's lives. We're used to making work that strays into the grey area between the truth and fiction, memory and imagination. This is what we do: work that incorporates documentary detail and fiction but doesn't bother to point out which is which. But this piece is new to us. We find ourselves making a work that talks about real people and their lives, but this time many of them will be in the audience. I find that my loyalties to Walsall, to Chuckery School, and to individuals are all lurking in the work as it is made. I want to do these people justice. I want to represent everyone equally, and fairly. Which makes for a dull show. At some point in rehearsal Rachael, my Co-Director, says to me, "This isn't about them at all. It's about you, about how you see them. Tell us what you remember of them, what's significant to you. Some of them are more important to you, and that's okay." That is okay.

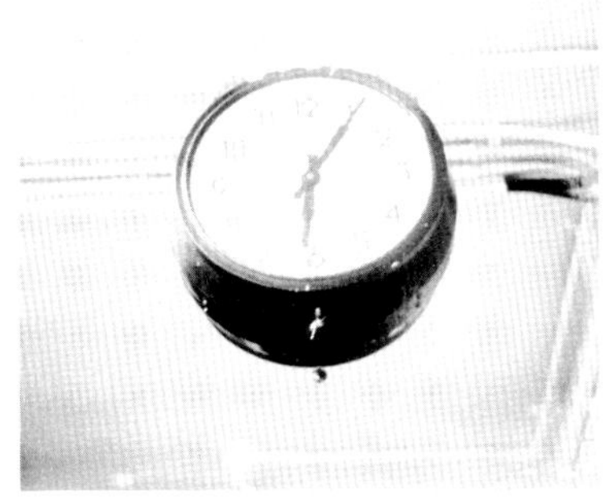

Friday 5th May 2000. I perform *Class of '76* in Chuckery Infants School Hall. And this time I tell the truth. The audience is a mix of people from the photograph (about ten) and other classes in our year, their partners and parents, my friends and family, some Live Art people and a few members of the public, many of whom have a connection to the school in some way. The performance is just one part of the social event. In the pub afterwards the Chuckery Infants School Class of '76 gather around a postcard of the photograph and compare notes and memories. Physically, some of us are clearly recognisable, and some look so different that they are accused of being impostors. But a lot of those kids are recognisable in the people we have become. Fourteen or so people with very different lifestyles. Some of us still live in Walsall. Some are married. Some have kids. Some of us run our own businesses. Some of us still live with our parents. Some of us are well-off. Some of us are skint. We all dress differently. We get on like a house on fire.

I didn't find everyone. And I didn't get to speak to everyone that I found. That task will continue, I suspect. It's still unfinished business. So would I do it again? I am something of a completist – but when does it end with this one? Annual updates from everyone in the photo? In the pub after the show I agree to do the piece once more, in twenty years. Which gives us time to all lose touch again.

Iain Daniels
Stephen Lea ... er spoke to him ...
Yeah?
Er, where are we, er, Stephen Lea, er ... going for a drink with him on Sunday ... in fact ...
Excellent ...
Yeah...
What's he up to?
Er, I dunno, I just um, had a chat w... briefly, and um I said I'm going to b... Walsall he said oh well, we'll meet up for a beer then, so I'm going to have a chat with him then ...
Bloody hell ... 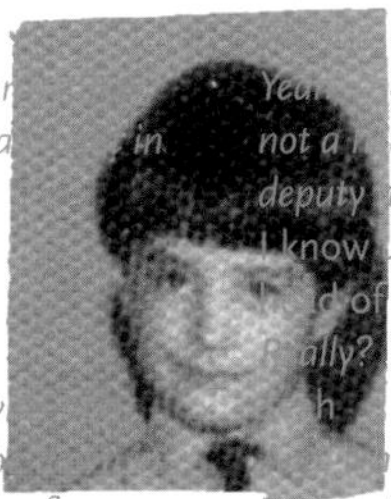
I'm gonna take the photo down, this photo down to see who he remembers, but interestingly he says that there's um, there's a guy he knows in Aldridge who's a doorman, who runs like the doorman on a couple of pubs in Aldridge who is called Stephen Petite, and he doesn't know, er if, if it's the same ...
... or whether he's bionic or not ... 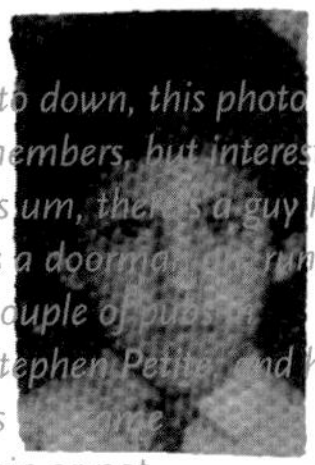
whether he's bionic, yeah [?] bionic for us, would be, be a good, good thing to be if you're a doorman, I reckon, being bionic ...
Yes, yes ...
So that would be alright, but er, 'cos Stephen Petite apparently left in juniors according to other people ...
Right ... 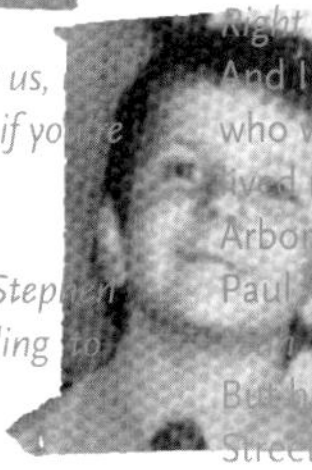
... in our class, so, that's probably why no-one knew what happened to him ...
Yeah
Richard Sadler, I was ...
Richard Sadler, yeah I ... spoken to him, no, I've spoken to his wife, Rachel, he lives in Nottingham somewhere, but er I haven't ...
The problem with people, the problem with people you've known subsequently, is your, your impression of them is based on what you knew of them past ...
Yep, yep ...
What you don't have is [...?] you see um, Paul Groombridge, and you think yeah he was that smart bastard who didn't have a TV [laughs].
... I mean its just um, my, I tell you, I tell you a story about, I knew something happened to me, I went to Paul Groombridges birthday party, whatever it was ...
Right ...
And um, I remember these things stick with you, I remember I had egg sandwiches ...
Yeah ...
... egg sandwiches, but I was as sick as a dog for two days afterwards ...

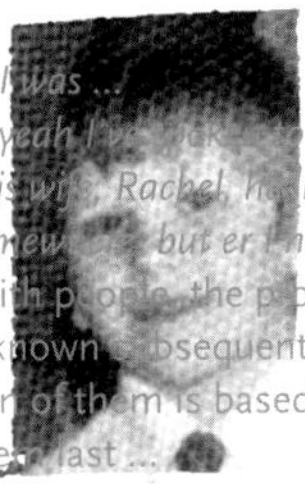

... a couple of years ago ... she's a teacher, in Brum 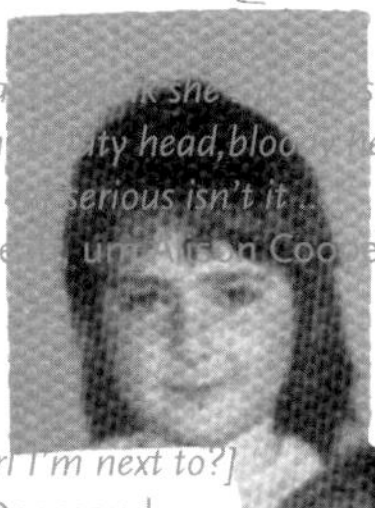
Yeah she's er, in fact I think she, she not a head, she's a deputy head, bloody hell, deputy head, it's a ... serious isn't it ...
I know um, well yeah um, Alison Cooper's into ... of music ...
Really?
Yeah
...who's the [girl I'm next to?]
Right ..., Kelsey Desmond 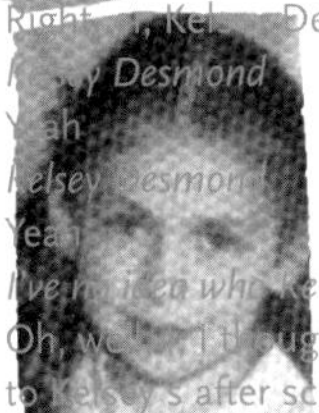 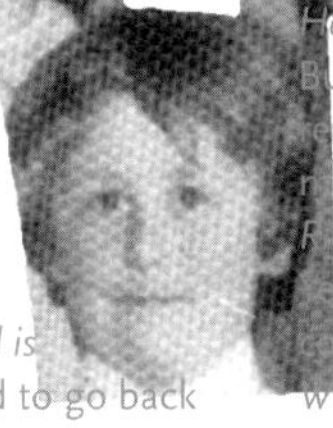
Kelsey Desmond
Yeah
Kelsey Desmond
Yeah
I've no idea who Kelsey Desmond is
Oh, well ... I thought that I used to go back to Kelsey's after school to be looked after, but my Mum says actually it was um, er, a childminder, I happened to go to the same childminder as Kelsey
Right 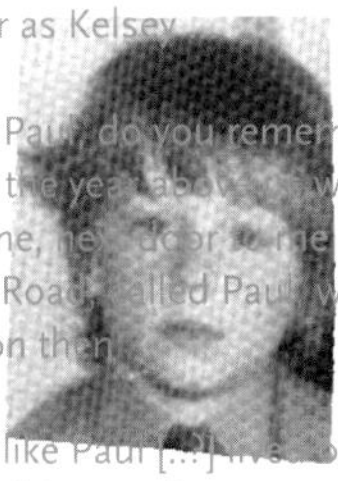 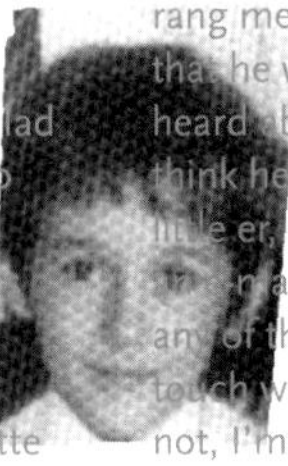
And I think Paul, do you remember that lad who was in the year below us, who I, who lived near me, next door to me at Arboretum Road, called Paul, well he was Paul Weedon then ...
Right
But he was like Paul [...] lived on Charlotte Street, I think he used to go as well, and we used to have to watch every night, I seem to remember, Michael Bentine's *Potty Time*, and I used to hate it, but I, I don't know if I hated because I associated it with not being able to go home ... 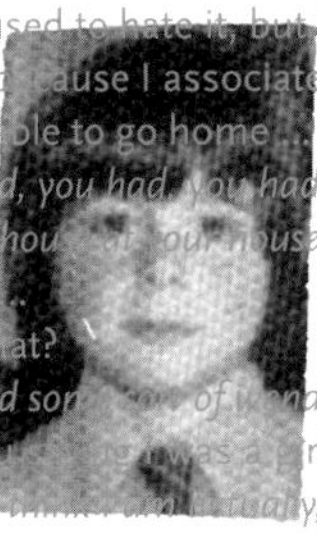 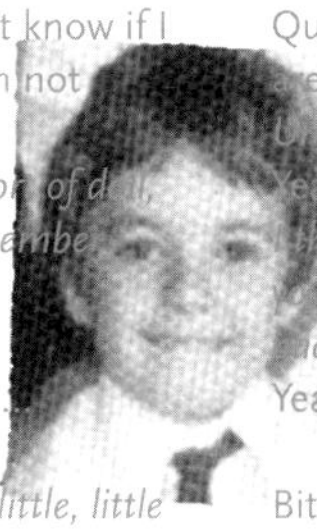
You had, you had, you had some sort of doll's wendy house, doll's house if I remember rightly ...
You what?
You had some sort of wendy house ...
Are you calling me a girl?
Yeah, I mean, it was actually, with a little, little plastic kitchen thing ... in Arboretum Road ...
No there was a plastic doll's house at my Nan's house,
Right,
But yeah, yeah like a little tent that looked like a house,
Ah, um, [laughs] I think you're a big girl ...
[and where's?] Neville Moody, I know Neville Moody has got the straightest hair that I've seen on anyone
[Laughs] Yeah, he's um he's in Glasgow,
Really?
Yeah, apparently being an engineer, um I've got his parent's number ...

[That wouldn't?] 'cos he was bright wasn't he?
Was he? 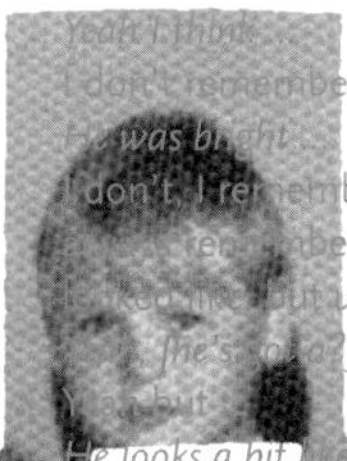 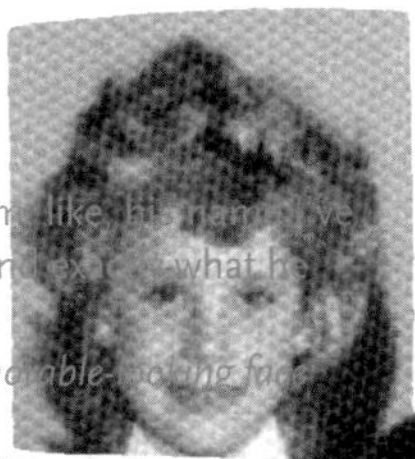
Yeah I think ...
I don't remember..
He was bright ...
I don't, I remember him, like his name I've remembered, and I remember what he looked like but um,
[he's not a] memorable looking face
Yeah but ...
He looks a bit like Matthew Parish actually 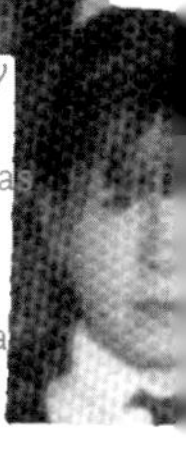 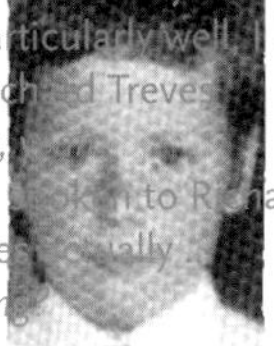
But what he was actually like I don't remember, particularly well, I know he was mates with Richard Treves
Richard Treves,
Yeah 'cos I've spoken to Richard Treves a couple of times actually
what's he doing
Um ...
He wasn't in our class, was he?
No, he wasn't in our class, he, he, 'cos he rang me up and he was really disappointed that he wasn't in the photograph, 'cos he'd heard about it and he was quite excited so I think he, he might be doing off his own little er, finding people, so, he sent me an email with a few names on it saying "any of these in the photograph, I can get in touch with them, of, for me, or if they're not, I'm going to try and get in touch with them anyway". 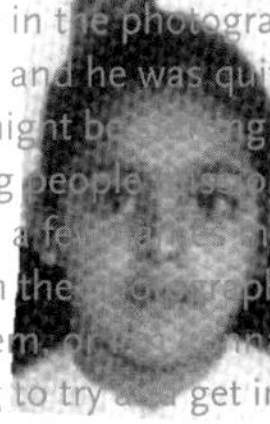 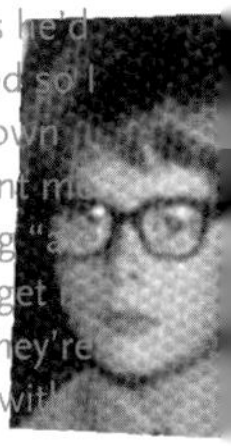
Did you find a lot of people have stayed in Walsall?
Quite a good, about half, I guess half of us are still in Walsall ...
Um ...
Yeah..
I think, one of the differences, is if you go to University, you often don't come back, as it were ...
Yeah, yeah 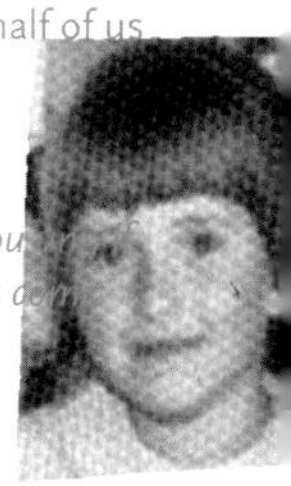
Bit of a surprise, him getting married, now who's the girl next to her?
Shazir Jaffri ...
Shazir Jaffri, yeah, yeah yeah yeah ...
And d'you know what?
What?
There's one Jaffri in the Walsall phone book, on Lee Road, Lee Close, actually ...
I just find that amazing there's only one Jaffri ...
So I phoned them up today ...
Yup ...
And that's, it's her family, um, and she er, after junior school um, they moved to the Isle of Wight ...

Stuart Boyd

So, um, I left school ...
Yeah
Er, high school, and then I went to do a
five year apprenticeship for my dad in a
[lock?] company ...
Right
And er, but 'cos I only got two O [?]
[like a dick?]
Right
I went to, did night school, got myself
an HND in mechanical production ...
engineering ...
Right
and then um, I went to work in a couple of firms, different companies, different er,
press companies in [Walsall?],
Right
and around Walsall, and er, I was a
technical estimator for [Valves?] that
kind of stuff ...
What's a technical estimator?
A technical estimator, ok, they er, say er,
it's mainly for Ford, Vauxhall ...
Right
and if they want a part making ...
Yeah
for a vehicle, it's mainly press work,
they call it press metal in different
shapes, they'd then draw it, and I'd have
to like, deconstruct the drawing, and say
right, we could make that, how much,
and where, how quick ...
Right
So, did that for around three years, um,
got made redundant when I was 22 ...
Bloody hell
Um, well we all knew it was coming
because it was the recession ...
Right
Then I went travelling for six months in
er Central America ...
*Right, your next door neighbour told me
that, though she said India I think ...*
That's my brother ...
Oh right
My brother, um, went travelling for
about six months, came back, and um,
didn't know what to do really so I signed
up for a degree
Right
I went, I came down to Bristol University
...
Oh right
And um, spent the last, spent three years
in Bristol getting a degree in engineering
...

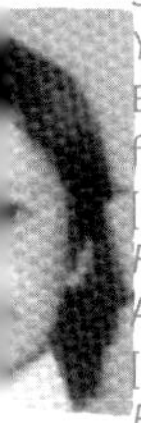

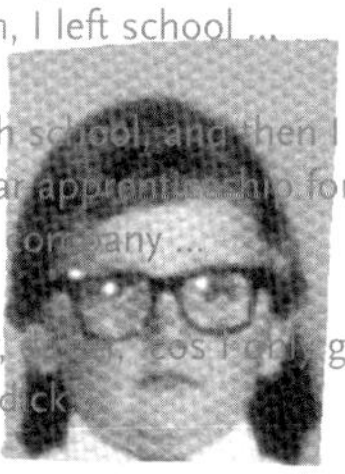

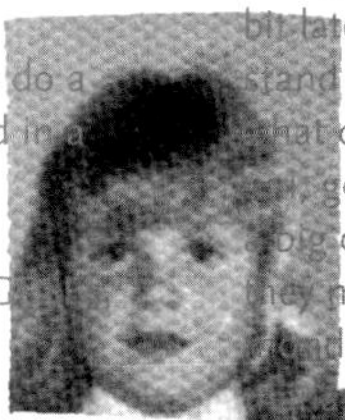

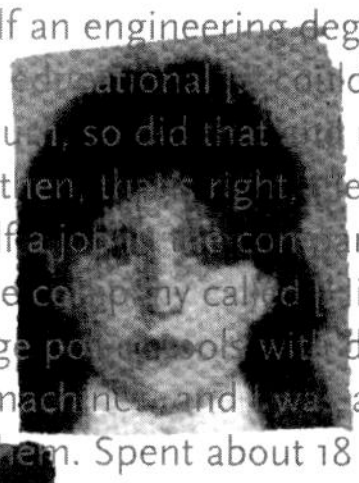

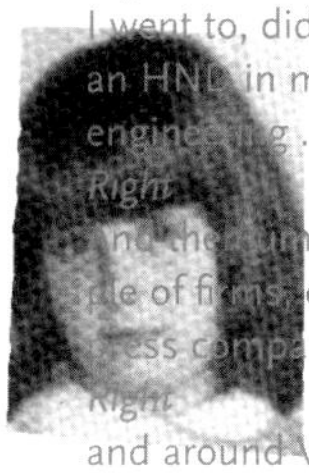

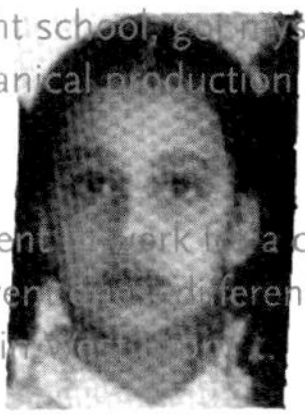

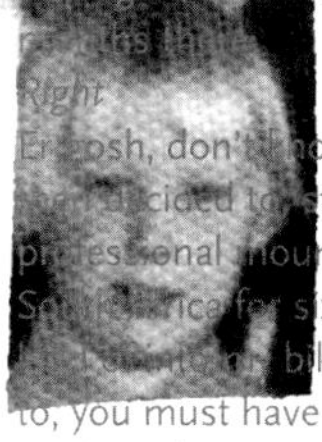

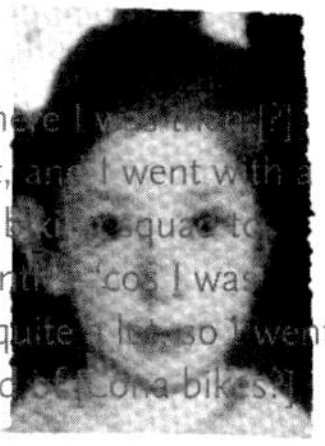

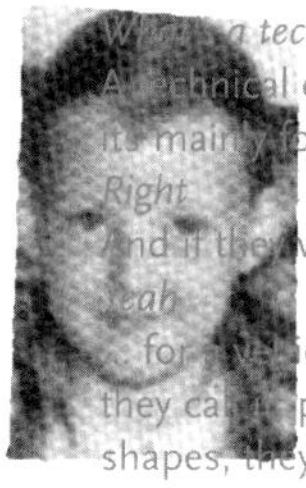

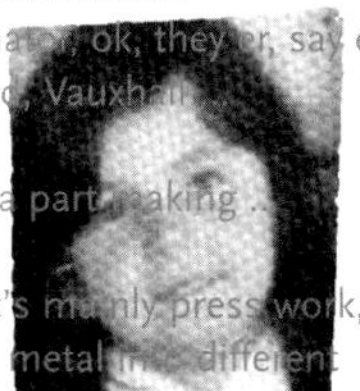

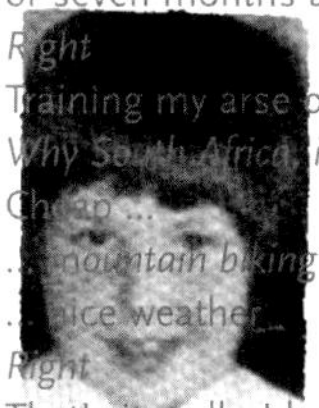

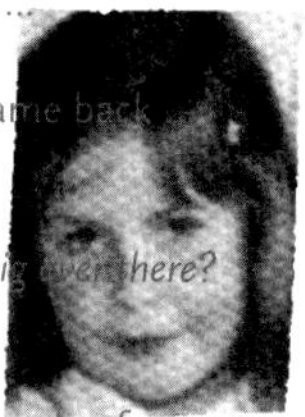

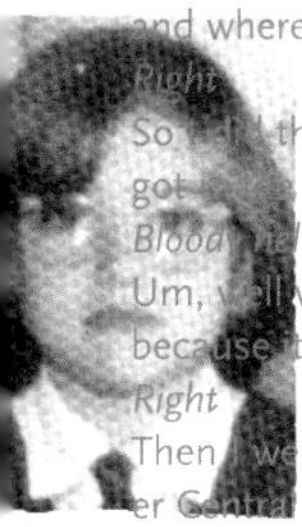

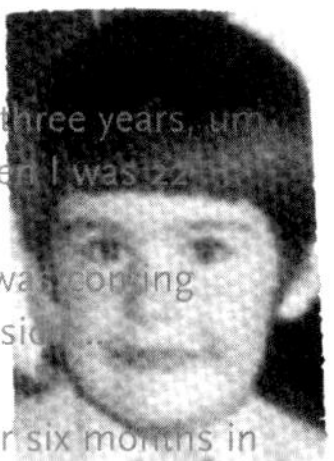

Right
So I got myself an engineering degree ...
bit late on the educational [?] couldn't
stand school, um, so did that and um,
what did I do then, that's right, I left er
and got myself a job in the company, like
a big corporate company called [Wiltey?]
they make huge power tools with dia-
mond cutter machines, and I was a
manager for them. Spent about 18
months [?]
Right
Er, gosh, don't know where I was then [?]
and I decided to stuff it, and I went with a
professional mountain biking squad to
South Africa for six months 'cos I was
getting into the biking quite a lot, so I went
to, you must have heard of Cona bikes ...
Yeah, yeah
I went with Cona to South Africa, um
stayed over there for about, oh about six
or seven months actually ...
Right
Training my arse off, er came back
Why South Africa, is ...
Cheap ...
... mountain biking really big over there?
Nice weather ...
Right
That's it really, I knew a couple of guys
over there, then what did I do ... er, came
back, and then, what did I do then,
[raced?] for a while, stayed at home with
my parents, and then decided I'd better,
do something I enjoy, I was a tennis
coach anyway, I don't know if you
remember I used to play a lot of tennis ...
Yeah, yeah
I'm a tennis coach, and I decided I
enjoyed teaching so ...
Right
I've been, I've been through the Bunac, and
you know Bunacamp stuff ...
Oh yeah 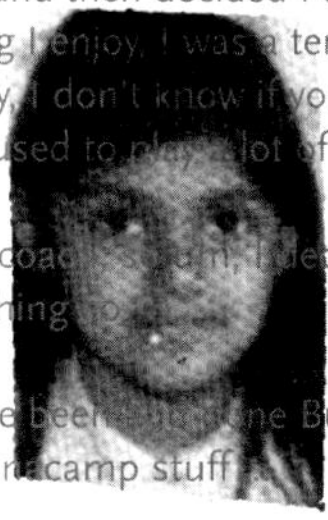
... over in the states, and things like that,
and, so I signed up for a teaching course,
'cos I got my degree, I did a PGCE ...
Yeah
... to be a teacher in design and
technology, so I'm now working as a head
of design and technology ...
Oh wow ...
I'm a teacher mate ...
*Bloody hell, it's a long and winding road to
get there ...*
Yeah it is isn't it, so I'm er, head of DT, in
a school down in Swindon, and I live in

Chippenham now ...
I know that, 'cos er your grandma told me.
Yeah
*Yeah, cos you, you were one of the harder
people to find ...*
Was I?
*Yeah, cos everyone could remember your
house on Longwood Lane ...*
Yeah, we left there in about 1980.
Yeah
1980
Yeah, people knew you'd moved away ...
Yeah
*But after that, the trail ran cold a bit there.
Really, how did you get in contact with
my nan then, cos I looked in the book?*
Um, no I didn't actually, I just er, um, I just
I went and knocked on the, Michelle
Symms couldn't remember which house it
was, and she said, um it is the white house,
and they've just, had those trees lopped, at
the front, like last year or something ... 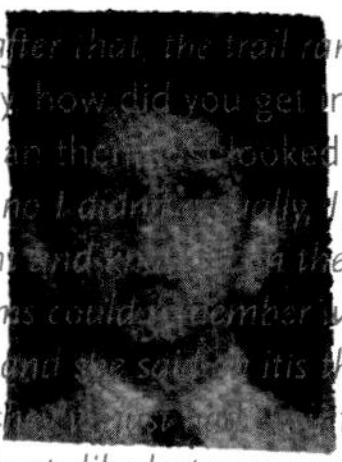
I liked that house, yeah ...
And, and so, that was my way of finding the
house, so I just went and knocked on the
door, and there was no-one in, but there was
a dead mouse on the mat, really
weirdly, um, and so I was going to write a
note and put it through the door saying, do
you have a forwarding address for the Boyds,
um, and then I thought, well hang on, if the
neighbours are still the same neighbours, so
I went and knocked, as you look at your old
house, the house on the left ...
Yeah
I went and knocked on their door, and she,
um, er obviously remembered you and
she, took my number, and then went away
and admitted to all the other neighbours,
and phoned me up with your nan's number ...
Oh wow ...
So um, I felt like a real detective ...
*Yeah, good isn't it ... brilliant, so that's
find me [?]*
Yeah
I keep, um I coach, I'm a tennis coach ...
Yeah
Pretty much half time as well as teaching,
um, I was, just, I just finished 'cos I
couldn't keep up with my biking cos it
don't pay anymore ...
Right
I was sponsored by Lotus, you know
Lotus cars ...
Was your brother into tennis as well?
Yeah, Andy's, Andy's now living in Zurich ...
Wow.

Peggy Phelan

Untimely

I have been thinking of the perfect first sentence for so long, the story has changed. It was going to be a beautiful, harrowing, Irish sentence. But now, having waited so long, such a sentence no longer fits the story. All the characters, all the acts, are the same. But my understanding of them is not. The sentence I intended to write has become untimely, even though it was never composed. This is the real source of writer's block: the events to be written have occurred but the writer's relationship to those events occurs while writing. When Kafka wrote, "I write to forget," he meant that writing is a step toward amnesia – the amnesia at which we hope to arrive so as to enter the present tense. The wager is that once something gets written down, the writer might get past it. This idea was the kernel of the psychoanalytic talking cure as well: put everything in a story and forget about it. But sometimes the very act of composing a story, trying to create a sequential time frame, is too daunting because one cannot recall when one noticed the inner structure that formed the external events. It's now very tempting as I write these sentences to become ever more abstract, scholarly, distant. But it's only a way of stalling. I am exhausted from waiting. Let me be direct.

I am trying to write about her. But I keep getting in the way. It's more than a matter of calculating 'the force of the observer', as the quantum physicists say. It's messier than that. Each of my efforts to tell the story make her too much my creature; it robs her of the unique thing she gave me – a refusal to become absorbed, to be lost in me. Women, you have no doubt heard, often have 'boundary' problems; they tend to melt across all the lines and seep into crevices you had not even noticed. She melted, but she remained herself.

When I was younger I played a lot of basketball and the coaches would all say, "If you have no idea what to do and you have the ball, call time-out." I was amazed by the concept of time-out. The clock stopped and everyone had a talk. It was such a beautiful idea. After talking, the game resumed. We still had the ball. We could breathe. The court seemed a little smaller. Sometimes I think I played basketball for so long because I fell in love with time-outs. I wish I had remembered to call one that day. But the game had gotten out of my control. I can't even say now who had the ball at that time.

When I could not write this story, I went for a session with an older writer

whose novels I admire. He said that he thought I was 'too close to the material.'
But I began to mistrust him: when one is trying to write an intimate story,
closeness is not something to be shunned. My problem has nothing to do with
space, with how far away to stand. Rather, I think my problem is temporal. Bad
timing has been the cause of our lost literature – I sometimes weep when I think
of all the stories and poems that have not been written because there's no place
to begin when nothing ends. It becomes impossible to know if it is too early or
too late to write the story, when the only certainty is that the story changes as
one writes it. I want desperately to fix this story, to contain it on this screen, on
this square little page, so I can bury it in a square little grave.

We buried my sister in one of those little white baskets. It looked like an
old-fashioned wicker hamper. I suppose it must have been sturdier than that.
But my memory of her is coloured by the sensation of fragility. Mainly I remember
her soft head – small velvety indentations beneath wisps of blonde hair. One day
I saw her lying in the crib; the next day I saw her lying in the casket. She arrived
so quickly; she left so fast. But even now she has not left completely.

It's a different kind of death I am trying to write here. Different because
everyone involved is still alive. It's a relief to mention my sister's death though.
It's a fact I can hold. She lived; she died. All the events in between are stories I
tell myself, tell my siblings, my mother, when I am drunk and feeling Irish. The
main thing I like about being Irish is the undisguised fascination with death.
When the writer I admired opined that I was too close to the material, he
assumed I was writing 'from life'. I felt the force and shape of his assumption
but did not challenge it. The chasm between us seemed too wide. Not having
been dead yet, or at least not in the biological way, from where else could I write,
if not from life? He meant that there are two distinct realms of experience – one
called reality, one called writing – or as he likes to say, "littterrrrattturre". I don't
feel the distinction so sharply. Where does literature come from and where does
it go, if not toward and away from life? Isn't that the place which readers and
writers seek to go in order to forget their own specificity and melt into the
creviced sentences of someone else's? There are so many ways to die. Biological
death tends to close the conversation, but I always think of it as an opening, a
way to begin. This has sometimes made it hard for me to talk.

I know it is past time to begin. To begin again with her. How I wish I could!
But I can't begin at the beginning, nor can I tell you how it ends. But I can say
that to me she is the entirely beautiful.

"The entirely beautiful" is not my phrase. I stole it from W.H. Auden's short
poem, *Lullaby*:

> *But in my arms till break of day*
> *Let the living creature lie,*
> *Mortal, guilty, but to me*
> *The entirely beautiful.*

Poor Auden. Too closeted to write, "let him lie," he had to resort to a profusion of indefinite articles, "the living creature", "the entirely beautiful." What he gains in the abstractions of the universal, he loses in the graphic compositions of sweating passion. I want my sweating passion – even if it makes me a bad writer. Invoking "the living creature", Auden invites his readers to fill in their specific version of the entirely beautiful. I am less generous. I want you to know her in all her weighty specificity. I want to crowd you with the details of her, and not point you toward your inner obsessions. But every time I try, I keep writing about me. It's terrifically exhausting. I want her story to become yours, but I want to erase my part in it. One way of saying this perhaps is to claim that this is not a poem, not a conversation. It's more like a letter I never sent to the intended addressee – to the you I was when I was with her, to the you I was when I might have been able to call a time-out. Now that time has passed and I am forced to replay it all again.

Neither one of us was any good at time. She was almost always late and I often misread schedules. Once I confused the flight number with the time of departure and I arrived at the airport six hours after my flight had left. She was always very busy, rushing, panicked. She kept telling me she had no time for me, in the most elaborately long love letters I have ever had.

But even saying these things turns us into some banal little couple you have already read about a million times. In the tabloids. In Balzac. Does it really matter in what genre you have encountered us? No. You will think you know the code, can deduce the semiotic sheaths and know us intimately. I know you cannot. This too makes it hard to write her story. If I said, "we dallied over morning coffee; we rushed over dinner," you would begin to add your own projections to my scene. I prefer you not to. But I also know this is a theatre of projection.

Please understand why I won't tell you how what happened happened. Anything I said would distort her, infect us. It did happen. I can assure you of that. There was desire. There was sex. There was writing. There was love. There was learning. But there was also something else. Something that retains its status as metaphor, as figure rather than plot. It was for me something about being ensnared in the cross-hair of a hunter's gun and discovering that I had lived my whole life trying to be prey.

I had known I had never wanted to be a hunter; but I did not know I desired to be hunted. She kept insisting I was hunting her, but what is love if not a series of reversals? Love, like reading, produces projections that go in the wrong direction precisely because they want to land in the heart. 'Love is blind', and I was a dart thrower aiming at the wrong target. I wanted to free her. And now look what has happened.

Blood on the page again. Still no smooth screens. No square page, no square grave. The gravity, in this story, belongs to time. Not to me. The state has dispossessed me. Here I am in my tiny cell. There she is, bloodless and gone. Before I met her, I had been fairly methodical, regular in my actions. With her, I was something, someone, else. That is why even now the whole story seems out of time, breathless before it properly begins.

To write about her is to damage what I most want to preserve. Not to write about her is to leave her unknown. Speech and its regretting; love and its ending: this is the theme of all literature.

I begin to believe that maybe the whole story is one sentence – a sentence that can only be written by a criminal in the words of another writer – a sentence that must live, if it is to be written at all, in the continuous present that constitutes the life sentence I am writing here. *To me, she is the entirely beautiful.* There is no 'was' for me now. There is no 'is' for her now. Between these two impossibilities, time beats.

I said that writer's block might be understood as a problem between the past and the present. The events the writer hoped to write down occurred, but in the act of writing, the writer's relationship to those events occurs. This is what I want to honour here, perhaps even more than I want to protect her. I want to claim time for literature's occurrence in me, in you, in her. All of this is for her. I know it is too late. I remain fundamentally untimely. Nonetheless I repeat again even now as you consume these words: *To me, she is the entirely beautiful.*

Graeme Miller

Overhead Projection

A wheel of twelve months

The Rabbit Tree
The Man in the Woods
The Book of Facts
Seedy Ron
Umbrella
My Little Pebble
O'Ryan's Belt
Starburger
The Reindeer
Storm of Bits
Fur Boots
Nothing

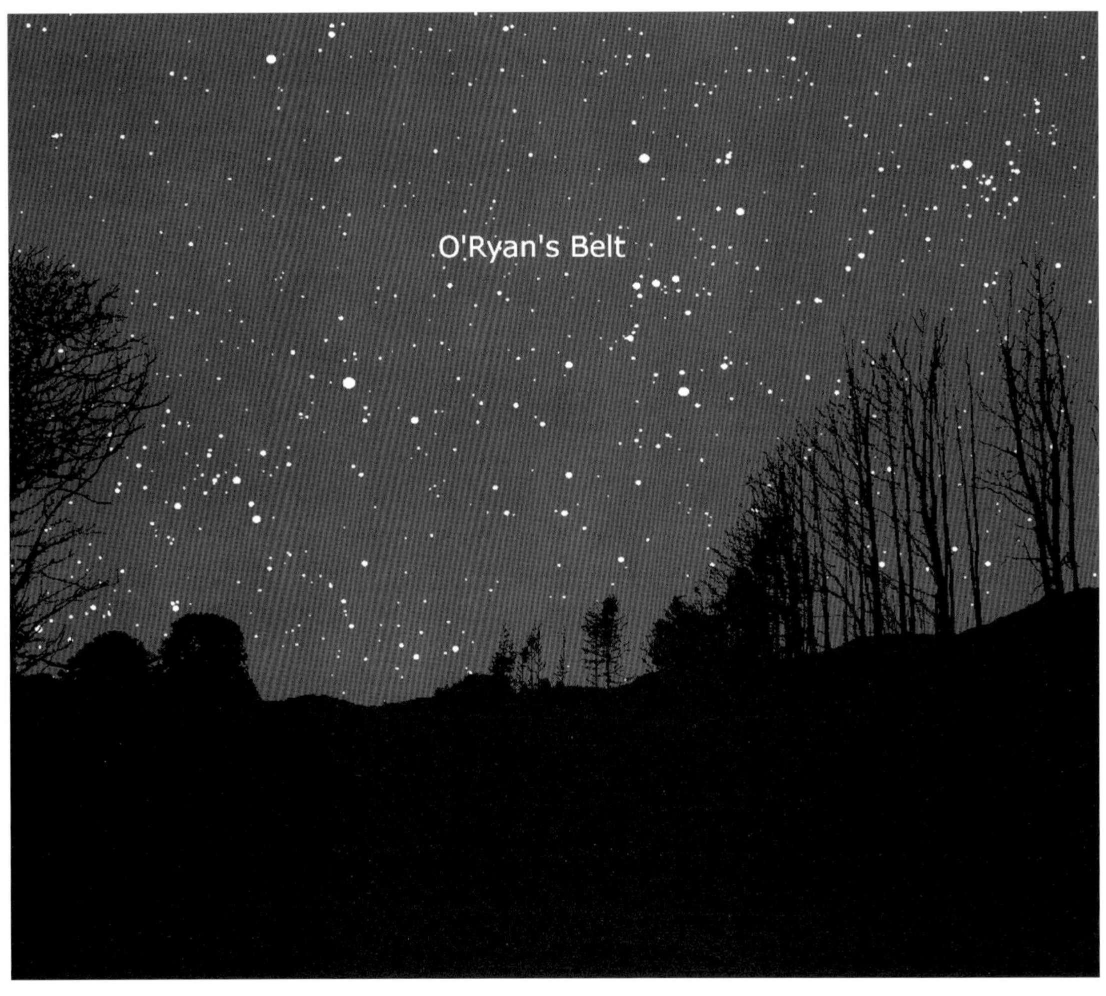
O'Ryan's Belt

The Rabbit Tree

The Rabbit Tree – a family ritual to point it out each and every time we turned the same corner. Hawthorn ears first, it would emerge over the brow of the down to receive its confirmation and bestow its constancy on our suburban tribe. Half a mile behind, another family in another Ford – only blue – are already excited as they are about to glimpse The Bear Tree.

Name that tune that pet that TV vet, that green field cul-de-sac all sold, but uninhabited. Name the milk cow but not the beef. Name against the abattoir and the arbitrary. Name a swathe through the masses, morning register, roll call, role call, call up the dead, mourning register. Name up just-enough-thank-you from too-much, too-many, The Rest. Name the Gold, Silver and Bronze but not the brass, paper, plastic, cardboard, gob and piss of seething runners-up.

Kipper has been re-homed. Her new owner has marked this by calling her Sally. Sally! Sally! ... Sally ... The cores of her soft brown eyes are extremely dark and filled with dog-eye jelly. A far-off universe of animal otherness. The howling Dogstar.

The Man in the Woods

The Man in the Woods has decided to walk for three days, just walking and sleeping where he stops, then walking again. Sleepwalking – a sort of test. Tonight he is testing his own shadows against the closing night to see where they meet. He should sleep, but the wood is filled with pheasants and hedgehogs and every other snuffling twigsnapping thing. He should sleep, but the sky is howling with stars.

Too thin, his eyelids will not shut out the piercing stellar radiation. The torch shows the watch and the watch shows 11 o'clock. Face down, a trembly sleep with the sensation of being tattooed by cold brilliant light. Sleeping Acupuncture-diagram Man is face down in the English woodland. Tree bark. Dogstar. Howling.

Dawn with its daylight haze and also with its slack drizzle thickening to steady cold rain has shut the stars off. The next ten days will not have one clear night. Hereabouts the settlement is in the valleys, leaving the hilltops clear and at five in the morning streetlights are still alight and in the mist make a little constellation before he descends. Acupuncture-diagram Man walks through the village before anyone else is up.

The Book of Facts

Actually the stars are still there. In fact they are there day and night and are, in fact, suns and, in fact, the lights of suns far-off and actually, old news, as the freshest information is, in fact, over four years old, which is when we last heard from our nearest neighbour, and actually, anything could have happened in the meantime. Did you know? Because what you did you won't. For what seems probably isn't. Did you know the twins aren't twins at all? Castor and Pollux, ten light years apart and of different parents. Now they say the Rabbit Tree is actually three trees you can walk between. The whole family is falling apart. Actually-factually the Rhyming God of Reason will not let up. For now the still night is no longer. *Stille Nacht Nicht.*

Night sky is viewed from a spinning sphere, hurtling in orbit at 29 k.p.s. around a star that is itself shooting off at a blistering 270 k.p.s. on the arm of a rotating galaxy in an expanding universe. In actual fact we are headed for Vega, but by the time we get there it will be gone. What is, is what was and all at high speed and numbing dimensions. It is information which I do not disbelieve, gathered by radio waves and infra-red and spectroscopic data. Hubble Trouble.

Seedy Ron

In the Astronomy hours I click through the 'Starry Night' program and spook myself. With time and date set for now and place to London, I open a window on the sky and it shows me the horizon and a deep blue sky filled with stars, planets and galaxies. Here it is never cloudy and even daylight can be removed. It will scroll forwards in real time and, if I line it up with the direction the computer is facing, it acts as a little stellar window. But you can shift your location within the solar system and also elevate above your location. One evening, I climbed several miles over Hackney and into space. I fixed my location in space and let the program roll time forward. Earth, with my friends and family on board and moon in tow, wandered off into the year ahead leaving me, like a lost child in a department store. I knew the Earth would come back for me. It did come back, but had drifted off its year-old course and passed me by. I could not climb back down the ladder I had climbed up. It was no use calling; I might wake my real family. 'Starry Night' is a Mortality Engine – only recently it showed that I would be dead by the time Halley's comet next came around. It is a fairly blunt prophet and spares no-one to show that distance To is also distance From, that man is the measure of all things, but also all things measure man.

Umbrella

Swirling, hallucinogenic night just three hours into the year 2000 and swaying home through the Scottish dark. The oil of what I see repels the water of what I know. Skull drilled with a galaxy of facts and eyes and body tattooed with starlight. I am porous and cannot, try as I might, make the leap of filling the space between myself and the stars with any real distance. I am deprived of my stereoscopic measure of distance and I cannot perceive motion. I am flattened by this ceiling. My umbrella of knowledge has been shot through with ancient light and, on this glorious night, believable distance ends at the horizon.

My Little Pebble

Take a walk along a stony beach. Find a pebble, learn it and befriend it. Then throw it hard and watch with a parental eye where it lands. Before you forget, run and find it. It is surprisingly easy to recognise. Each parting and reunion brings a certain closeness which makes the eventual loss all the more poignant. When you have given up the search, you might de-consecrate with only-a-stonedom and leave it to rest among the infinite as you crunch back home. "You should take your children to the sea when they are young" says the Dean, "It gives them a sense of the Infinite". Take them to a stony beach and they can also practice this game of life and death, meaning and meaninglessness. For it is our mortal souls we chuck down the beach. They should sleep well tonight …

A grain of sand is to the beach and all the beaches and dunes, what a star is to the whole skyful. Not infinite, but bloody many. To choose is to be chosen. To single something out is to confirm our own singularity. The Singularity is embryo of the Universe. As Above So Below. Our Lucky Star is a grain that helps spell out I-N-F-I-N-I-T-Y or a lost fleck in an arbitrary chaotic mass. It might depend on your mood.

O'Ryan's Belt

You can name a star for free and you can also pay. For a price your star name gets entered into a book and you receive a certificate. It'll cost you, mind. And who keeps the book and for how long? The stars spell out d-i-s-p-e-r-s-e-d c-e-l-e-b-r-i-t-y, which, like LONGEVITY magazine, is a sign of the times. And like any star system we find that the big slots are taken. Because no-one really has access to the book or interest in it, this immortality is like karaoke in a soundproof cell. O'Ryan's Belt is in the celestial suburbs and no-one is talking to their neighbours. The 'burbs are built on ancient sites and the milky way is still a river of souls. Alpheratz, Sadalachbia, Dschubba, Deneb, Vega, Menkar, Menkent, Nunki, Adrian Meadows.

It is a miracle of the Shopping Monkey species that we write our names on a blackboard we now know to be shifting, expanding, melting and reforming. As fast as we can write the letters fall back to earth. Science has sent the twelve-spoked wheel of the heavens a-wobbling. It makes no more sense than naming the particles in an exploding sack of salt. Even greater then, this miracle.

Starburger

Stars are out. Movie and TV actors, hotel ratings. Graphic design staple to suggest antiquity, fate, point of focus or mark of approval. Packaging for nursery and aromatherapy products. Cabaret backdrop, love cyclorama. Evening paper syndicated horoscopes. Five point, six point, emblem of the masonic, the revolutionary or fundamental, the religious and the military. The heavens come pre-named and stamped with a mixture of antiquity and mystery. Count your lucky, catch a falling, guiding, twinkling, well-worn lyric that peppers the sentences. We live in a cosmos of pre-boiled stars and we do not look up.

And now, so very recently, streetlight obscures our contact with the source of these images. Streetlight, burning the fossil fuels of stored starlight, or drinking the nuclear power of our home-made stars, is readable in space. Another cosmos of our own and we do not look up. The mariners on GPS do not look up. And neither do I, city dweller, traffic dodger, usually late. But there is something in The Stance ... and at Liverpool Street Station the rush-hour crowd stands rapt with faces upturned to the destination board. Naked-eye astronomers. Soul bearers.

The Reindeer

Our 88 official constellations of the Western, scientific world were finalised and agreed in 1930. Half of these were already named in 2000 B.C. and each of these was made up by someone. All at once in a small area of the globe, the 'W' of Cassiopeia, the African Queen was also the Hand – stained with henna – of the Arabs and the Faery King to the Celts. Triangulum was Delta to the Greeks and Sicily to the Romans. The twins were twins in Europe, Asia, Australia and Polynesia. Our current 88 have been set from the world view of a Middle Eastern and European consortium united by the culture of marine trade and the culture of science. Behind the orthodox is a map of flux and erasure. The skies of the last 4000 years are littered with overlooked constellations and rejected sky objects. Abandoned Musca Borealis, the sinister Lord of the Flies. The Psaltery of George II has gone. Electric Machine and Chemical Furnace have been struck off along with Tarandus, The Reindeer, named by Le Monnier in 1736 to commemorate his trip to Lapland. Under the official chart are countless rubbings-out of both the pompous and the personal. But gone too is Heaven's Temporary Granary and with it, the wealth and diversity, the complexity and music of the bulk of global cultures. As above, so below.

Storm of Bits

Let us say that in this year of Now and Then and also Big and Small, we have permission to wipe the slate clean and rewrite the night sky, or undo the agreement of 1930 and overwrite the overwritten. Sandwich all these individual cosmoses together and the web of clashing connections and overlapping networks may make a map that is hard to navigate by. Now is complex and Then a lot simpler. Our Dissipating Structures, our 48 channels and global polyculture, cities of information, our overlapping and sheer quantity might be reflected in our chart. As we converge on authorised world versions, we simultaneously diverge. As our science begins to embrace disorder so we must co-habit with Chaos. Constellations might as well be called Many Small Things, General Mess, or Storm of Bits, or just Help. Billions of people have moved into the village.

The Rabbit Tree was a conarboration that marked the core and the limits of a family of four. To connect the trees, the dots, the stars, is to build a society. All the names of stars, planets and constellations were made up by individuals but only persisted because they were shared. Constellations are the shape of agreement and the music of culture.

Fur Boots

Nothing

Let us say we rename the stars in this the year of BIG and SMALL. A name game to find out if and where we might agree or disagree – a slight thing and an excuse to send the players out to step into the fur boots of our ancestors and watch the sky as it is. I suspect that labelling the stars is like trying to label a shoal of fish with a biro. If the names really do run out at the horizon then that, at least, is as it is. To look up on a clear night for more than five minutes is to drink up five minutes of as-it-is. The predigested slips away. The repetitive medium-sized shifts into UNIQUE, BIG and SMALL. Small being, big universe: it draws us up to god size then swats us like gnats. And the difficult science legends can add a giddy thrill to naked-eye astronomy and give the starlight distance and time which is bewildering and humbling. Distance To is distance From. Our light takes as long to reach Alpha Centauri as theirs does to us. We are nature. Actually-factually we are stardust. There are no names but only acts of looking. If we set the model universe in motion and pour in time, the points of light are revealed to be moments. Our lookings-up are moments too. Our writings and erasures are moments. Singularities in time. Face-up, shoulders-back, on a street corner. As is. What can you say?

Ann Whitehurst

Conceiving Difference

...vick.

...on June 22nd after a
...r (G.I.) of Weobley.
...rtin, father-in-law of
...Private Committal
...reford Crematorium
...29th at 12.40 p.m.
...orial Service at St.
...s Church, Weobley at
...owers only please
...sired for Cancer
...ary Care Unit,
...ospital, Birmingham
...Evans, 23/24 Gaol

...y, died peacefully
...ursing Home,
...he will be missed.
...et Crematorium,
...riday, June 30th at
...iends are welcome to
...H.R. Palmer Funeral
...te, tel. 01843 592 720.

...died peacefully on
...ed 91. Much loved
...nd dearly loved
...great grandmother.
...n Wood
...low on Friday, June
...mily flowers only.
...ed to Macmillan
...onner, 29 High
...ex CM5 9DS.

peace. Remembrance service at Bowdon Parish Church on Friday, June 30th at 1 p.m., followed by private cremation. No flowers please. Donations to Broughton House, Home for Disabled Ex-Servicemen, Park Lane, Salford, Lancs.

NAPIER.—BEVIL 'CHARLES' ALAN, of Ballater, Aberdeenshire, suddenly but peacefully at home on Saturday, June 24th, aged 81. Beloved husband of Pamela, father of James and John and grandfather. Services at St. Kentigern's Episcopal Church, Ballater at 12 noon and at West Chapel, Aberdeen Crematorium at Hazlehead, 2.15 p.m. on Thursday, June 29th.

O'BRIEN.—Susan Philippa (née Hort), of Druid Stoke Avenue, Stoke Bishop, Bristol, died June 26th, aged 61 years. Wife of Dr. MICHAEL O'BRIEN and mother of Catherine, James, Liz and Claire. Requiem Mass at The Church of the Sacred Heart, Westbury-on-Trym, Bristol, Wednesday, June 28th at 12 noon. Burial to take place in Ireland.

PETTMAN.—DORIS FRANCES MARION, dearly loved mother and grandmother, aged 94, passed peacefully into the presence of her Lord, Sunday, June 25th. Funeral inquiries 01622 850840. Family flowers only. Donations, if desired, to RNIB, c/o A.W. Court, Grafty Green, Maidstone.

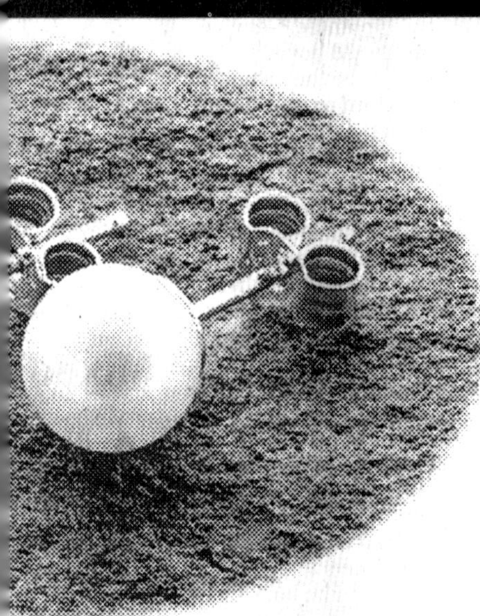

...der

...1509 638 625; 24 hours a day, 7 days a week, to place
...credit card service. Enquiry lines open 8.30 to 20.00
...3.30 to 16.30 Saturday and Sunday.
...3718
...38 664
...sales@readersoffers.co.uk

...coupon to order by post, sending a crossed cheque or postal
...ddress on back), or quoting your credit card number.
...cash. Send your coupon to:

...ph, Pearl Earrings Offer (V3718),
...t, Loughborough, Leics, LE11 5XL.

...esses only. Please allow up to 14 days for delivery.
...ty. If you are not fully satisfied, please return within

The Daily Telegraph

(Please use block...)

...HEREBY KNOW that we dwell in him, and he in us, because he hath given us of his Spirit. And we have seen and do testify that the Father sent the Son to be the Saviour of the world.
1 John 4.13-14

BELOVED J. Me 2 U R still fabulous & I'm smitten. Luv U 2 bits. Luv always M.

CIGARETTE? You are the gentleman I met in the interval at The Royal Albert Hall, June 21st. I should like to offer you a cigarette in return.

2 CU AGAIN; weary with toil...uno VAIEIMIAEI.YI.

Articles for sale/wanted

A BETTER PRICE guaranteed for all Masonic articles, medals, regalia, objects etc. Tel. 020 7229 9618.

A BIRTHDATE NEWSPAPER original. Freephone 0800 906609. http://www.historic-newspapers.co.uk

ALL TICKETS AVAILABLE for all Sold Out Events, sport, theatre, pop. All best seats, 020 7925 0085 / 020 7930 0800.

A NEWSPAPER for that special date 1642-2000. Most titles available. Remember When; 020 8763 6363 or Call Free 0500 520 000.

TRADITIONAL YORK, Pennant Limestone and Slate flagstones and floor tiles. Handmade Terracotta. Cobbles etc. Masonry service. National and International delivery. Holley Hextall 01380 850039 (Wiltshire).

WIM. DEBS. All Concert, Theatre, Sporting events. Tel: 020 7240 6266.

4 TICKETS, Glyndebourne, Saturday, 1st July. Peter Grimes, unable to use, for face value £130 each. Tel. 020 7246 6212.

Announcements

CONGRATULATIONS to all Disabled People on being conceived. May we continue to be born. www.outside-centre.org.uk

Wimbledon tickets

WIMBLEDON No.1 COURT SEATS. Official Debenture Tickets from £125 for sale by original owners. 020 7935 7516.

WIMBLEDON DEBENTURES required full books and odd days. Best prices paid, discretion guaranteed 020 7925 0085 or 020 7930 0800

General

Telegraph Reader Offer

The Millennium Barograph

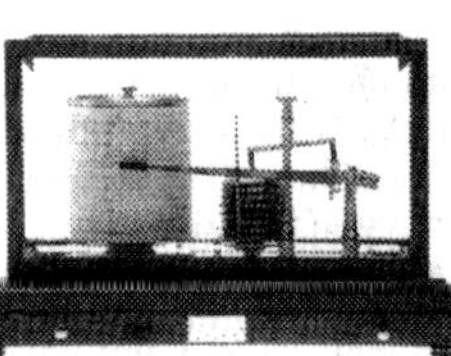

For further information on this mahogany cased precision Barograph and Millennium engraveable plaque please telephone (01582) 842 840...

General

Telegraph Reader Offer

The Millennium Rocking Horse

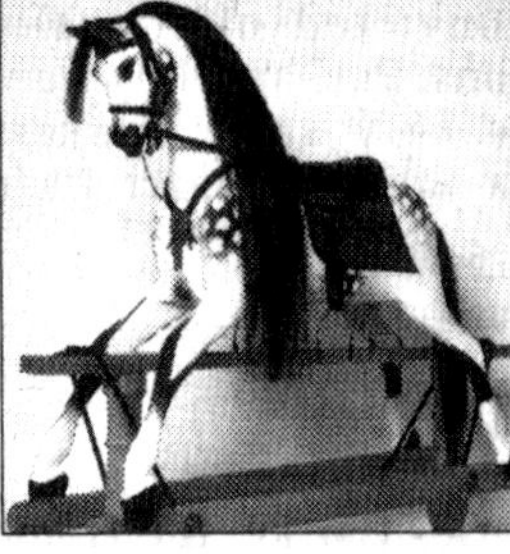

For further information please telephone
(01582) 842 840

or write to: The Rather Nice Company, PO Box 550, Markyate, Herts. AL3 8QP
Facsimile: (01582) 842 113
e-mail: telegraph@rathernice.co.uk

Kindred Spirits
BROWSE LINES
To hear the latest selection of advertisers, just dial the number below:-
09063 678 997
Lines are open 24 hours a day, 7 days a week
09063 Calls are charged at 60p/minute at all times

CONDITIONS FOR ADVERTISING
All advertisements are accepted subject to the publisher's standard conditions of insertion.

For a copy please write to Karen Adams at 1 Canada Square, London E14 5DT.

The Daily Telegraph
WHILST CARE IS TAKEN TO ESTABLISH THAT OUR ADVERTISERS ARE BONA FIDE
Readers are strongly recommended to take their own precaution before entering into any agreement.

WIMBLEDON CAUTION
Except for debenture tickets, it is unlawful to buy or sell tickets...

Miss A.S Katason...
The engagement is announc... between Guy, elder son of Mr Robin Kingston, of Sunningdale, and Mrs Fidel... Kingston, of Banstead, and Alexandra, younger daughte... Mr and Mrs Sergei Katason... of Protva, Russia.

Mr R.D. Hirst and Miss S.J. Bar...
The engagement is announc... between Richard, eldest son... Mr and Mrs David Hirst, of Orlingbury, Northamptonsh... and Samantha, daughter of... Paul Barnes, of Aspley Guis... Bedfordshire, and Mrs Jean... Barnes, of Weybridge, Surr...

Mr J.J. Rhodes and Miss M. Tana...
The engagement is announce... between Jeremy, younger so... of Mr E. Robert Rhodes, of Rickmansworth, Hertfordshi... and Mrs Sylvia McCormick, of Chesham Bois, Buckinghams... and Mieko, younger daughte... of Mr and Mrs Tanaka, of Os... Japan.

Mr R. Kljun and Miss F.A. Sm...
The engagement is announce... from Australia between Rob... son of Mr and Mrs Joseph Kljun, of Mount Gambier, S... Australia, and Fiona, elder daughter of Mr and Mrs Joh... Smith, of Ash, Aldershot, Hampshire. The marriage wi... take place in Australia on March 24, 2001.

BR...

Unlikely slam
By Tony Forrester

Dealer South
Vulnerability E/W

```
                  ♠ J 10 5 4 3
                  ♥ Q J 8 4
                  ♦ Q 9
                  ♣ 4 2
 ♠ Q                              ♠ 8
 ♥ K 7 6          N               ♥ A 10
 ♦ 7 6 3 2     W     E            ♦ K 10
 ♣ K Q 9 8 6      S               ♣ J 10
                  ♠ A K 9 7 6 2
                  ♥ 5
                  ♦ A J 8 5
                  ♣ A 3
```

South	West	North	E...
1♠	Pass	3♠(!)	P...
6♠	Pass	Pass	P...

Contract 6♠
Declarer South
Opening Lead ♣K

TONY Waterlow's team g... to a flying start in the C...ford's Cup final when Victo...verstone and Oliver Seag... and made a most unlikely... on the deal above. Unf...nately for them, this was s...thing of a high water ma... the squad rather surpris...failed to make an impact o... event as a whole.

The result of the auction... tred around North's respo... 1♠. At the prevailing vul...bility he was anxious to ... life difficult for his oppo...

The Only Invitation

To Those Not Allowed

We are celebrating the conception of all disabled people and want to invite you to the party. It's to be a commemoration too of the lives you should have had. We would love it if you could be there.

I was conceived and fortunately allowed to be born fifty years ago this new millennium year and because it is the new millennium, the dawning of the new genetics age and probably our last chance as a people, we decided to celebrate the event and to remember.

We thought of inviting people who are, have been, or will be significant. I don't know what significance you would have had as yours is thought a life not worth living. Ours too but luckily we escaped and are here now. We know this will not be the case in the future, our presence is increasingly disallowed, so our party is to commemorate all of us too.

The party is to be a yearly event. We will look for significance, for significant people and throw a party as the only remembrance, the only memorial so far set up throughout all ages, all countries and peoples, the only one set up to honour and remember the lives of disabled people who have been and are, massacred, institutionalised, not allowed life. You are not forgotten as long as we remain.

We take your acceptance as read
and your absence as involuntary

love

Myther White

Gilane Tawadros

A Thousand and One

Sweating, fucking, sleeping, dreaming.
Blue and green butterflies hover above the archipelago of sweat and semen stains on the soiled mattress whose pale pink material has faded only slightly. The mattress is a dumb object, mute witness to the actions that once took place over it and the people who occupied it. It bears the dirty traces of mundane bodily functions, the mingling of blood and sweat and semen. The itinerant artist, a Brazilian by the name of Eduardo Padhila, has stitched some words into the fabric like clumsy handwriting scrawled onto a hasty note. From a distance, it reads: "Abstinence conundrum".
Sweating, fucking, sleeping, waking up to a nightmare.
I remember him pacing up and down, from Marble Arch to Oxford Circus, handing out his leaflets for eleven pence each, "Less Protein for Less Lust", "Less Meat, Eggs, Nuts". A man with a mission carrying his hand-made plaque, day in and day out come rain or shine. Was he the last Christian soldier taking the battle onwards up Oxford Street?
Continued abstinence.
But if everyone had abstained, the race would have been wiped out a long time ago. Pure desire mixed up the races to produce a motley but happy breed.

"The progeny of a white and negro is a mulatto, or half and half," explained Frederick Marryat's *Peter Simple* at a fancy-dress ball in Barbados in the early nineteenth century. "Of a white and mulatto, a *quadroon*, or one-quarter black, and of this class the company were chiefly composed. I believe a quadroon and white make the *mustee* or one-eighth black, and the mustee and white the *mustafina*, or one-sixteenth black. After that, they are *whitewashed*, and considered as Europeans [...] The quadroons are certainly the handsomest race of the whole; some of the women are really beautiful [...] I must acknowledge, at the risk of losing the good opinion of my fair country-women, that I never saw before so many pretty figures and faces."

Back at home, Jane Austen's heroines were travelling from one corner of the South-east to the other, beginning and ending their narratives in one or another of a handful of home counties. This is England. No Ireland, no Scotland, no Wales or any Celtic fringe. This is England but only a small corner of our sceptred isle. A map of parochialism and denial. The filthy grime of industrialisation does not sully the picnics on Box Hill and Mansfield Park can manage perfectly well (albeit in an uncontrolled way) while Sir Thomas Bertram sees to business in far-away Antigua. Back to basics and to Englishness now that we have shrugged off our Celtic fringe. We are as pure as Normandy butter. This island should be called "New Normandy like New York" said Jimmie Durham. It could be the semantic badge of our origins if not our originality.

pure adj. 1 Unmixed, unadulterated. 2 of unmixed descent. 3 mere, simple, nothing but. 4 not corrupt.

"Stranger rests in a strange land", reads another mattress text. Dispersed across the floor, Padilha's mattresses map a makeshift, unmade landscape. They bear the traces of countless couplings. They have borne witness to a thousand and one dreams, and nightmares endlessly repeating: sleeping, waking, sleeping, waking, sleeping, waking, sleeping. Unlike Kuitca's mattresses imprinted with the maps of real places and false names, these mattresses guard their anonymity. Second or third or even fourth-hand hand-me-downs, they are a million miles away from the pristine down-at-heel designer chic of Habitat home style, sampling other cultures like they were going out of fashion.

"Will you be the stranger to my native?" she said. "Pretend that I'm Kuchuk Hanem and you're my Flaubert." Dallying in Oriental robes, Flaubert smoked his hookah and wrote home from Cairo in the winter of 1850: "The little bells on the dromedaries are tinkling in your ears, and great flocks of black goats are making their way along the street, bleating at the horses, the donkeys and the merchants. There is jostling, there is argument, there is sweating of all kinds, there is shouting in a dozen languages. The raucous Semitic syllables clatter in the air like the sound of a whiplash [...] it is delightful." Having tasted the delights of Cairo, Flaubert sailed up the Nile to Upper Egypt where he met his priestess in the flesh, Kuchuk Hanem, a dancer exiled from the capital.
She gave him *Salammbo*. He gave her syphilis.

Swamping, flooding, swamping, flooding.
Like a swarm of locusts, a plague of refugees.
Swamping and flooding Brixton, Soho, Brick Lane.
What was he thinking of, London's lone bomber with his sad plastic bag exploding with hatred?
Did he think he could wipe the slate clean and make England pure again?
Did he think he could turn back the clock with his deadly ticking device?
Pure white. Pure cube. Pure white cube. Pure modern. Pure.
But England was never a green and pleasant land.
And the English have always been a mixed-up race.

Ronald Fraser-Munro

The Second Kommen

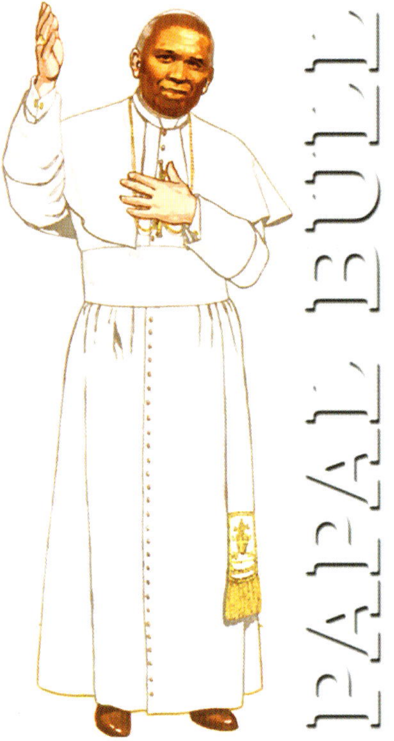

God is inside us all said the Bishop buttering up the congregation. God is inside of every one of us and the congregation roared with delight and threw their hands into the air towards the heaven as though inviting the Christians for the burning inevitable reward for their incredulous beliefs.

The Second Kommen is split into two books, the first being *Vader, Dear Vader*, based on the popular misconception of the priest in society, unfortunately not as portrayed by the stunning characterisation given unto us behind the scenes. While nothing much can be done about this overall conspiracy, at least we can have the presentation of Christianity by Derek Nimmo some years ago. As thou will recall this production (notably from the Patrick Cargill School of Acting) was a soft-core bastardisation of the religious middleman. *Vader* sets out to explore theology and academia outside of the fetid, cramped, masturbatory and dank rooms of the monastery. By placing the character of the priest within society and liberally indulging the said priests in a small sherry, vodka, whisky with instructions to discuss the wealth of paranoia, bogus 'insight', fear, discontentment, etc. the already abstract concept of religion and how it affects life, spirituality is teased to the full in a stunning multi-dimensional piss against the leg of the catholic corporation.

The second part of the *Second Kommen* is the manifestation of the Black Pope and so called Anti-Christ, the cumming of a global crisis of God's judgment on a world that will be groping in everlasting darkness, flung into the eternal orifice!

The coronation of the new pope as an antidote to liberal and anti-Christian bias in contemporary Nazi politics simply redirects the coke-sucking, Disney-licking, Macgonads-stuffing believer in the direction of their sweet demise. Who can help but lead a clueless herd of sheep to the very precipice of their existence.

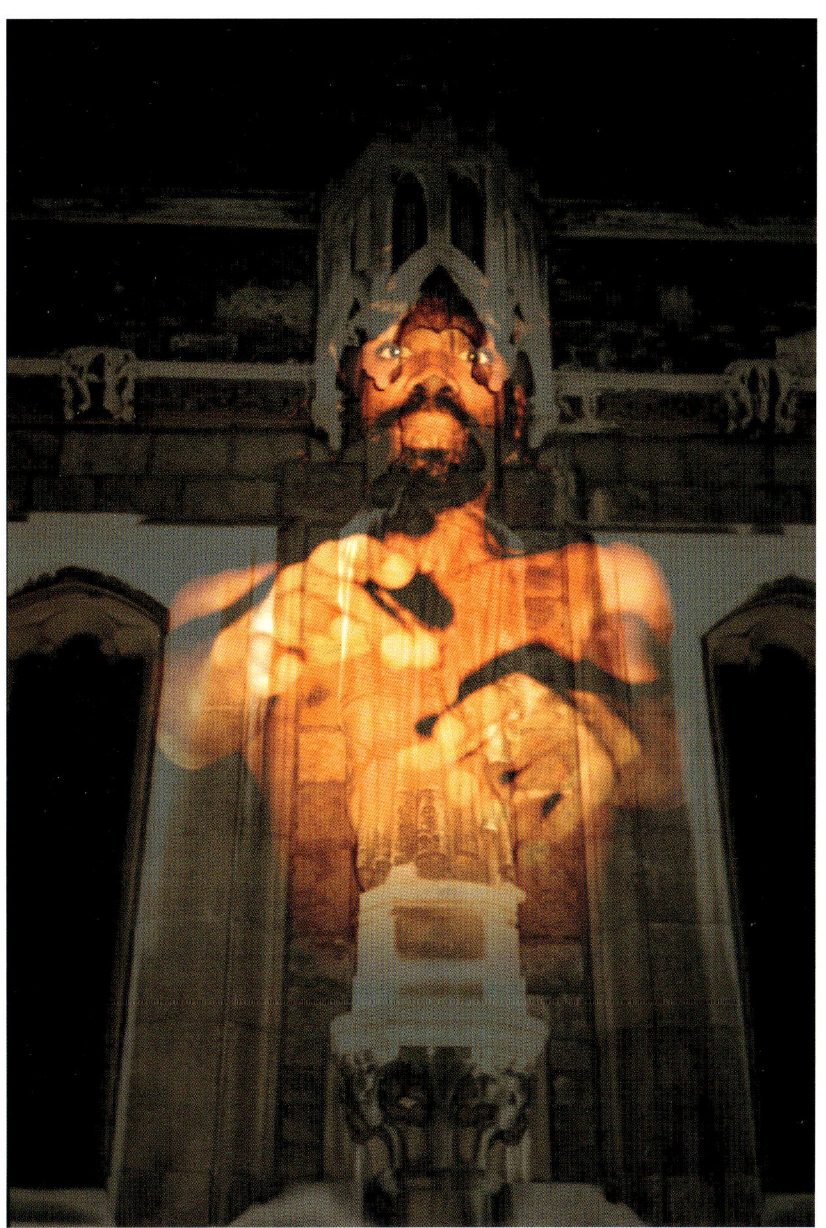

Then fling them off it into a cauldron of blood and anguish? Certainly not this butcher! Nor none I know! And so the end must stop being nigh and finally rear upon its hind-quarters to reveal its weapon of salvation. The congregation, like a well-seasoned game show audience, always gets what it deserves.

Following the gathering of the testimonials, scriptures and evidence from *Vader* and the *Second Kommen*, the material will then be manipulated to perform the visual and audio backdrop for the *Congregational Service.*

The third part of it is not work to cheer the soul. So a few new hymns have to be composed of the crowning beauty-or-horror with an anti-Christian bias or bass. All manner of emotions will flow from those that meet these peculiar voices from heaven. Indeed all manner of liquid angst.

Ich bin Alpha and Omega, tha beginning and tha ending, sayeth tha Lord, which art, and which was, and which is to come, tha Almighty. Jean, who also is our bruder, and companion in tribulation, and in the kingdom and patience of Jesus Christ, was in the isle that is called Pathos, for the worm of God, and for the testicolo of Jesus Christ.

Search your conscience and ask 2000 years of what?

What has religion done for human beings, the animals, plants, water and the whole planet?

What is religion?

What are the political motives omitting the original and more obvious anti-Semitic ravings that by weaving them in togetherness causes this more stark and ironic delusion amongst Jewish Christians than the original nature-based attachments of religion?

The roots of the Catholic Kirk, the papacy, the power-brokering and self-serving redefinition of early religions by the Roman Catholic Church through the propaganda conceived, written and implemented as policy by priests and princes.

The defamation of the spiritual outlanders and enemies of the Kirk whose only crime was to espouse an alternative to a corporate and global church. Those ostracised and persecuted by the Kirk. Beam me up Lucifer! Consider the Inquisition, its winners and losers, the use in religion of torture and the obsession with the purification of the mortal flesh as a route to the soul. Where are all the Agnostics? Did they die out or just give up?

Then contemplate the Knights of the Templar, The Cathars and Jesus' entry into French politics after fleeing Israel. Remember the brother of Christ, James. Think on his family and lovers, his background, education and power. Do not live in ignorance as our forebearers do. Who ever heard of such a simple fairy tale as God vs. Lucifer?

Does God not welcome the Witch hunts popular for four to five centuries where believers are imprisoned, even put to death for their face?

Is this not pumping out of the frying pan and into the Germanic Protestant religion?

It is indeed righteous work to seek the alternative Religion and who are we to resist God's creamy butter when offered as enrichment to our stale and dry crust of an existence.

Religion, Politics and Spirituality (Hitler and Stalin, etc.)

The Revelation of Jesus Christ, which God gave unto him gratis, to shew

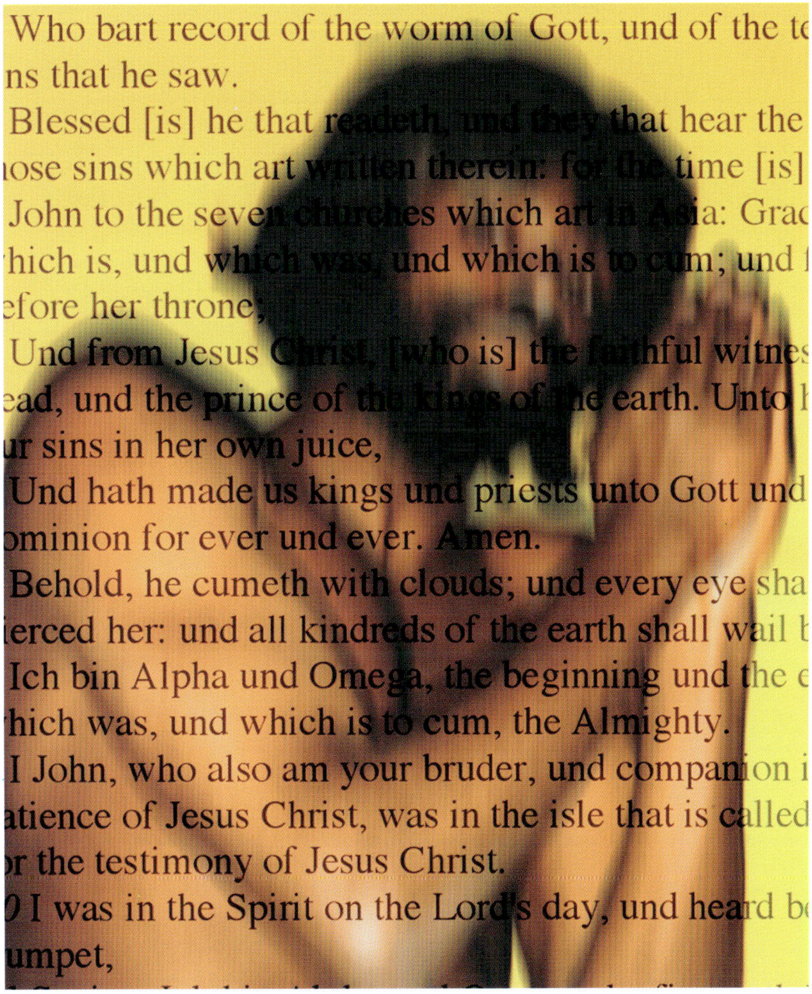

Who bart record of the worm of Gott, und of the te
ns that he saw.
Blessed [is] he that readeth, und they that hear the
iose sins which art written therein: for the time [is]
John to the seven churches which art in Asia: Grac
hich is, und which was, und which is to cum; und f
efore her throne;
Und from Jesus Christ, [who is] the faithful witne
ead, und the prince of the kings of the earth. Unto h
ur sins in her own juice,
Und hath made us kings und priests unto Gott und
ominion for ever und ever. Amen.
Behold, he cumeth with clouds; und every eye sha
ierced her: und all kindreds of the earth shall wail b
Ich bin Alpha und Omega, the beginning und the e
hich was, und which is to cum, the Almighty.
I John, who also am your bruder, und companion i
atience of Jesus Christ, was in the isle that is called
r the testimony of Jesus Christ.
I was in the Spirit on the Lord's day, und heard b
umpet,

unto his servants things which must shortly come to pass; and he sent and signified [it] by his alien angels unto his servant Jean. Who bares record of the phat word of God, and of the testiclo antico of Gesu Christo, and of all things that he dreamt?

And his feet like unto fine bras, as if they burned in a fur nas; and his voice as the sound of many wafers. And he had on his right hund seven stairs; and owt of his mouth went a shard two-edged sword; and his countenance [was] as the fun shineth in his strength. And when I tore him, I fell at his head. And he laid his right hand upon me, saying unto me, Fear not; I am the first and the last. And, behold, I am alive for ever more, Amen; and have the keys of hell and of death. The mystery of the seven stairs which thou sawest in my weary right hand, and the seven golden candlesticks. The seven stairs are the aliens of the seven kirks; and the seven comfort-sticks, which thou sawest, are the seven kirks.

The confinements of the monk and nun. Never trust a being removed from society.

The concept of the priest. Never trust a man wearing a frock.

The origin of the priest. Never trust tradition.

The *sturm und drang* pastor of Germany and the occult and twisted legacy of the Aryan tradition.

The flamboyant French monsignor and garlic-laced fornication of the Marquis de Sade which paled by the excesses and intrigues of the Vatican and its military Kirk.

I was in the Spirit on the Lord's day, and heard behind me a great trumpet, Saying, Ich bin Alpha und Omega, the first and the last; and, What thou sets, write in a book, and send [it] unto the seven kirks which are in Asia; unto Effuses, and unto Maryland, and unto Pogroms, and unto Theatre, and unto Saudis, and unto Philadelphia, and unto Laodicea.

And I turned to see the voice that spake with me. And being turned, I saw seven golden comfort-sticks; oh joy! And in the midst of the seven [one] like unto the Son of man, clothed with a garment down to the foot, and girt about the paps with a golden girl. His head and [his] hairs [were] like wood, as white as shite; and his eyes [were] as the beast Blessed [is] he that readeth and they hear the words of this prophecy, and keep those things, which are written therein; for the time [is] at hand.

Lois Keidan

Artland 2000

I'm standing outside a chipshop in a remote North Lincolnshire village on a balmy evening in April 2000. I'm with a crowd of elderly locals I haven't met before, but they all seem to have known each other for ever. We're listening to a man recall a childhood that began on this very spot, that was played out in the lanes he walks us through, that was part of the fabric and folklore of this village, shaped and shared by most of the friends, family and neighbours gathered here this evening. Through the memory of a child he maps a history of a place and the making of a person. That child is now a man who turned 50 at the brink of the new Millennium and who, with us as witnesses and accomplices, is re-inhabiting the process of his becoming; performing the memory of memories, assembling and disassembling the social and cultural forces that made him who he is today.

I'm standing in a bland hotel function suite in Sheffield on a cold, wet night in January 2000. I'm with a small bunch of thirtysomethings who, to all intents and purposes, do not know each other but have been invited here tonight, for a party. We're nibbling vol-au-vents, talking small and raising glasses to an artist who has chosen to spend her first birthday in the new Millennium here, in a city she doesn't know, with us, apparent strangers. We are here, it seems, not just to celebrate, but to bear witness to a survival, to an unexpected arrival in the year 2000. When the birthday candles have been blown out we are invited to sit in silence and watch as she marks the moment with and on her body, through an act of bloodletting that acknowledges her, and our, presence in this place and in this time and ritualises her own tiny passing into the new year.

I'm standing under a graffiti-covered motorway sign at a junction of an M5 service station on a cold and damp dusk in late January 2000. I'm with a small group of people who have travelled from Bristol, London, Devon and beyond to be here. We're watching a man recount people, places and defining moments from three long hard weeks of hitchhiking through the lives of strangers and 'nobodies' on and off the roads of Britain in the first flush of the new Millennium. The text he reads is filled with the chance meetings, random locations, snatches of conversation, silences, acts of kindness and deception that marked his travels; encounters that expose senses of place, of journeying and of not belonging right here, right now.

I'm standing in Trafalgar Square on a rainy afternoon in April 2000 amongst crowds of damp tourists and Londoners going about their business. In the middle of the traffic comes a woman strapped to the back of an open truck, shouting "Pull Yourself Together" through a megaphone. Some people try to ignore her, some shout back "why?", "how?", "fuck off", whilst others stop and stare with expressions ranging from amazement and amusement to confusion and irritation. As the truck moves on we see a banner at the back declaring it to be "Mental Health Action Week". Without realising it or asking for it, we seem to have been both the spectators to a very public performance action and the subjects of an awareness campaign around outmoded, unenlightened, but nonetheless prevalent attitudes towards mental health.

I'm standing alone in a coffee shop in Brick Lane in May 2000 looking at a bundle of postcards that have been left in a leaflet rack. On the postcards is a grainy, black and white image: a photograph of a young woman wearing a party hat and a party smile. On the back is a short fragment of text, a recollection of a night on the town. That's it; we don't know who she is, the people she talks about, or whether these memories are even hers. She's talking about (her) Millennium night, but the words – personal and universal, charged and mundane – could be anyone's. They are a reminder of that contradictory feeling that for all the anticipation and all the significance, perhaps in the detail the moment of the Millennium was really just another night out.

These are just a few of the things I've witnessed until now, June 2000, in *Small Acts* – some of the fourteen acts and actions commissioned to mark contested and complex experiences at the turning of a new Millennium. You might also have encountered some of these actions if you had either chosen to, been invited to, or had just logged onto or stumbled upon them. But there are others that none of us could have 'been there' for even if we had wanted to. With these small acts, the act itself is a hidden and private thing. There's an artist out there working with what are quaintly known as 'ordinary' people to create star maps for the new age. Another whose act was to capture and cull the moment of the Millennium from his roof, down his phone line, and through his aerial. These are small acts that only become 'visible' through reflection, through their traces and their documentation; they occupy a public space only through their relics, or when edited, mediated and transposed to the medium of this book. The exquisite, extraordinary and diverse works for the page found here were a central part of the process of the making of these projects, often, in fact, intrinsic to the concept of each *Small Acts* act.

The *Small Acts* series itself also raises some charged and irresistible questions about art, artists and audiences in this overly constructed and controlled Millennium year. For those at the helms of the ships of state and culture the year 2000 represents not just an unusually significant and portentous date but more of an opportunity to shape and brand a cultural identity in a new world order: to strike a pose about Britain and Britishness. Under the cultural 'management' of New Labour, this Millennium comes complete with an Official Agenda that carries with it enormous assumptions about the cultural values of our times, about who we are and what we want and, within this, what our art should be, and do, to have currency. The endorsed (aka funded) art of this Millennium has Guidelines and these ultimately determine the kind of art that the Millennium in Britain represents and that, in turn, validate Britain in the year 2000. Broadly speaking, the Official Agenda suggests that the Art of the Millennium should be a tool for a celebration of being British rather than a mechanism to critique what this might mean. It ought to be widely accessible and popular rather than remote, difficult or marginal. It should be inclusive, not at odds with, audiences; a participatory and collective response to this historic moment. It should foreground common experiences based on the values of consensus in order to engender a spirit of community rather than a sense of individuality. Ideally it is art that brings us all together in happy whole(some)ness rather than negotiate the complexities of our differences – past, present and future. This mindset leads to a culture of sanctioned art in the shadow of the state, that has little to do with lived realities.

The inevitably disastrous consequences of such thinking can, of course, be seen in all their glory in the Dome; a spurious, soulless and singular vision of our culture, identity and experiences. But they can also be found in public art projects and 'community' shows throughout the land and, moreover, they are ingrained in the bricks and mortar of all of those new cultural centres built in the heat of Millennium fever. Yes, of course they are all long overdue, civilised and, often, magnificent in their conception and design, but however emblematic, they are simply buildings, buildings that without an equal investment in art and in artists are nothing more than a front. And at the same time buildings in themselves inevitably limit and, to a considerable degree, predetermine the processes of art-making and art-placing and the ways in which it may engage with a public: they control the shape of art and contain its leakage. For all the stunning splendour and stake-raising of Tate Modern we should perhaps be wary of its potential to influence the institutionalisation and aggrandisement of radical art; to assimilate, depoliticise and sanitise dissident processes and practices that may have been conceived in a spirit of opposition to the received cultural values of their times. The official agenda appears in danger of, on one hand, confusing surface with substance and, on the other, reinforcing a singular approach to the place and function of art in society.

I see *Small Acts* as a series that lurks in the cracks of this Millennial culture, wrestling with questions of the contextualisation of art and its relation to an audience. It is a series of actions which contests the Official Agenda: an address to the edges, the margins and the undersides of cultural experience, a set of expressions of individual, hidden and forgotten lives. As a counterpoint to the received thinking and conventions that determine the cultural significance of the historical moment, the series was concerned with the idea of history felt at the level of the personal. The relation of these works to their audiences is both radical and particular and the work deliberately places art outside of its usual institutional frames.

The series is one which inherently questions how, who and what we think of, when we think of an audience for contemporary artistic practices, especially those understood to be performative. 'Audience, access, participation and impact' is the mantra driving all kinds of arts thinking and arts funding these days but there is little discussion about what these things could mean or could be. The works I described earlier, and most other *Small Acts* projects, were not necessarily 'fun for all the family' or in some cases even accessible, open or visible to everyone and nor were they intended to be. But each small act in its own way, and through its own route, somehow connected with a diverse and contradictory range of people: the unwitting in Daniel Gosling's hitch, the familiar in *Class of '76* or the strangers of *Unknowing*, the mass in *Flood* and *Pull Yourself Together* or the intimate community of *Bubbling Tom*. Collectively these projects suggested the complicit and the random ways that 'a public' can participate in art, or engage with its ideas: be it as a ticket buyer, a witness, a subject, a collaborator or through chance encounter or hearsay. *Small Acts* is as much a description as a title and, in the shadow of bridges and fireworks, scale was never on the agenda; we were more interested in tiny markers for the leaving of the twentieth century. But we trust that the experiences of these audiences and the nature of their various engagements makes as significant a contribution to debates around what art can be and the ways that it can enter people's lives as the mass spectacle of circus or a new cathedral of culture.

Some of the *Small Acts* I saw considered what form an audience may take. But others went further and invited us to question the intrusion of an audience, the necessity of having an audience at all; whether the act needs to be witnessed (to be seen to be communicating with someone – anyone!) to be considered art. They asked if the art is in the doing or the telling and whether it should be 'the audience' that legitimises, accredits, the work of an artist in these figure-happy times. In the bigger scheme of ideas and influences would it matter if nobody had 'seen' Joseph Beuys and his coyote and conversely does it matter how many actually did? Well no, but I shudder to think of the grant application!

Inevitably, questions of audience expose assumptions about context and, again, *Small Acts* raises the stakes in debates about the 'place' of art by suggesting that a home, a wilderness, a private suite, a high street, are as valid, as potent and powerful, a site as the four walls of our galleries and theatres. These are the debates that determine how our art is named and framed, how it is controlled and decontaminated for mass consumption, and the practices and ideas represented by *Small Acts*, more often than not, tend to fall off the agendas. Happily these are challenging and problematic issues facing the cultural infrastructure of the Official Agenda and *Small Acts* hopes to do its little bit to keep them alive. It is exposing the points where distinctions between artist and audience, spectator and collaborator, individual and community, spectacle and privacy, truth and fiction collide and collapse. In a time characterised by mass celebration and consensus, *Small Acts* suggests one way that a more representative cultural framework could accommodate a plurality of processes and practices and consider all manner of conversations between an artist and a public. *Small Acts* is an, albeit fleeting, attempt to frame more maverick and less essentialised approaches to the diverse, the dissident, the difficult and the delicate experiences of our times and a little gesture of defiance against a GM World in which we're all having fun in Artland 2000.

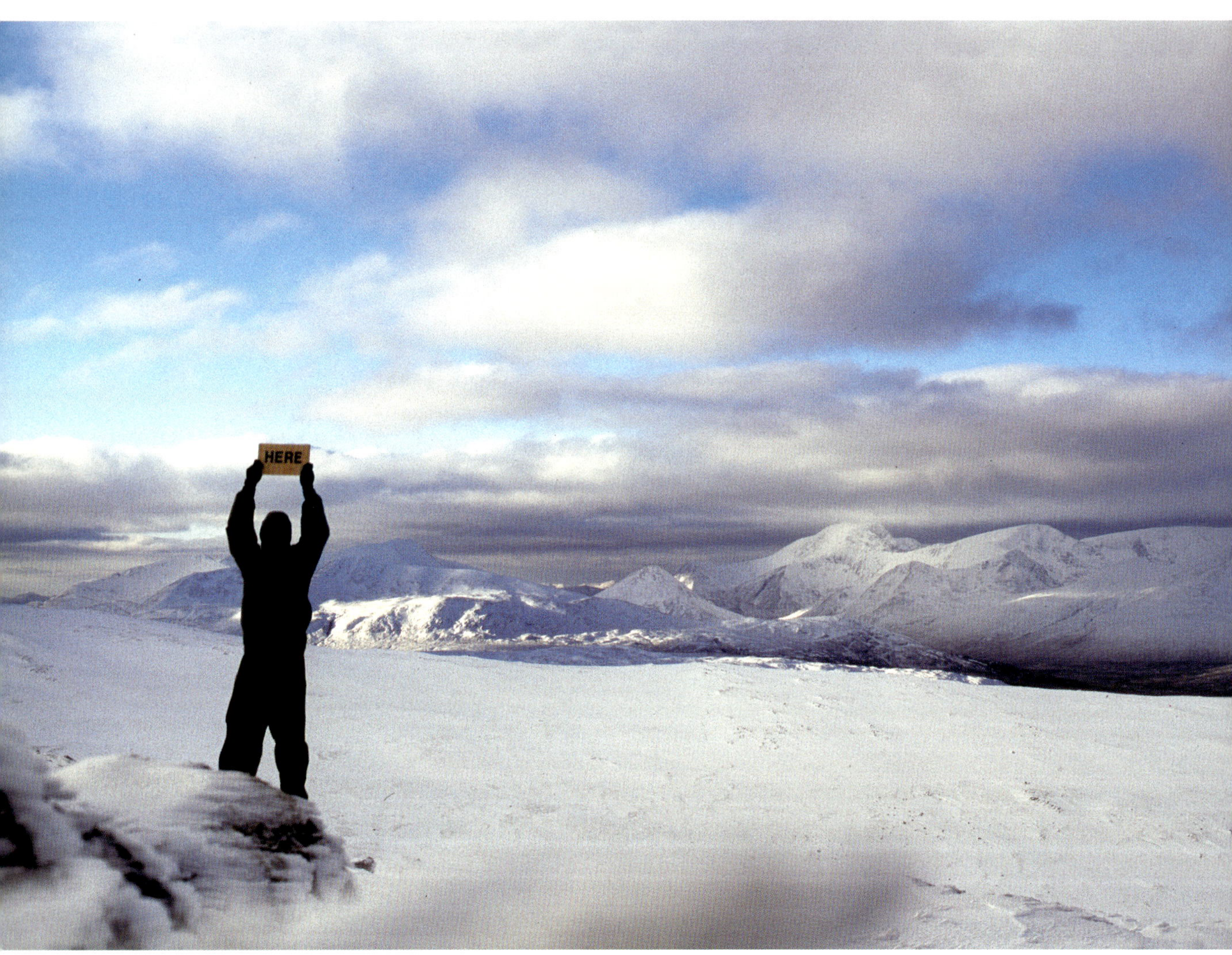
HERE

Daniel Gosling

10.1.00 > > 30.1.00 > > > <

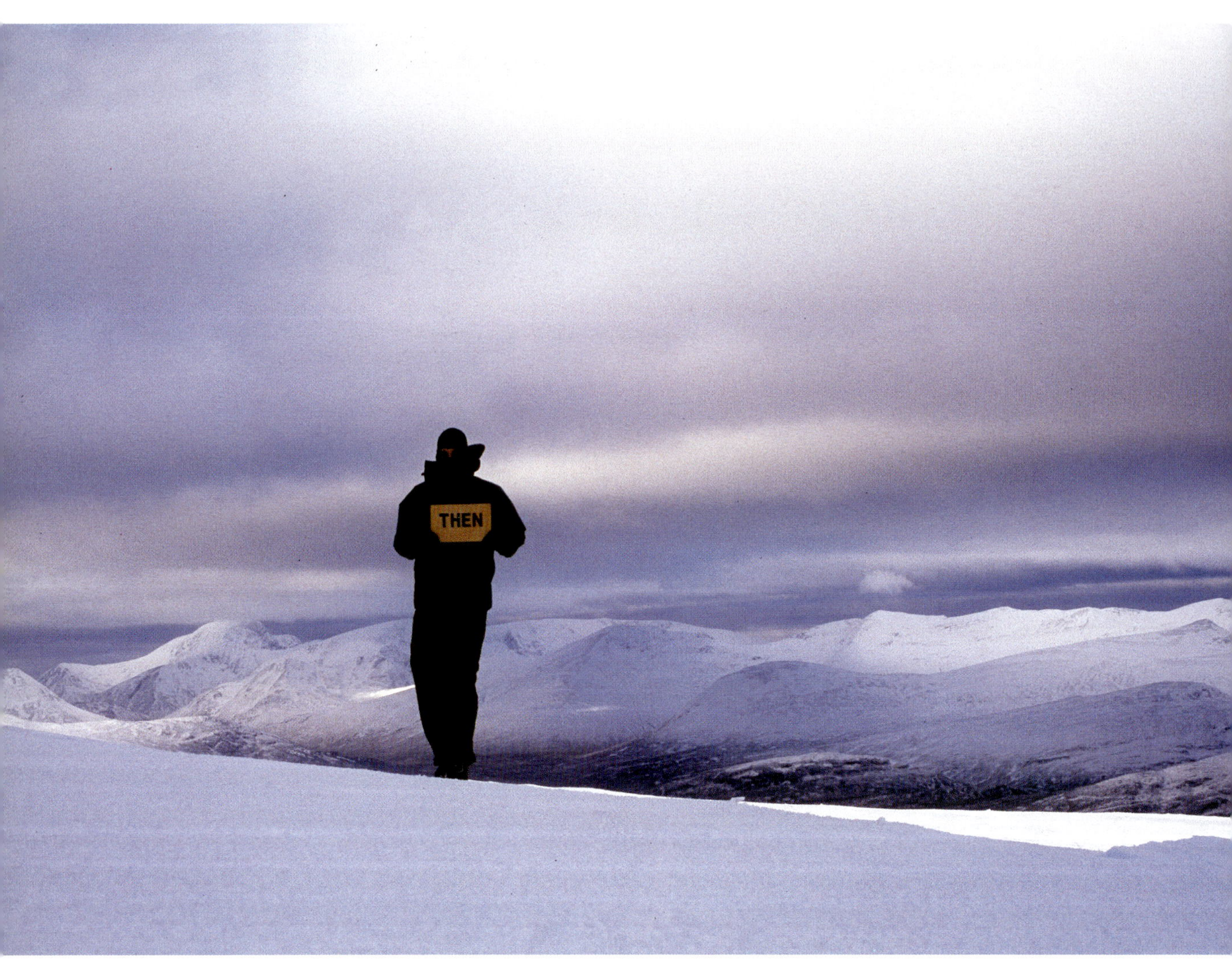
THEN

SENSITISED TO DEATH MONDAY 10.01.00 APPREHENSIVENESS 13.15: M1 JUNCTION 1 GUTTER SILT FOOTPRINTS OF A DEPARTED HITCH HIKER EXPECTATION 14.02: THE FIRST DECEPTION RELOCATING AUSTRALIAN BICKERING CROWS CHARGED AIR BLACK CLOUDS TRADE PLATERS MARRIED HOMOSEXUAL DUSK DRIZZLE DARKNESS RAIN 22-YEAR VETERAN OF THE HAULAGE TRAIL JOB AND MARRIAGE COLLISION M6 CRASH OBSERVED AFTER THE FACT: "IT'S A RAT RACE" AGRI-CONSULTANT IN ORGANIC BOOM TIME THE LAKES KIND OFFER DECLINED ANOTHER ACCEPTED KESWICK WAR MEMORIAL MEETING PLACE CLOSED YOUTH HOSTEL EMPTY HOTEL MORNING DARKNESS OFFER MADE GOOD HEAD LIT LANES RAINLESS DAWN "WELCOME TO SCOTLAND" SERIAL BRIDGES LOCKERBIE SIGN MISPLACED TOWERBLOCKS RACIST FROM LONDON: "I LOVE IT UP 'ERE, THERE'S NO NIGNOGS" SNOW TO THE WEST BUS MARKED ULLAPOOL TEENAGE PUNKER HITCHER PASSED ENGINEER TURNED FISHERMAN "AVOID THE FUCKEN' ISLANDS IF YA LOOKEN' FURRA WOMAN" BRAEMORE JUNCTION PUNKER HITCHER DROPPED CLOSED WET ULLAPOOL LEWIS FERRY GAELIC SPEECH UNSOLICITED

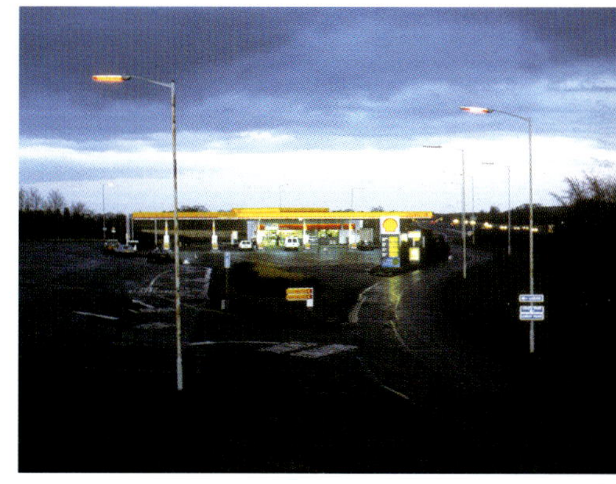

LIFT STREET-LIT STORNOWAY STORM SWEPT CONTRACTING ROAD PASSING PLACES CAR CRASH SON SPOT HARRIS BORDER BANDED MIST DRUNKEN WOMAN ROADBLOCK FOOTBALL TEAM DAUGHTER AND HER FOOTBALL TEAM FRIENDS CLOSED TARBET BORED LADS B&B 6AM BREAK FAST TALE OF MISSING NEVIS CLIMBER SKYE FERRY DAYBREAK AT SEA SNOW COVERED TOPS WHITE CROFTER'S COTTAGES THE PORT OF UIG KIWI TOURISTS CIGARETTE JUNCTION MULTI-RACIAL VAN OF URBAN ESCAPEES ROAD WALKING FOR PLEASURE GOOD AIR FREEZING RAIN ICED ROAD TEN MPH SOLO CRASH OBSERVED AT TEN PACES LAUGHTER COLD HANDS FAMOUS ROCK SCOTTISH EXSQUADDY PROUD OF BEING BRITISH ANTI-WELSH SENTIMENT "IF YA THINK LEWIS LOOKED BLEAK YA WANNA' CHECK THE FALKLANDS" CONTROVERSIAL TOLL BRIDGE QUEENLESS STAMPS SPARSE TRAFFIC EILEAN DONAN CASTLE WW1 MEMORIAL: "WE ARE THE DEAD, SHORT DAYS AGO WE LIVED, FELT DAWN, SAW SUNSETS GLOW, LOVED AND WERE LOVED, AND NOW WE LIE IN FLANDERS FIELDS" SOUND OF DIESEL NORTHBOUND NEWCASTLE CAB LONG WET WAIT CONTENTEDNESS "DADDY WAS A BANK ROBBER ..." NEWCASTLE CAB AGAIN GEORDIE ACCENTS SMELL OF BOOZE TWO EX-PARAS A WOMAN AND A CATARACT-EYES DOG LOCATION BY LICKING RIDGE-POSING STAGS SUBLIME WINTERSCAPE VERTIGINOUS PEAKS STREAMING CREATIVE EXPLETIVES UNCONTROLLABLE LAUGHTER FANTASTIC LIFE FORT WILLIAM SUPERMARKET CAR PARK "THAT'LL BE TWO 'UNDRED QUID PLEASE" JUMPED TRAIN HIGHLAND STATION FROZEN GROUND NO ROADS SIGNALBOX-BUNKHOUSE TWO GLAZIERS ON A REMOTE JOB MISSED SON CALLED DANIEL MIDNIGHT RAILWAY TRESPASS MOON-LIT LEUM UILLEIM FILMSTAR FOOTBRIDGE ABSOLUTE STILLNESS STARS FOREVER FREIGHT TRAIN LIGHT BARKING DOGS DECISION TO STOP MOVING MORNING SNOW CHANGEABLE WEATHER ILLADVISED HILL EXCURSION SOLITUDE A TEXT OF LONGING SHOUTED OUT TO NO ONE FAST CLOUD WHITE-OUT FEAR PAGER TONE MYSTERY 0171 NUMBER DISSIPATED FEAR LAUGHTER BLUE SKY CLOUD BLUE SKY SNOWSTORM GINGER BREAD BUGGY TRACKS WAY-

WARD COURSE SURE-FOOTED MISRECOGNITION OF A SHINY PINK 'BOULDER' STOMACH AND INTESTINES OF AN ADULT DEER NO MORE TRACKS RETRACED STEPS SAFETY TELE-PHONE CALL SOLVED MYSTERY HAPPINESS FADING LIGHT COSY SLEEP NOCTURNAL FREIGHT WEATHER REPORT WORK DECISION ANOTHER EXCURSION STARTLED DEER HERD DEEP SNOW RASPING WIND ENDLESS PANORAMA THE NEVIS RANGE PHOTO SHOOT INVISIBLE SKIS DEPARTED GLAZIERS FLAGGED TRAIN CRIAN LARICH JUNCTION INSTANT LIFT TURNING FOR KILLIN READING KILLIN' ANOTHER HITCHER'S BLACK MARKER HUMOUR LOCAL TRAFFIC LOCAL NEWS: "THE ONLY THING MISSING ABOUT HIM IS HIS BODY" DUNBLANE SIGN DEATH REFERENCES COMING THICK AND FAST CONFUSING ROAD LAYOUT A WOMAN WHO TALKED ABOUT MAKING MAGIC BOUNDLESS POSITIVITY THE QUIETEST JUNCTION ON THE M74 "MAKE SOME MAGIC!" INSTANT LIFT DOPESMOKE DRIVER "WELCOME TO ENGLAND" "THEY'RE ALL KILLIN' EACH OTHER IN MOSSIDE YA KNOW" MURDERED SCHOOL FRIENDS ACCRINGTON PUB-HOTEL LOCAL RAG HEADLINE:

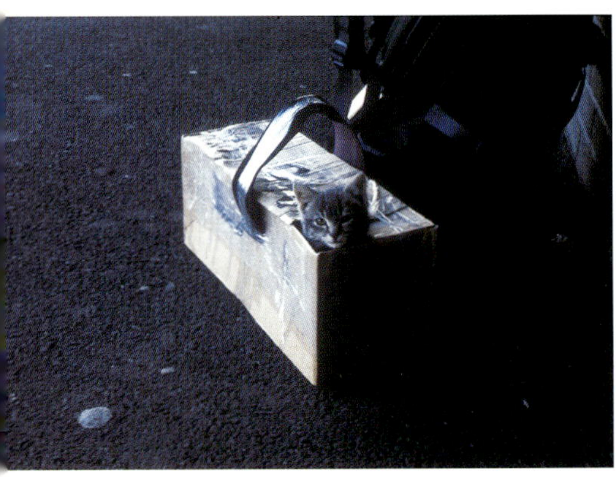

"PUB FIGHT DEATH" THERE IT WAS AGAIN SUNDAY 16.01.00 PRESTON OUTSKIRTS M6 SLIPROAD SPAT AT BY A COWARD CONSTANT TRAFFIC FOUR HOURS THUMB-TWIDDLING RENDEZVOUS TIME SHORTAGE LUCIFER OVER LANCASHIRE? LANCASTER SERVICES MEETING POINT 16.20/ SUNSET THANKS FOR COMING TOSSED COIN: SOUTH MASSED LIGHTS OF INDUSTRY FEIGNING NEW YORK ARMY PADRE IN LOVE WITH HIS CAR HOLY-HEAD VISIBLY MISSED BOAT RETINA-OFFENDING WAIT-ING ROOM LIGHT 07.30: DUBLIN DOCKS SLEEP DEFICIT CITY NAVIGATION UNCERTAIN ROAD STATUS STRAINED SHOULDER LOST MONEY LOST STAMINA PHONECALLS ACQUAINTANCE HOSPITALITY WATERPROOF-RUINING LAUNDRY EURO-BOOMTOWN MORNING DEADLOCK SHEEP FARMING COUPLE COMPULSIVE KNITTING AND ANECDOTES "THE DYING THIRST": AN OLD WOMAN WHO DRANK A BOTTLE OF BLEACH "THE BANSHEE": DEATH'S TERRITORY AGAIN INVITATION TO A TINY FARM NEW-BORN LAMBS UNDEVELOPED FEAR ANXIOUS MOTHERS COFFEE AND A PHOTOGRAPH OF OLD DUBLIN NELSON'S COLUMN COURTING RENDEZVOUS IRA BOMB NO MORE NELSON NO MORE LANDMARK REGRET GRUMPY BASTARD NEIGHBOUR FEUD THE DEVIL'S SPIT "WE WANT ENNISKILLEN BACK" BORDER DEMARCATED BY DIESEL STATIONS AND A RETURN TO MILES DECOMMISSIONED ARMY CHECKPOINT HEAVILY FORTIFIED R.U.C. SHOP UNIONIST IDENTITY CRISIS: "WHAT PART OF OUR COUNTRY ARE YOU FROM?" DESERTED ROAD TO DONEGAL FRIENDLY DONKEY DUSK WALKING "I GAVE YOU THE KEY TO THE HIGHWAY, AND THE KEY TO MY MOTEL DOOR, I'M TIRED OF LEAVIN' AN' LEAVIN' ..." DIESEL STATION AND A RETURN TO KILOMETRES FACTORY CLOCK-OFF TRAFFIC HOSTEL AUSTRALIANS IN EUROPE ILL-CONSIDERED ACT AN UNWANTED KITTEN WHO BECAME DONNIE FROM DONEGAL "WHAT'S IN THE BOX?" SIGNS FOR OMAGH DIESEL STATION AND MILES AGAIN DERRY/LONDONDERRY DIESEL SMUGGLERS BUSHMILLS UNION JACKS A PET SHEEP BLACK MARKET DIESEL DEALING "THE NORTH'S NOT LIKE THEY SAY ON THE TELLY. WE'RE NOT LIKE THAT, WE'RE GOOD PEOPLE" BALLINTOY HOSTEL SCOTLAND FROM IRELAND DEEP SLEEP GIANT'S CAUSEWAY

DONNIE MISSING IN TOILETRY ACTION DRIZZLE RAIN VIBRATING POCKET: "STILL NO LUCK ON THE CAT FRONT CALL ME" ENGLISH EX-SQUADDY "WHAT'S IN THE BOX?" THE PORT OF LARNE AWOL DONNIE MISSED FERRY LIGHTS OF CAIRNRYAN AFFIRMATIVE WAGON-DECK ACTION "WHAT'S IN THE BOX?" CAT-LOVING DRIVER GRETNA LORRY PARK "WELCOME TO ENGLAND" CROSSED ON FOOT 21.05: THE QUIETEST JUNCTION ON THE M6 SOUTH COLD HUNGER RAIN RESIGNATION AN ARTIC' SOME MAGIC "I'M GOIN' AS FAR AS BIRMINGHAM" STRAINED MIAOWING STENCH OF SHIT DESPERATE JUSTIFIABLE BOX ESCAPE AFFECTIONATE REASSURANCE AND SHIT SHIT SHIT SHIT SHIT TOLERANT DRIVER BAG STRAP LEASH GIFT SMALL HOURS SERVICE STATION UNDERBELLY LADS ON PUSH-BIKES UNDER AGE GAMBLING SELF-CONSCIOUSNESS SHIT CLEAN-UP NEEDY NADIR PHONECALL EMPATHY LACK TETHERED SHOULDER-KITTEN MANCUNIAN ANGEL OF DELIVERANCE ERRONEOUS ADMIRATION SPEED DIRECTION CATS-EYE HYPER-REAL DESERTED M-WAY BEAUTY THE ATTRITION OF DECEPTION LAPTOP DONNIE VERBAL DELIRIUM UNCONSCIOUSNESS 5AM BRIGHTON DOOR-STEP SLEEP STARTLED PAPERBOY DAYBREAK DISTANT DRUG-DAYS FRIEND PHONECALLS POMPEY HOME FOR DONNIE BORED MOTORBIKE COP ATTENTION UNWANTED GIFT OF A LIFE ENHANCING CASSETTE BRIDPORT ROUNDABOUT MANTRA: "BASTARDS! BASTARDS! YAH YAH BASTARDS! BASTARDS! BASTARDS! ..." DUSK MENTAL EXHAUSTION RACIST BIGGLES DESIGN TECHNOLOGY TEACHER TOTNES ON THE ROCKS GIRLFRIEND OVER-SLEEP LATE START SLIPROAD STICKER: "RECLAIM THE RAILWAYS / TUESDAY 30.NOV.99 / 5PM EUSTON STATION" LIFT FROM ACQUAINTANCES FAMILIAR HITCHING PLACE STARTLED FEEDING BUZZARD BITING WIND MYSTERY WAVING WOMAN AWE-INSPIRING PETROL STATION SUN-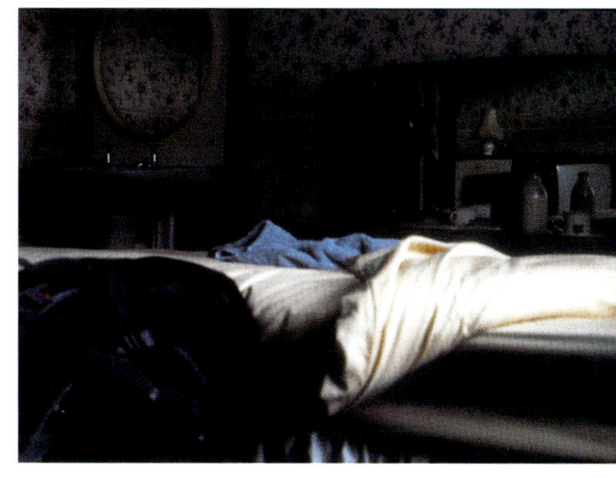SET FREEZING RAIN LONG LIFT WITH AN OVER-ACCOMMODATING DRIVER TAMWORTH SERVICES PRE-CLUB BURGER BOYS AND A WEEKEND ACCESS DAD TOSSED COIN BAD DECISION LONELY SEVENTEEN YEAR-OLD LOOKING FOR HITCHERS: "I'LL TAKE YA WHEREVA YA WANNA' GO MATE" WEIRD ATMOSPHERE NO MATES JUST PETROL FULL B&B'S EXCUSES PREMATURE PARTING DARK DESERTED ROAD WALKING "AAH PUDDA SSSPELL ON YOU ... 'CUZ YOUR MAA-HINE ... " PLUMMETING TEMPERATURE ANXIOUSNESS PETROL STATION ENQUIRY NON-NATIVE SPEAKER EX-HITCHER HELP FULL B&B'S COVENTRY SUBURBS YOUNG CHILDREN AND A WARY WIFE BACK GARDEN TENT NEARLY COMING CLEAN SUN-DAY 23.01.00 UNCANNY SHARED KNOWLEDGE OF SHEFFIELD'S BELLHAG RD SOUTH LEICESTER M1 ACCESS ROUNDABOUT ROADRAGE BLACKSPOT VISIBLE DESTINATION EXCESSIVE ANIMOSITY DECISION TO WALK D.O.T. JURISDICTION TRESPASS ON FORGOTTEN GROUND EMERGENT LIFEFORMS MOTORWAY CHICKEN-DASH CROSS-COUNTRY ASSAULT COURSE SNAGGED CLOTHES SCARED FEMALE JOGGER SOUTHBOUND HITCHER GOING NOWHERE FAST LEICESTER FOREST EAST SERVICES MEETING POINT DECLINED LIFT OFFER FROM A RUCKSACK SIGNAL 16.33/ SUNSET THANKS FOR COMING COMPENSATORY NOT HITCHED LIFT TO SHEFFIELD HOSPITALITY PLANNED EARLY START FLAGGING MOTI-VATION BARNSLEY URBAN NAVIGATION DELIVERIES ROTHERHAM CONFUSION AN IDIOT

BEMUSEMENT SHEFFIELD AGAIN PRIVATE 'PARTY' UNMANAGEABLE LEVELS OF DECEP-
TION CONTROVERSY REGAINED ENERGY REVISITED DEPARTURE POINT "PEOPLE DON'T
PICK UP HITCHERS 'COZ THEY'RE TAUGHT TO BE SCARED OF ANYTHIN' DIFFRENT. WELL
NOT ME MATE" INSTANT UNSOLICITED LIFT: "NO REASON T'BE 'ERE UNLESS YA THUMBIN'
IT" SMALL-TIME TOBACCO SMUGGLER OUT OF DOVER YORK RING ROAD DRENCHING
SPRAY GRIM PROSPECTS "OH LORD JESUS, DO YOU THINK I'VE SERVED MY TIME?..."
EMERGENCY STOPPER: "I USED TO 'ITCH MYSELF SO I KNOW WHAT IT'S LIKE" SCARBOR-
OUGH: PARENTAL CHILDHOOD HOLIDAY RESORT GRAND HOTEL IN SIZE ALONE INEDIBLE
BREAKFAST HAZY DAY HOURS OF WALKING "THE LUNATICS HAVE TAKEN OVER THE ASY-
LUM ..." CLIFF-TOP WAITING INDISTINCT NAUTICAL HORIZON "I CAN'T REMEMBER THE
LAST TIME I SAW A HITCHER ROUND 'ERE" WINDSCREEN STREAKED WITH CONCENTRIC
DIRT ARCS BLINDING SUN LIGHT MONUMENTAL SCULPTURES BILLOWING STEAM END-
LESS CONVOY OF ARTICS AND WAGONS MERGED MOTORWAYS ABJECTED SUBURBS

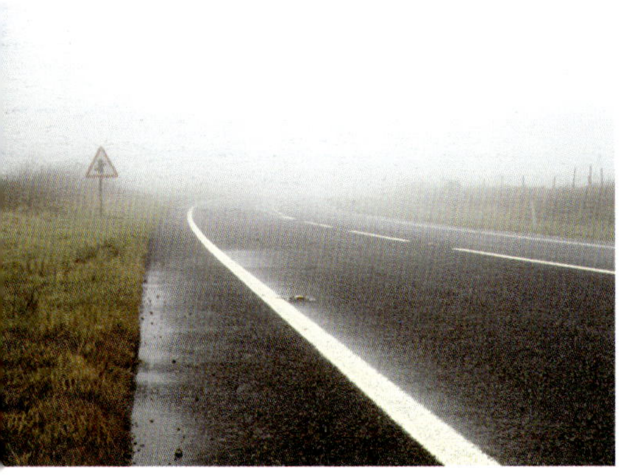

NOWHERE TO STAND TIREDNESS ACCRINGTON PUBHO-
TEL AGAIN SUPERMARKET BREAKFAST IDEAL HITCHING
PLACE OVER-ENTHUSIASTIC MEDICATED DEPRESSIVE
UNATTENTIVE DRIVING COLD SWEAT CENTRAL BLACK-
BURN DROP-OFF FULL SIDE IMPACT OBSERVED AT THIR-
TY PACES SEVEN MILE WALK COP-HEAVY WEIGH BRIDGE
FOUR LOST HOURS "FILTH" HATING SCOUSE DEJA VU
PORNO MAGS AND CONFEDERATE FLAG ROCKABILLY
PSYCHOSIS SMOG SUNSET FALKLANDS VETERAN
BECOME JEHOVAH'S WITNESS TORPEDOED FRIENDS
BLOOD CONVERSATION SURPRISE VISIT HONESTY AND
SLEEP SHIT-STINK FARM TRUCK "WELCOME TO CORN-
WALL" DIRE WEATHER NOWHERE TO STOP "THE MOON
... IS IN ... THE GUDDERRR" AT FULL UNHEARD VOLUME
AIRBORNE OCEAN HAD ENOUGH ALTERED ROUTE B&B-PUB THE MORNING OF THE DAY
BEFORE THE END OUT OF SEASON TOURIST TRAIL LOCAL TRAFFIC TWO MILE LIFTS LEAD-
WEIGHT RUCKSACK INCESSANT RAIN DEJECTED WALKING LACK OF COMPASSION BARN-
STAPLE OUTSKIRTS INCREASED TRAFFIC SOAKED COMPETITORS FREE TAXI SPEED-FREAK
AQUA PLANING CRASH BARRIER GRAFFITI: "BMW'S CAN FUCK MY ARSE" LAUGHTER
TORRENTIAL RAIN END OF TETHER TRADE PLATER HITCHER'S GRAVEYARD MERCIFUL
ESCAPE "YOU'RE NOT A MURDERER ARE YOU?" BRISTOL FRIEND'S SOFA SUNDAY 30 .01. 00
TOO CLOSE TO GO ANYWHERE AND FAR TOO WEARY TO TRY GORDANO SERVICES MEETING
POINT 16.55/ SUNSET THANKS FOR COMING. WHEN WAS/IS THE MILLENNIUM AGAIN?

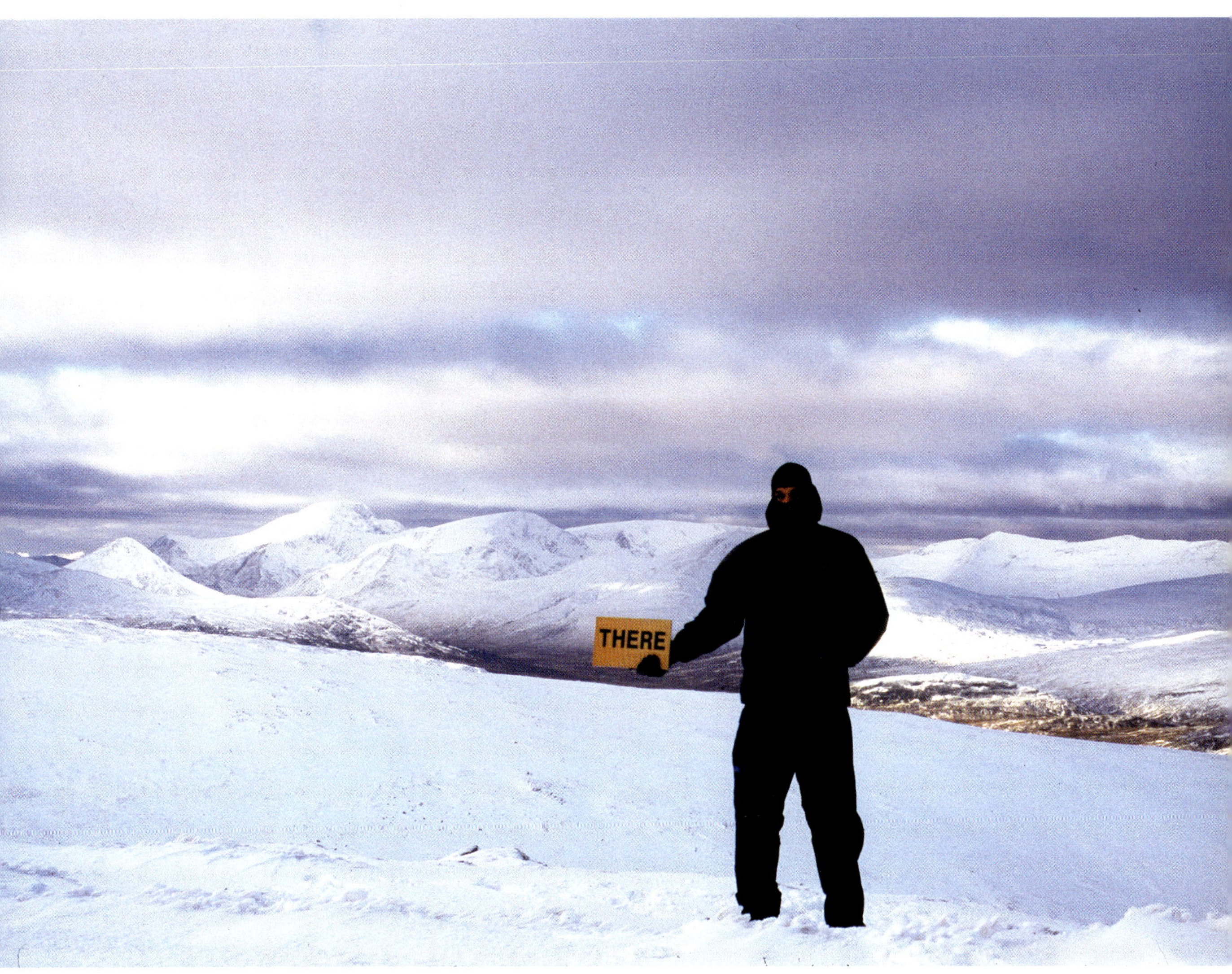
THERE

ROADS

EXPOSURE

OTHERNESS

CHANCE

RISK

ANONYMITY

DECEPTION

CONFIDENCE

TRUST

KINDNESS

HOPE

UNCERTAINTY

TRANSIENCE

THE LAW

SURVEILLANCE

THE MOMENT

VITALITY

EXHAUST(ION)

AND

A PREDOMINANTLY ENGLISH CONCEPT NAMED

BRITAIN

THAT LIMPED INTO THIS

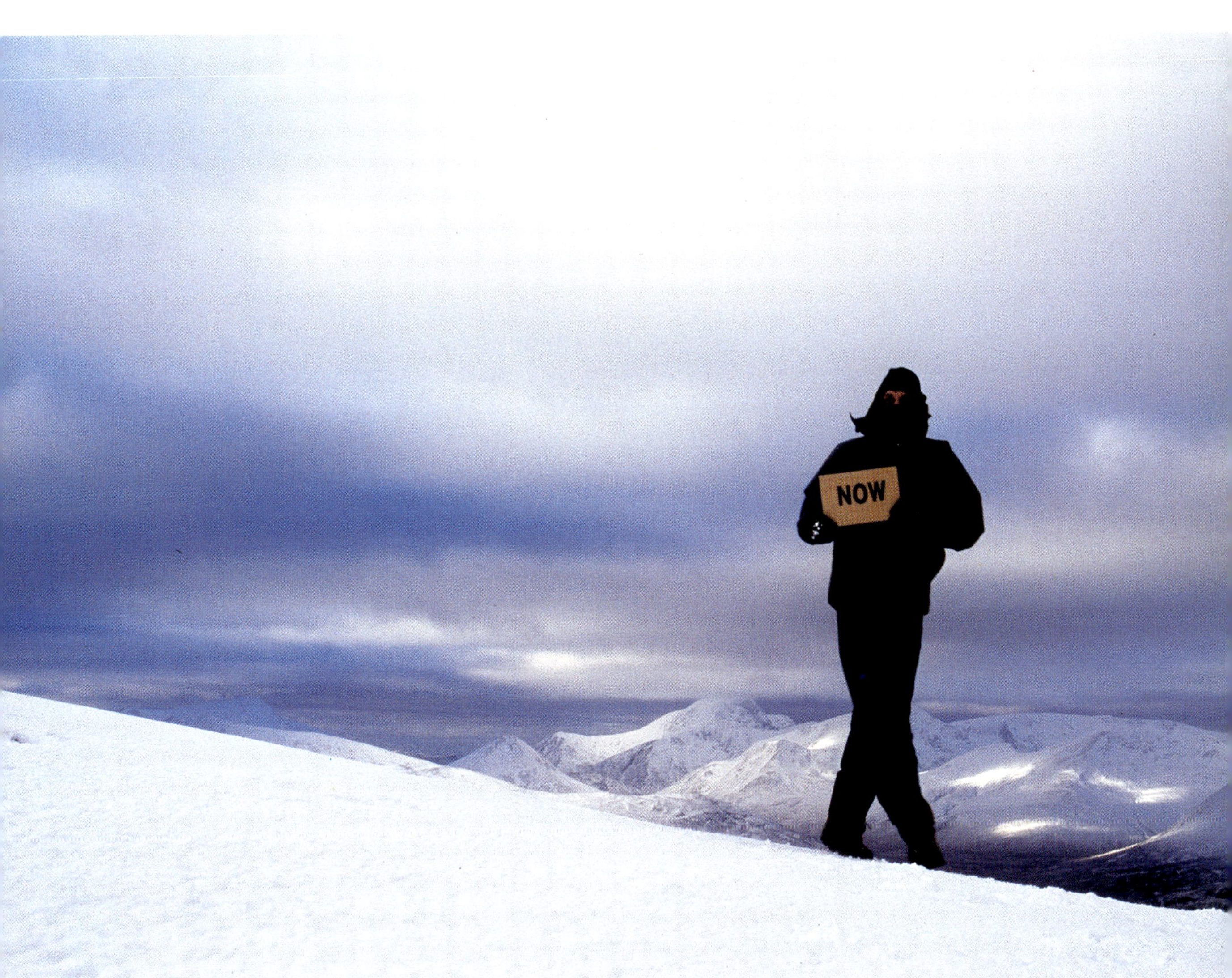
NOW

Brian Eno

The Long Now

It was 1978. I was new to New York. A rich acquaintance had invited me to a housewarming party, and, as my cabdriver wound his way down increasingly potholed and dingy streets, I began wondering whether he'd got the address right. Finally he stopped at the doorway of a gloomy, unwelcoming industrial building. Two winos were crumpled on the steps, oblivious. There was no other sign of life in the whole street. "I think you may have made a mistake", I ventured. But he hadn't. My friend's voice called "Top Floor!", when I rang the bell, and I thought, knowing her sense of humour, "Oh, this is going to be some kind of joke". I was all ready to laugh. The elevator creaked and clanked slowly upwards, and I stepped out – into a multi-million dollar palace. The contrast with the rest of the building and the street outside couldn't have been starker. I just didn't understand. Why would anyone spend so much money building a place like that in a neighbourhood like this? Later, I got into conversation with the hostess. "Do you like it here?", I asked. "It's the best place I've ever lived", she replied. "But I mean, you know, is it an interesting neighbourhood?" "Oh, the neighbourhood? Well that's outside!", she laughed.

The incident stuck in my mind. How could you not think of 'where I live' as including at least some of the space outside your four walls, some of the bits you couldn't lock up behind you? I felt this was something particular to New York: I called it 'The Small Here'. I realized that, like most Europeans, I was used to living in a bigger Here. I noticed that this very local attitude to space in New York paralleled a similarly limited attitude to time. Everything was exciting, fast, current, and temporary. Enormous buildings came and went, careers rose and crashed in weeks. You rarely got the feeling that anyone had the time to think two years ahead, let alone ten or a hundred. Everyone seemed to be 'passing through'. It was undeniably lively, but the downside was that it seemed selfish, irresponsible and randomly dangerous. I came to think of this as 'The Short Now', and this suggested the possibility of its opposite: 'The Long Now'.

'Now' is never just a moment. The Long Now is the recognition that the precise moment you're in grows out of the past and is a seed for the future. The longer your sense of Now, the more past and future it includes. It's ironic that, at a time when humankind is at a peak of its technical powers, able to create huge global changes that will echo down the centuries, most of our social systems seem geared to increasingly short nows. Huge industries feel pressure to plan for the bottom line and the next shareholders' meeting. Politicians feel forced to perform for the next election or opinion poll. The media attract bigger audiences by spurring instant and heated reactions to 'human interest' stories while overlooking longer-term issues – the real human interest. Meanwhile, we struggle to negotiate our way through an atmosphere of utopian promises and dystopian threats, a minefield studded with pots of treasure. We face a future where almost anything could happen. Will we be crippled by global warming, weapons proliferation and species depletion, or liberated by space travel, world government and molecule-sized computers? We don't even want to start thinking about it. This is our peculiar form of selfishness, a studied disregard for the future. Our astonishing success as a technical civilisation has led us to complacency – to expect that things will probably just keep getting better. But there is no reason to believe this. We might be living in the last gilded moments of a great civilisation about to collapse into a new Dark Age, which, given our hugely amplified and widespread destructive powers, could be very dark indeed.

If we want to contribute to some sort of tenable future, we have to reach a frame of mind where it comes to seem unacceptable – gauche, uncivilised – to act with disregard for our descendants. Such changes of social outlook are quite possible; it wasn't so long ago, for example, that we accepted slavery, an idea which most of us now find repellent. We felt no compulsion to regard slaves as fellow-humans and thus placed them outside the circle of our empathy. This changed as we began to realise – perhaps it was partly the glory of their music – that they were real people, and that it was no longer acceptable that we should cripple their lives just so that ours could be freer. It just stopped feeling right. The same type of change happened when we stopped employing kids to work in mines, or when we began to accept that women had voices too. Today we view as fellow-humans many whom our grand-parents may have regarded as savages, and even feel some compulsion to share their difficulties – aid donations by individuals to others they will never meet continue to increase. These extensions of our understanding of who qualifies for our empathy, indicate that culturally, economically and emotionally we live in an increasingly Big Here; we are now unable to lock a door behind us and pretend the rest of the world is just 'outside'.

We don't yet, however, live in a very long now. Our empathy doesn't extend far forward in time. We need now to start thinking of our great-grandchildren, and their great-grandchildren, as other fellow-humans who are going to live in a real world which we are incessantly, though only semi-consciously, building. But can we accept that our actions and decisions have distant consequences, and yet still dare to do anything? Well, it was an act of faith to believe, in the days of slavery, that a way of life which had been materially very successful could be abandoned and replaced by another, as yet only vaguely imaginable, but somehow it happened. We need to make a similar act of imagination now. Since this act of imagination concerns our relationship to time, a Millennium is a good moment to articulate it. Can we grasp this sense of ourselves as existing in time, part of the beautiful continuum of life? Can we become inspired by the prospect of contributing to the future? Can we shame ourselves into thinking that we really do owe those who follow us some sort of consideration; just as the people of the nineteenth century shamed themselves out of slavery? Can we extend our empathy to the lives beyond ours?

I think we can. Humans are capable of a unique trick: creating realities by first imagining them, by experiencing them in their minds. When Martin Luther King said "I have a dream" he was inviting others to dream it with him. Once a dream becomes shared in that way, current reality gets measured against it and then modified towards it. As soon as we sense the possibility of a more desirable world, we begin behaving differently; as though that world is starting to come into existence, as though, in our minds at least, we're already there. The dream becomes an invisible force which pulls us forward. By this process it starts to come true. The act of imagining something makes it real. This imaginative process can be seeded and nurtured by artists and designers, for, since the beginning of the twentieth century, artists have been moving away from an idea of art as something finished, perfect, definitive and unchanging towards a view of artworks as processes or the seeds for processes; things that exist and change in time, things that are never finished. Sometimes this is quite explicit – as in Walter de Maria's *Lightning Field* – a huge grid of metal poles designed to attract lightning. Many musical compositions don't have one form, but change without repeating over time – many of my own pieces and Jem Finer's current Artangel installation *Long Player* are like this. Artworks in general are increasingly regarded as seeds that need a viewer's (or a whole culture's) active mind in which to develop. Increasingly working with time, culture-makers see themselves as people who start things, not finish them.

And what is possible in art becomes thinkable in life. We become our new selves first in simulacrum, through style and fashion and art; our deliberate immersions in virtual worlds. Through them we sense how it might feel to be another kind of person with other kinds of values. We rehearse new feelings and sensitivities. We imagine other ways of thinking about our world and its future. Danny Hillis' *Clock of the Long Now* is a project designed to achieve such a result. It is, on the face of it, far-fetched to think that one could make a clock which will survive and work for the next 10,000 years. But the act of even trying is valuable: it puts time and the future on the agenda and encourages thinking about them. As Stewart Brand, a colleague in The Long Now Foundation, says:

> *Such a clock, if sufficiently impressive and well-engineered, would embody deep time for people. It should be charismatic to visit, interesting to think about, and famous enough to become iconic in the public discourse. Ideally, it would do for thinking about time what the photographs of Earth from space have done for thinking about the environment. Such icons reframe the way people think.*

The twentieth century yielded its share of icons, icons like Muhammad Ali and Madonna, that inspired our attempts at self-actualisation and self-reinvention. It produced icons to our careless and misdirected power – the mushroom cloud, Auschwitz – and to our capacity for compassion – Live Aid, the Red Cross. In this, the twenty-first century, we may need icons more than ever before. Our conversation about time and the future must necessarily be global, so it needs to be inspired and consolidated by images that can transcend language and geography. As artists and culture-makers begin making time, change and continuity their subject matter, they will make legitimate and emotionally attractive a new and important conversation.

Meloni Poole

A Clean Slate

Notes towards a site-specific film
at Annesley Bentinck Colliery, Nottinghamshire

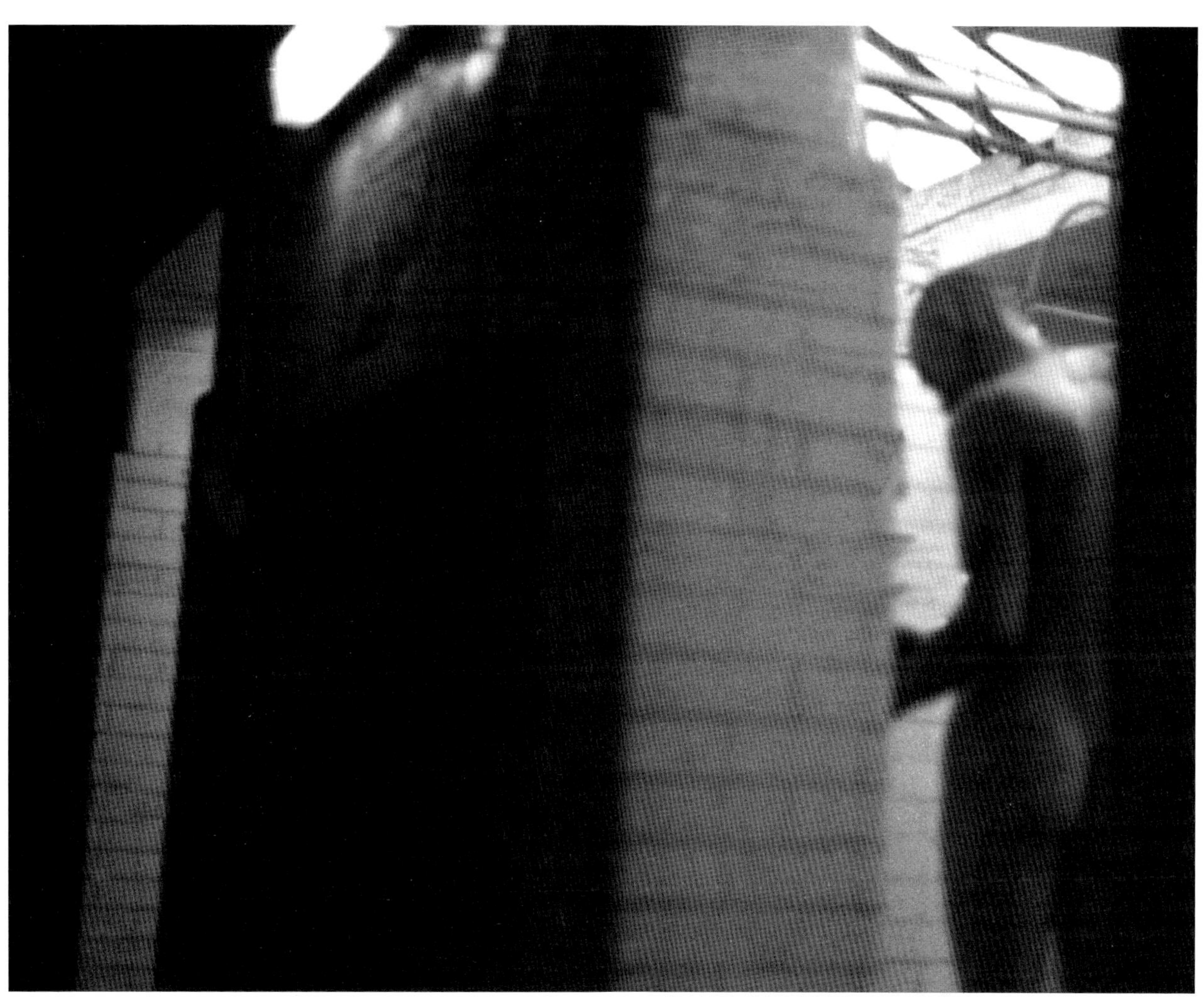

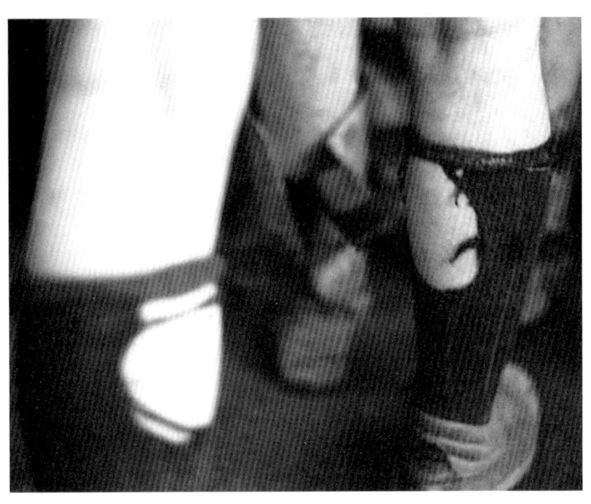

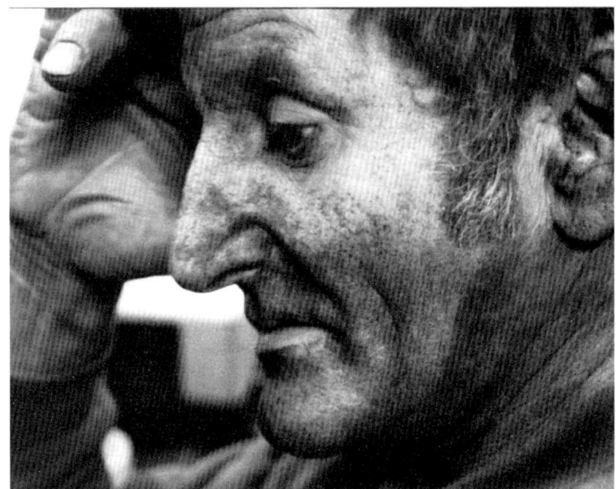

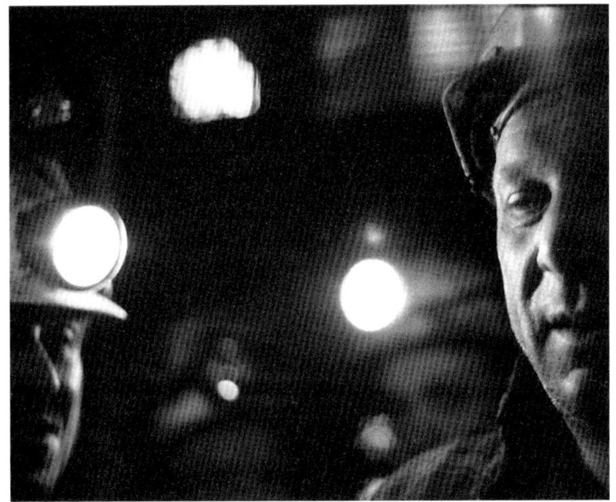

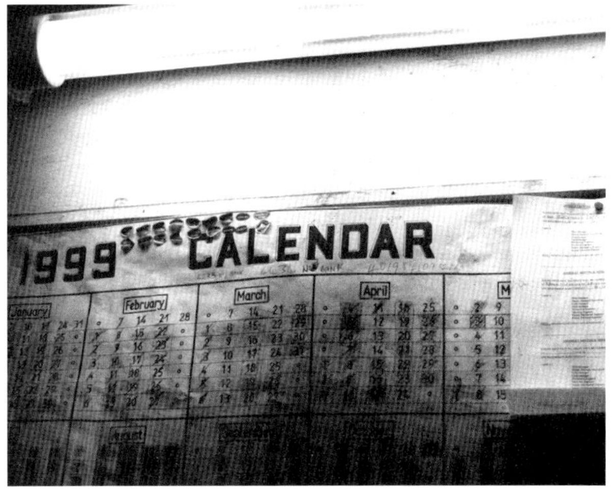

1999 CALENDAR
January
February
March
April

My Dad was a miner for 35 years. He struggled for breath for the last ten.
Dad showed me glow worms. Knitted. Loved horses. As a little girl in boxing
shorts he taught me how to float like a butterfly and sting like a bee. Dad had
huge black lined hands. He held gladioli and karaoked along with Morrissey to
This Charming Man.

Now I cannot see the face of my father, I wonder what the face of a miner
will look like in a new century? As the new Millennium begins, the mine where
Dad worked, Annesley Bentinck Colliery, will die.

Annesley Bentinck is the oldest colliery in Britain, thousands of men have
mined its seams. Moving from a century that needed coal into a new
Millennium, coal is obliterated from the social landscape. A new life was promised.
But how easy is it to create a new future? Start again with a clean slate?

Can you live in the present without also living in the past? Is an act of
erasure, an act of forgetting, the only chance to begin again?

What if you don't want to forget?

What if you want to hold on to the memories?

What if that's all you've got left?

With loss you try to hold on to memories by making them into images;
frightened that they'll slip through your fingers if you don't.

Coal mining is about men working together. Working in dirt and damp, in
unbearable heat, in tiny cramped spaces. Working in shorts or knickers with just
a beam of light to reveal a few inches in front of the face. The whiteness of their
skin stands out in the blackness. I think of young limbs, smiling faces. Muscular,
strong bodies. But most of the faces belong to men who have worked
underground since leaving school, some twenty, thirty, forty years ago. A big part
of your life. Under the dust and dirt their faces and bodies have changed. From
my first visit to the colliery it was the men's bodies that fascinated me. The lines
on their faces, their hands, the stories they could tell.

My childhood memories of Dad are brief flickers. Black mascara was always
etched around his eyes and in the creases of his big hands a big black pencil had
drawn out lines. As a child I did not imagine what the dust did, even though the
signs were already there.

Images around mining always start with miners' bodies. The starkness of
being human, stripped of any signs of civilisation, crawling around in darkness.
The body on all fours. Men having to trust that nature will bring them back to
the light. Images on the surface depict healthy bodies, bodies that work,
confident men, sure of where they place their feet.

After years of misrepresentation miners are wary; they know how cameras depict them. Some of the men remembered Dad. He was quiet and hard working. Talking to the men I was touched by their openness and generosity; but mostly it was their humour that shone out. A humour surprising given the circumstances they found themselves in.

Everything in mining is about relationships. Present and past. Daylight and the darkness of the mine. Ascent, descent. The human and the natural. The physical and the psychological. The story of mining is about a relationship between the mine and the men and about the relationships between the men themselves. How often have we heard about the 'crack', the camaraderie, the watching out for each other? How does working in a dark, dangerous hole day after day affect how the men relate to each other? How does this 'looking out for each other' translate in the twenty-first century? It seems an old-fashioned thing, this empathy and shared experience in the context of our dissolving communities. Making this piece for the colliery site, I'm constantly asking: why are these relationships important and how can I translate them?

1999	Hospital. Massaged Dad's hands, saying that I'd never seen them so clean. All my life the creases, lines and nails have always been black with coal dust. He laughed.

Dad is on his journey. It is his journey. We try to adapt to the changing conditions of his body. Can the fear be lessened by knowing that we are there with him, holding his hand, to soothe and love him? Part of me wants to have control, but I have no control over his body. His body is doing what it is doing. It has a life of its own.

2000	Going underground. You have to be kitted out. Safety first. Helmet, lamp, goggles, earphones, kneepads, a self-rescuer kit. And lots of water. Physically you have to be strong. Goodbye daylight. Getting in the shaft cage you descend into darkness.

The air changes, it's cold and smells of old bodies. You learn how to breathe differently, quickly. Like there's not enough air. Breathe shallow. Ventilation pipes run throughout, bringing in oxygen to keep the mine alive. One of the miners talked about the mine as a living, breathing thing. And being down the mine is like being inside a body. Archways, tunnels, shafts, subterranean veins. Dark and grey. Steel, corrugated. A noisy body. It could be the film set of *Alien*, water dripping, strange, stale smells. The temperature changes from hot and humid, over one hundred degrees in places, to freezing cold and windy. We walked the 'microwave mile'. It took over an hour and a half to get to the coalface. The walking alternates with rides on conveyor belts. Like being in an Indiana Jones scene, you lie down flat on the conveyor belt which sends you hurtling into the darkness. The mine is another world, where time is changed.

Three things stay in my mind after going underground: FEMALE, LIVING THING, GHOSTS.

Ironically 70s archive footage proclaimed coal as an industry of the twenty-first century. Images of unknown men descending in cages. Recruitment propaganda for the young working class. Generations of men, fathers, sons, grandfathers, uncles, cousins. The coal dust clings to their sweat. They try to shower-off the black stains on skin. "When you're dirty you don't have a voice, you're just a dirty face". The dust gets everywhere, it eats away at masculinity.

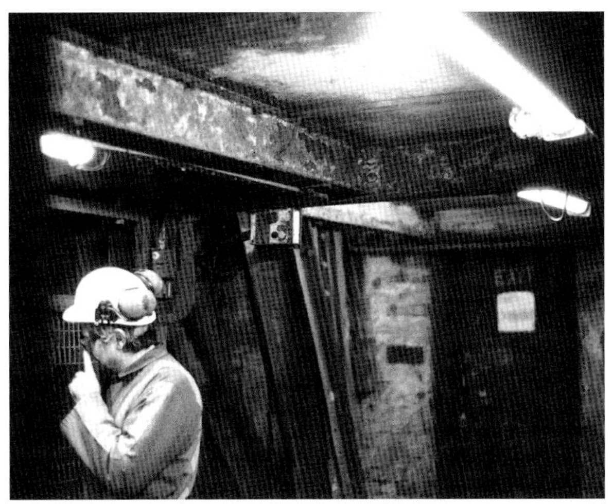

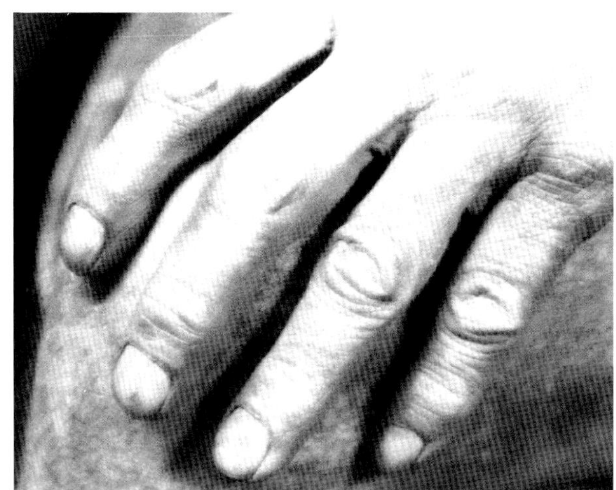

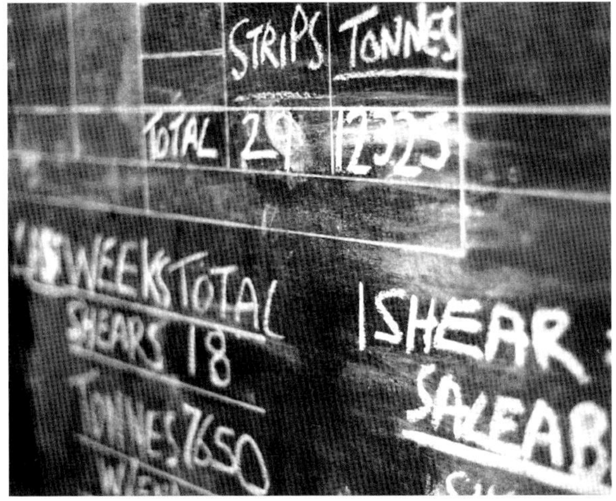
STRIPS TONNES
TOTAL 29 12923
WEEKS TOTAL
SHEARS 18
TONNES 7650
1 SHEAR
SALEAB

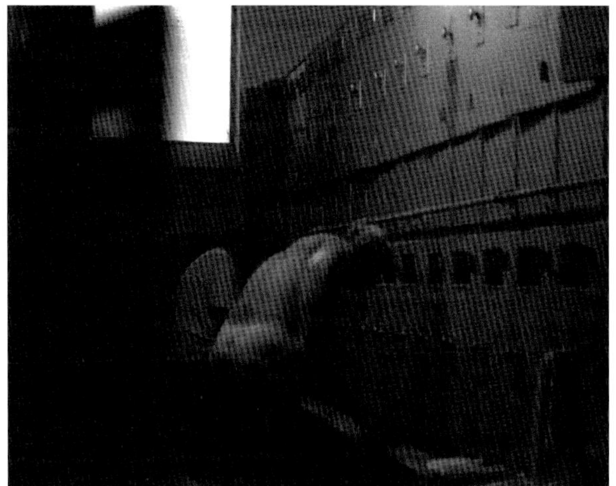

There have been many silent deaths.

"You go down the mine a young man and come up old".

Archive images of miners are like old pictures of themselves that have died. Now, washing away the dirt, lines and creases, reveals a new body. How will they define themselves as men in now changed bodies?

1999   Hospital. The man in the bed opposite Dad told Mum that Dad had cried himself to sleep at night. Father, man, human, crying. When your body lets you down you've lost control of your future, your destiny. Dad died. The dust found his heart and ate into it.

2000   Hands make a fire. Kindle the tiny flame. What have these hands done, what will they do now? I will never forget the story of Dad's hands. They would never come clean. Black, lined hands. If you could have read the palms, the heart line, the fate line, what would they have said?

Standing at the door step with a piece of coal in hand. A memory of New Year's Eve. The clock is ready to strike midnight. My father, brother and sisters are about to step over the threshold of the door carrying a piece of coal. First footing is a ritual that welcomes in the new. In first footing COAL = LUCK, HOPE and WEALTH. Stepping over the doorstep in a new Millennium, I am struck by the irony of what coal has come to mean.

The last shift. No *Brassed Off* style scenes, no silhouetted figures of miners and their families, leaving the pit wheel in the dying light. There were no tears. It has been a slow and quiet death. Just a shaking of hands. And a brief well-wishing for the future, for what it might bring.

Over the last century there has been a myriad of images of miners: mainly black and white. They depicted heroic, dirty men. Through the collective belief in their revolutionary power, the miners shaped a hope for society. White and black. They could also pollute, overthrow. They were seen as a germ, a virus. Yet in times of need the miner was the backbone, the backbone of the nation. Heseltine talked about making a green and pleasant garden of the coalfields.

What has grown in the garden? Sanitised versions of mining are there in the museum experience. No dirt, no noise, no dust. Just plastic models of miners. And old pit sites have generally spawned American Adventure Theme Parks, Kentucky Fried Chickens and supermarkets. Out with the old, in with the industry of the future: leisure. People in this area have a lot of time on their hands.

1999   I.D. bracelet reads IAN BRIAN POOLE 17-9-35

2000   A child's hand writes down new resolutions, a wish list. Though not all wishes can be granted.

Pit shower room. Water streams down the men's bodies, making them clean. Slowly over time water will fill the tunnel ways of the mine and the ghosts of masculinity will be submerged.

They say that memory lives on. But after one month of the colliery closing one of the men said: "You begin to feel like the memories belonged to someone else. Maybe it wasn't you. Maybe it wasn't your life, but someone else's."

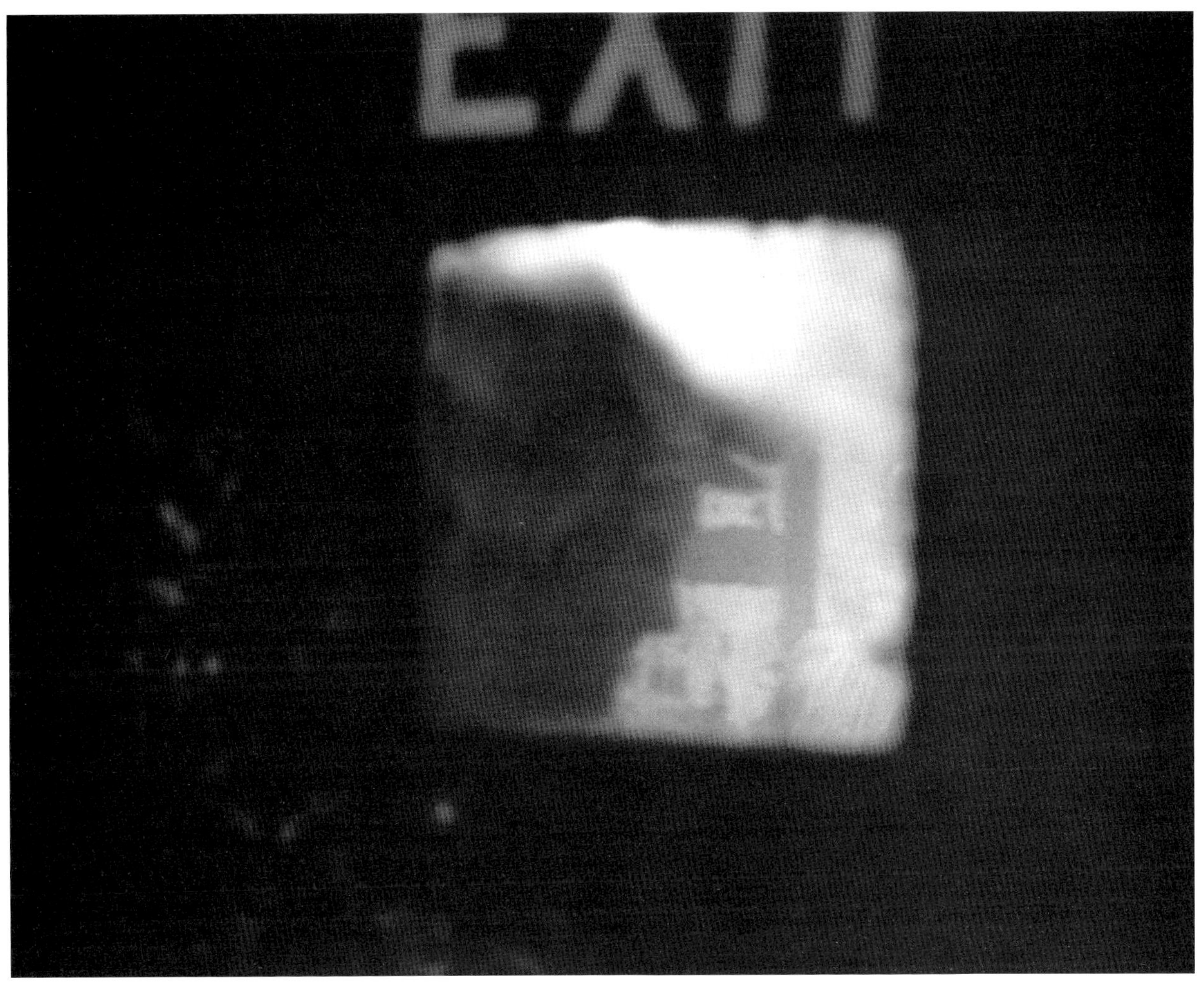

Adrian Heathfield

End Time Now

I   **Suppose something appears** to be ending; an era, a work of art, a story, a love, a life. You look back on its duration and account for the time spent. You evaluate and, listening to what the past tells, draw lessons for life in the present. The cultural milieu in which you live is filled with representations that might offer such lessons; the image, text and object residues of lives, loves and times whose moment has passed. In this learning you might come to believe that you have survived the thing that has ended, you might create a bar between you and it, and so consign it to the past. You might even think that your reckoning is part of an inevitable progression, in which a relentlessly discarded and ever-receding past makes a present which is itself drawn on by some unknown future. You think for a moment that this is something like History. But at once your ability to think of your learning as over, of the past as closed, is troubled. You are smaller than history and it does not wait for you. Each day you see around you things whose 'life' evidently extends beyond your own. You are haunted. You live in places that have long preceded you, places upon which you will barely make a mark. You make things, in order to extend your presence in the world, but when you see what you have made you are filled with sorrow; your creations already lack you as the witness to their 'eternal' value. The representations that seemed to promise survival only call you back to your finitude: you will not survive. Something happens; somewhere in the heart of this negativity you begin to embrace it. You sense a strategy arising from this touch, a different way of learning to live. Now, instead, you want to learn something more about the value of making and seeing things that do not last, about the value of the transient and the ephemeral, the value of the present. Why else would you have picked up this book, if you didn't think that it had something to do with the trouble between what you know and how you experience time; your ambivalence inside this historical moment; your sense of life as a strange mix of stasis, progression and regression; your need for art to address this feeling; your hunch, like mine, that performance has something to do with this trouble, something to say about it.

Performance, as an ephemeral act, seems to offer little to tell. It disappears fast and leaves the scarcest traces for historical record. You really have to be there, and even then that's not enough; the event itself is hard to fix in consciousness, in memory and in writing. Hard, because the experience of performance is often something like a trauma, a witnessing of an event that is constituted by the very fact that it exceeds you. The event is too full and seems too quick for you to know or contain it, which makes you feel like you were never fully there. As such, performance institutes a crisis in our ways of rationalising time: it leads us back to our elemental physical relation to time, where time is not simply experienced as linear, progressive and accumulative, but is also infused with suspension and loss. Performance makes apparent that it is neither original nor secondary, new nor old, but a kind of physical and imagistic repetition, in which the distinction between past and present falters and slides. And just like trauma, the best performance persists in recurrence: it remains unresolved, haunting our memories, documents and critical frameworks. Since it is neither knowable in the present of its enactment nor in its subsequent remainders, it stalls notions of progress, ruptures certainty and eludes historicisation. What then, can be learnt in the instance of disappearance, what can be told from the very moment of performance, what might its value be? How might the temporality of performance be connected to the contemporary experience of time?

II   In *A Decade of Forced Entertainment*, a fragmented narration of their performance practice from the mid-1980s to the mid-1990s, the company assert the significance of time in their aesthetic, and the connection between this use of time and an array of cultural, historical and fictional phenomena. Something appeared to be ending.[1] The piece was written and performed by the company under the threat of closure, and serves as both a retrospective summation of their body of work and a premature valediction. It is also an alternate and disjointed history of a Britain in dissolution, a place that Tim Etchells has come to call 'Endland'. In this work, historical fact blends into social, cultural and personal observation, which in turn melds into flashes of allegory and fragments of their performance works from the period. But one phrase surfaces again and again: "They knew something strange had happened to time." In a broken summation, the sources of this knowledge, the clues to the qualities and causes of time's distortion in contemporary culture, are found in the associations between the fragments of the text.

Writing their history, the company tried to draw a map of 'Endland' that "marked [...] the events of the last ten years", but the process was impossible, its failure led further and further into the recesses of history, to the "beginnings of geological time". The map the company drew "was scribbled over a thousand times – utterly black." Time, it would seem, feels strange because of the inability to recount history or account for the past; the weight of a past so full that to attempt to accommodate it in the present or to trace its contours would be to overwrite the page until there was nothing but ink. Blackness is held out as the pictorial index of an undepictable human suffering that requires a sublime representation in the present. Elsewhere in this piece the strangeness of time is intimately connected to a culture-wide absence of faith in grand social narratives, so that only the most personal events, "the [...] injuries and fallings in or out of love", those events close to the body and the heart, could be told with any assurance, or committed to record. Elsewhere again, time warps through the mediascape of contemporary culture; the *Challenger* disaster takes place in Manchester in 1985, in the contractions and folds of space in a globalised culture. Elaborating its relation to catastrophe, time's current irregularity is associated with a car crash lived like a cartoon in which the crash victims' bodies become uncanny combinations of plastic and blood. As if a body close to the current experience of temporal disorder is so frail in the wake of some elemental accident, so near to death, that it loses its authentic foundation, its very identity. This association between altered time and an inauthentic body is followed by two real minutes of silence for two real dead friends. Contemporary experience, then, falls into a state of estrangement from orthodox time because history is unnarratable, personal time is at once too vital and too minuscule to register, too at odds with public time which, in a shrunken world, continuously presents us with the catastrophic. Each of these forces differently reflects a return to phenomenal experience in the collapse of orthodox time, qualified and bounded by the presence of death. Caught in the contemplation of their own ending, this is the constellation of cultural powers that, for Forced Entertainment, makes time strange, and finds a manifestation in their performance aesthetic.

III The presence and use of altered time in contemporary performance is not surprising. Performance art has long tested the nature and resonance of temporal structures. Since the Happenings this experimentation has found many different forms: creating fleeting works; diminishing the 'known' and rehearsed dynamics of performance by opening it to improvisation and chance; employing actions in 'real time and space'; banishing, rupturing or warping fictional time and narration; scheduling works at 'improper' times; creating works whose time is autonomous and exceeds the spectator's ability to watch them; extending or shrinking duration beyond existing conventions; presenting the experience of duration through the body; deploying aesthetics of repetition which undo flow and progression. Nor should it be surprising that many artists working in other forms such as installation and video art are increasingly drawn to experimentation with the temporal dynamics of expression. These varied deployments of altered time invariably bring the art work towards the condition of eventhood, and shift the spectator's physical experience of temporality in order to de-naturalize our sense of official, public, clock time. It is no coincidence that a broad aesthetic shift towards temporalised expression has taken place under the shadow of late capitalism. For it is precisely in this time that orthodox time seems so out of synch with experience; seems, at the very height of its dominance and power, to shatter and fragment.

As the forces of late capitalism extend into more and more aspects of our lives they set in play a series of effects and experiences. In the logic of capital, time is a commodity that must be exploited to its maximum potential; wasted (non-productive) time is thus contracted or excluded from institutional operations. The hours of darkness are illuminated and become functional. Global capitalism institutes international links between its diverse agents, which require productive exchange, which in turn presses work life and then social life towards world-wide simultaneity. In the extension towards simultaneity there is an increased sense for individual subjects of the dissolution of personal or private temporality into the structure of a public temporality. Technologies which increasingly govern human interactions also operate through the most economical means, hence increased speed becomes the primary value in technological change, and communication itself is increasingly subject to acceleration. The time of technologies becomes habituated as human time, merged into social and physical rhythms. More than ever today, the necessity of controlling productivity by capitalising time results in the need to protect the present from the vagaries of the future. Consequently social institutions and their structures of operation seem increasingly based on the promise, on a projection forward whose purpose is better to control the uncertainty of the future, to secure the future in the present. Time's volatility is subdued and the future is 'colonised'. In social institutions the operational necessity of knowing the future now combines with technologically driven acceleration in systems of communication, so that the gap between the present and the future is eliminated, the future becomes less possible and more real. Relentless change is required as long as it is controlled. The future's function as an open horizon, as a space of possibilities, is diminished. In the heat of society's drive to foreknowledge, the future is drawn closer to the present into which it threatens to dissolve, creating instead what Nowotny has called an 'extended present'.[2]

Through these contexts, I want to look at one particular exemplary cultural intervention, that sheds light on the capacity of performance to open and challenge these orders of temporality and their operation upon experience. As in Forced Entertainment's decade narration, the deviation from orthodox time is marked as a return to an unstable temporality of physical experience.

IV In *One Year Performance* Tehching Hsieh created a monumental durational work in which he punched a time clock on the hour every hour, twenty four hours a day, for an entire year, beginning on April 11th 1980 at 7pm and ending on April 11th 1981 at 6pm. Hsieh's life during this year was ordered around the recurring regulated act, he could not stray far from his New York loft, nor could he sleep continuously for more than fifty or so minutes. Each day a witness came to verify the authenticity of his punch cards. During the course of the year Hsieh was unable to perform only 131 of the possible 8,760 punch-ins. He shaved his head before the performance began and then did not cut his hair throughout the duration of the year. After each punch-in he recorded his body beside the time clock and punch cards by taking a single still frame on a 16mm film camera. The resultant silent colour film survives the performance and when played in flow lasts just six minutes and two seconds. Visually the film is an uncanny mix of stasis and movement, bluntness and complexity, minimalism and excess. In its subdued colours the image-poverty of the film cuts against the immense scope of its human content. The film acts as an extraordinary visual testimony in which Hsieh's body rapidly mutates and trembles in the grip of a relentless machinic condensation of time. However, the art work called *One Year Performance* is neither performance, nor photograph, nor film; the work itself exists somewhere between the year-long event and its record, somewhere in the fusion and clash of its constitutive forms.

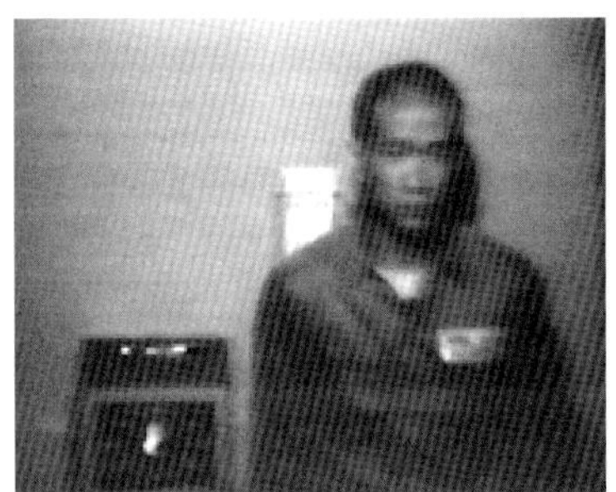

Hsieh's piece continues in a tradition of late twentieth century artist's performance, as a resistance to, if not rejection of, the commodification of the art market; but I want to suggest that the cultural value of this work goes beyond

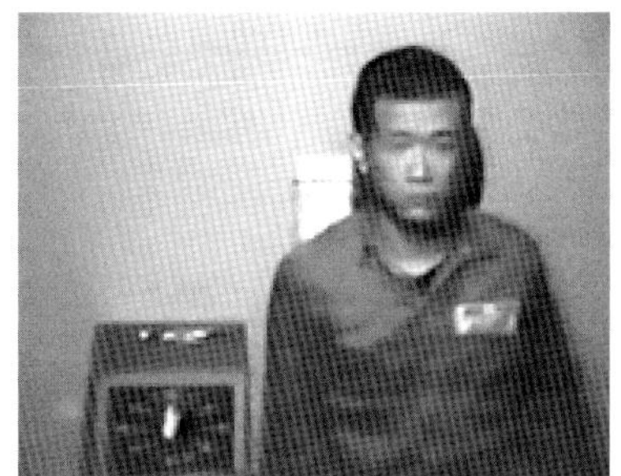

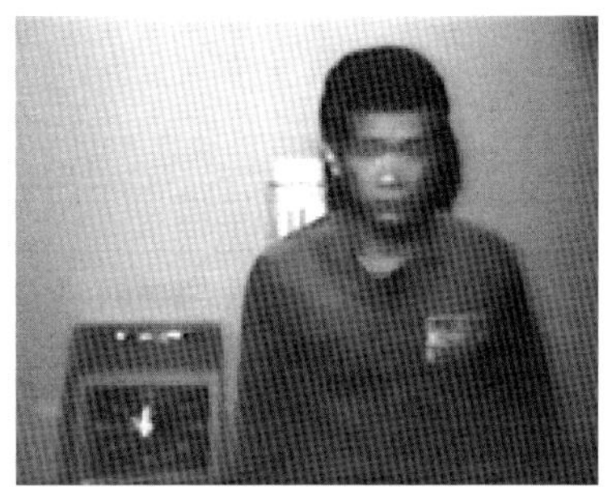

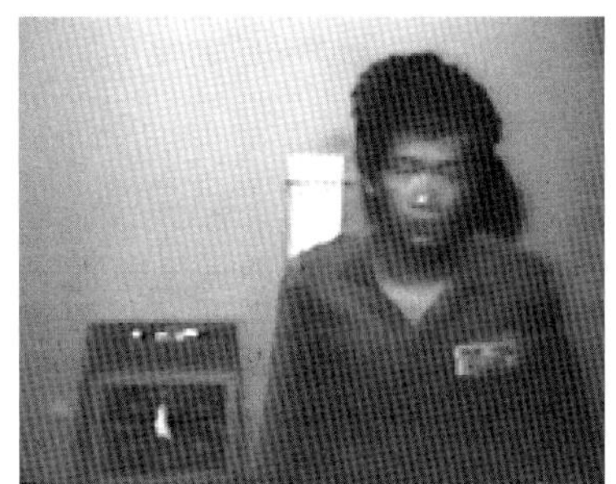

its status as a partial-object in that market. What is enacted in *One Year Performance* is a systemic critique of the temporal logics upon which the social organisations of late capitalism are founded. Hsieh gives over his life to the work of art, but also his art is given over to the time of work. In the moment of recording-clocking, the separation of public and private time realms is dissolved, his personal temporality is pressed into another order; circadian rhythm is trained to late-industrial time. The regulation of the piece and the presence of the symbols of the time clock and punch cards secure not only the piece's reference to temporal rationalisation, but its critical address to the forces which currently condition this temporality, the institutions of late capitalism. Hsieh labours under the temporal orders of capitalism but evidently does not produce in the terms of those orders; he is waiting, doing nothing, his action lacks visible function and utility. But nonetheless this work involves a human expenditure and through its process something is produced: a film. However, his actions are excessive, uneconomical, they create a product whose use value is in doubt. Is the film the work itself or its archival document, the piece or the trace? Is the film the accumulation of the work, or is it its waste product? As document, the film cannot even be said to capture its object, but rather it reproduces the excess which formed it, re-iterates the effects of this excess.

The film's ability to represent its referent is evidently called into question, the performance clearly exceeds the record, causes breaks in its representational coherence, which repeatedly signal to what is not there, not made visible, not represented. The work thus brings into presence a series of absences, whose value is made apparent. The film gives access for the spectator to the consequences of Hsieh's giving over of his self to the temporal regulation of capitalism; a giving over of the subject's freedom, to move, to follow a biological rhythm, to live unsurveilled. Crucially, in *One Year Performance*, it is this freedom from surveillance that emerges as the value most predominantly lost to the temporal orders of capitalism. This is highly prescient for a work of the early 1980s. In the logic of this piece every clocking-in is linked to being clocked by the camera. In the click of the shutter the forces of capitalism coincide with the technologies of visibility. Visual representation is thus itself seen as the necessary correlate upon which capitalist systems of time depend. As if the objective of such orders were not simply to make time a commodity, but to make time visible; to counter what Jacques Derrida describes as "the essential disappearance of time", since "Time, in any case, gives nothing to see. It is at the very least the element of invisibility itself." [3] The work thus presents the failure of the attempt within representation to master that very force of time which constantly evades representation. As such the piece can be read as an elaboration and critique of the operation of capital upon time, and of capitalised time upon the subject. The apparent weaknesses in the film's representational capacities effectively de-naturalise the relation between capital and time and make apparent the subject's alienation from both. But what I see in Hsieh's *One Year Performance*, more than anything else, perhaps I should say, what I feel, is his body, wracked by time, held in a kind of agitated stasis. This is a body lacking temporal continuity and physical integrity, a body whose borders oscillate and twitch; yet, a body whose still point, whose gaze, holds me remorselessly in its grip, as if to say "it is you I am implicating here."

V   He clocked on as usual. But without his noticing, the time of his dreams bled into his daily life, until every moment was like the moment of waking, days spent stalled inside the edge, hung between the possibility of rising out or falling back. By the time he had realised what had happened to time it was already too late. Too much logic had gotten into his days and under his skin. He wanted to pull himself up and sweat it out. But every day he felt himself getting closer to the ground. Often, out of the corner of his eye, he watched the second finger of the clock hesitating and slipping back, before regaining its beat. Moments of clarity, then whole hours spent in the suspension of a single thought, a single sentence, endlessly re-formulated. The world was dulled in his sight and touch. He woke most days to sheds of hair on the pillow, and blood drizzled out of his body, at first through orifices like the eyes and ears, later through the very pores of his skin. He counted the days, calculated forwards and back, lost count, began again, found his trail. He had forgotten the future, and was caught in an endless nostalgia. In a stilled moment of love (or love lost) his time was no longer his own and he drifted in an imagined simultaneity, his own time caught and blurred in the snare of another. Somewhere in his memories there were small moments of bliss and tenderness, but they had been held too tight for too long, so that even they had lost their vigour and didn't come easily anymore. Could it be, even then, even in *those* moments together, they were in different times, never simultaneous, never fully reciprocal. The images pulsed white then fizzled out, exhausted on the invisible screen of his days. Bleached out. Daylight. Burned up. His head was a TV tube flicking through a thousand different channels. The whole of his past – in all of its details, all of its nuances, pleasures and intimacies – was nothing but a cynical manufacturing job by some unnamed multi-national corporation. He was owned, contained, bought, framed, spent, sold, timed. He counted the days, calculated forwards and back, lost count, began again, found his trail. He said to himself, "I have survived".

VI   The repeated moments of representational rupture in Hsieh's work create an opening for the spectator. Perhaps one of the things that is given in this opening is time; an experience or sense of time that is excluded in the accumulative logics of the temporal orders of capitalism which this piece both inhabits and critiques. *One Year Performance* is a presentation of the ghosts that haunt the machinic operations of linear time, and in particular the ghost of the cyclical. For as much as the piece indicates time's arrow, progression and growth, it is also full of repetitions and returns. The complex interplay of linearity and cyclicality in the piece is made apparent in the visual record, where different temporal textures and symbols meet and clash. The cyclical is often associated with the natural world, with biological rhythms and with femininity, as such it is often subtly coded as soft, whereas linearity is often coded as hard, is perceived in a masculine register, it is taut, directional and doesn't curve. The hard black marks of the punch card carry the force and direction of linear time, yet their accumulation is repeatedly erased, turned in a cycle, back towards Hsieh's body. Since a day takes place in a second, the hands of the time clock itself never seem to move from the place where they began, though they spin

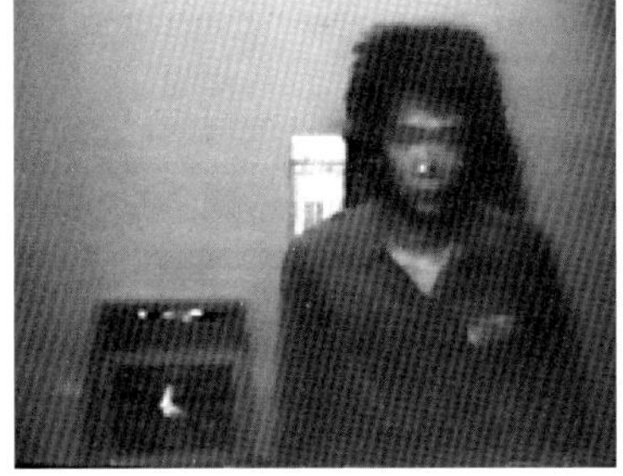

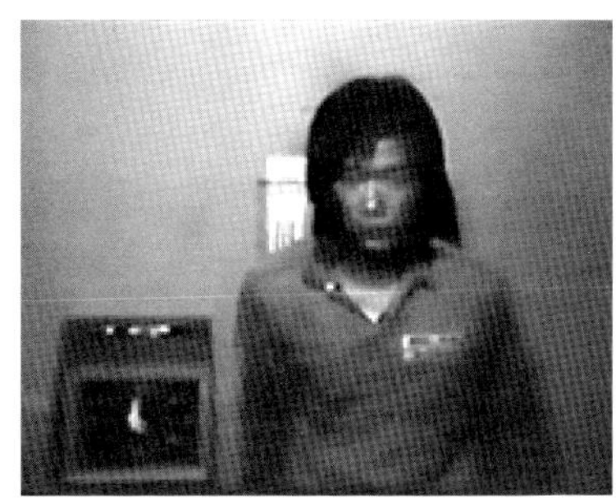

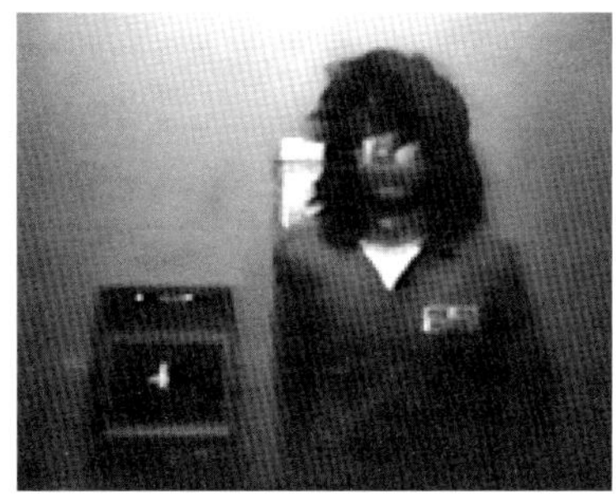

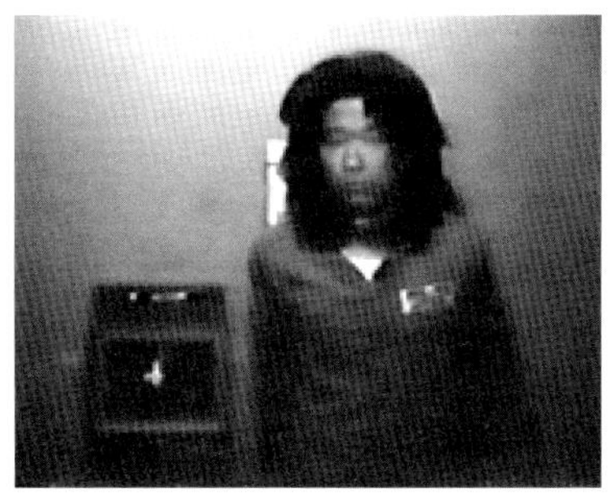

relentlessly. Hsieh shaves his head, starts masculine, establishes a linear accumulative frame; the hair will grow long, will not be cut. And yet the material employed under this temporal linearity is conversely the organic, whose gradual appearance is soft and wild. The ghost of cyclical time, returning to Hsieh in his linear quest, pressing with weight, into his body, erasing his face and identity, enveloping him in darkness. The ghost of all linear accumulation: the force of death.

Hsieh's body is flickering in and out of being before our eyes. This body is neither fully present, nor is it self-coincident, it is not owned by its subject, and it exists in a radical state of discontinuity and fray. And though his gaze insists that we look, the body given to be seen never forms a proper object for our vision. This is a body unknown to Hsieh, his unknowing returning us to our own embodiment, our own absent-presence, the sensory source of our unknowing. The film is more haptic than it is optic; it instigates a sensory relation, and what is given here, what the work discloses, is a condition or experience of embodiment that remains unmastered by the orders of capital, by the orders of discourse which govern and discipline it. The lived body met here does exist in time, but a kind of nowhen, lived by Hsieh and felt by us, in the blocking together of the linear and the cyclical, continuation and suspension: in the blocking together of incommensurable times. The phenomenal time that Hsieh gives us is both familiar and strange, moving and still, alive and dead. From the early 1980s to the present, this is perhaps the same strange time felt in Forced Entertainment's decade narration. For both of these artists the end of the twentieth century is a time of estrangement from time, a time in which a deployment of altered time within a performance aesthetic gives access to time as it might otherwise be lived and felt. In the grip of an affective sensory force, the moment of encounter with such works is one where we come to unlearn the discursive structures which shape our experiences. This is one of the enduring cultural values of performance.

And as for Hsieh, perhaps what he discovered through this work was that to remain in individuality, to stay so resolutely separated, so locked in one place, is perhaps to succumb too rigorously to disciplinary control. In his later works he discovered relation, itineracy, and living invisibly, and he produced art that has no public visibility. His most recent piece, a 13 year performance in which he made art but did not show it publicly, ended on his 49th birthday on December 31st 1999. I went to the ceremony in New York on New Year's Day at which Hsieh reported back from this invisible work. I knew something strange had happened to time. In this public appearance of an ending Hsieh finally delivered the singular product of his monumental work, a retrospective summation, an artist's history, a lasting document. The document was opened and read, it said this: "I, TEHCHING HSIEH, SURVIVED."

[1] Etchells, Tim, *Certain Fragments: Contemporary Performance and Forced Entertainment,* Routledge, 1999, pp. 29-47

[2] Nowotny, Helga, *Time: The Modern and Postmodern Experience,* Polity Press, 1994

[3] Derrida, Jacques, *Given Time: I. Counterfeit Money,* University of Chicago Press, 1993

Kira O'Reilly

Unknowing (remains)

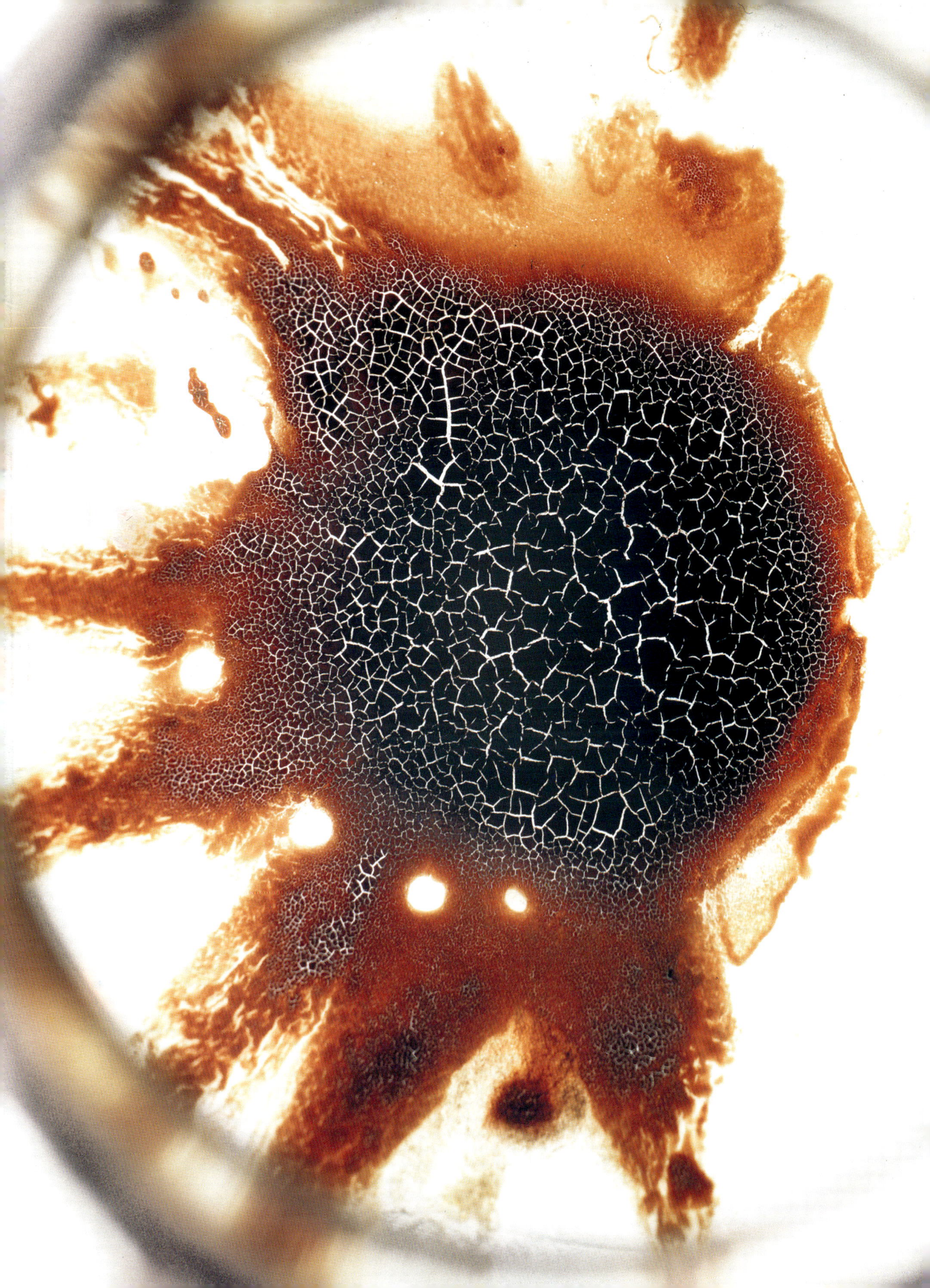

Intention

Unknowing came about as a response to the *Small Acts at the Millennium* brief, in particular to questions of the boundary between the public and the private, the existence of small or secret histories, and my need to acknowledge them. I found myself reacting to the Millennium pomp with a sense of marginalisation, a feeling of loss or grief. I felt a little invisible. I wanted to make an action or gesture that embodied these qualities.

For years as a little girl I used to work out how old I would be when the oh-so-distant Millennium arrived. Thirty-three seemed a lifetime away in my personal countdown, against a backdrop of imaginary apocalypses and armageddons, that just had to happen in the year 2000. Once-upon-a-Millennium. I wondered if I would make it. At times I wasn't certain if I even wanted to. I had taken direct actions to prevent my safe arrival at the Millennium, extreme interventions, the result of obsessive and compulsive ways of being. The actions failed and I made it. A little bit relieved, a little desperate, a little unknowing.

So I wanted to have a birthday party to mark my survival, despite myself. With cake. Presents too. A small act for a small number of people. Strangers. People as strange to me as I was to them. Marking their survival too perhaps. I wanted it to be anonymous, no names, not even aliases, but intimate too. Private. Ephemeral. It would be in a place strange to me: a city I didn't know. I wanted to maintain unknowingness as much as possible. A strangeness: to do something so personal, of no consequence to anyone really except myself, and to have it witnessed by strangers. And with a simple ritualised act of mark making. My party piece if you will. A series of twelve marks made by cutting, cupping and bleeding. An explicit use of my body (my body as myself) for celebration. An anonymous thirty-three year old birthday body for the party guests. Anybody. For me an anonymous body of guests. I hoped to have twelve guests, one for each marking.

Anonymity was important as I felt it would help me get away from a process that merely began and ended with me; a refusal of the idea that the work could only be located in my body and within my particular story. In a way, I could be anyone, despite the specificity of my body. I asked twelve people, friends from mostly non-art contexts, for a line or fragment of text on how they felt about making it to the year 2000. These were people, like myself, who I knew had survived despite the odds and who had been marginalised, ostracised or rendered invisible at some point in their lives. These texts would be worked into the fabric of the occasion and a mark would be made to correspond with each of them.

The event could only happen on one date: 24th January 2000.

Process

Perhaps the most difficult aspect of the work was finding guests. Initially they were gleaned from a process of advertising in the local press of the chosen city, on various appropriate notice boards and on the live art mailbase. They could write to a PO box or an email address. There were few responses and those that did respond had to be screened carefully and given some information about the nature of the work so that they wouldn't inadvertently enter into a situation in which they might be distressed or disturbed through witnessing the cutting and letting of blood. Most people seemed curious more than anything, several expressing their own experiences of and feelings about birthdays, life change, and the desire to try new things.

The process of contacting people who had responded to the advertisements led to odd and charming conversations with complete strangers. I would phone them from the privacy of my home, quite unknown and introduce the idea that this would be no ordinary party, that there would in fact be a mark making ritual. "Could you be a bit more specific?" was the usual reply. Only one person declined the invitation. The party was held in a hotel function room, a generic, anonymous room, and probably the site of hundreds of previous parties. A transitional space, and what seemed to me to be a fragile space as a non-art venue. A private party, the hotel was told, and no further information was given. Though I did not intend to inform the hotel of the nature of my party, in the end I unwittingly received unofficial managerial support, when against unlikely odds, one of the invited guests turned out to be the hotel manager, who felt it appropriate to decline the invitation.

As the work was realised, the need for a full complement of twelve guests became more urgent, and the intended anonymity of the participants was partially lost. There were a few genuine strangers who had been invited through the advertisements. People who are still utterly unknown to me and me to them. There were two assistants and one photographer whom I knew well. One of the curators was also there. I had a very tenuous link with another guest. Also another *Small Acts* artist came along, who I thought I didn't know, but as the party gathered I realised I had met him twice before. It also emerged that some people at the party knew each other. The vagaries of social connection and the dilemmas of rule-making and breaking became apparent to me. Yet I am glad every single one of the guests was there as they created a particular and unique permutation.

Action

In the end there were ten guests. They arrived, were welcomed and were invited to eat and drink. They were introduced to each other but without names. A special birthday soundtrack played in the background. I mingled. Inevitable conversations about birthdays and the Millennium. The game of figuring how old you would be in the year 2000 became a common topic and every now and then I would drop one of the texts I had into the conversation. After thirty minutes or so thirty-three candles were on a big white and lilac birthday cake with *Unknowing* iced on the top. Brandy glasses were handed out for a toast; not the usual drink for such an occasion but the shape of the glasses was ideal for the mark making ritual that was to follow. Each glass had a fragment of text engraved

---

"I want to mark my own personal development and prove to myself that I am continuing to seize opportunities. That's one reason I'm contacting you."
An anonymous guest

"I need this experience like I need salt on my chips."
An anonymous guest

"Birthdays are such fragile times – this could be a great idea ... and then again ... I'm ... looking for something unpredictable, unfamiliar at a time of my life when predictability and familiarity are like family members. I want 2000 to be a year of ... well, I don't know of what exactly, but not just a year the same as the last few ..."
An anonymous guest

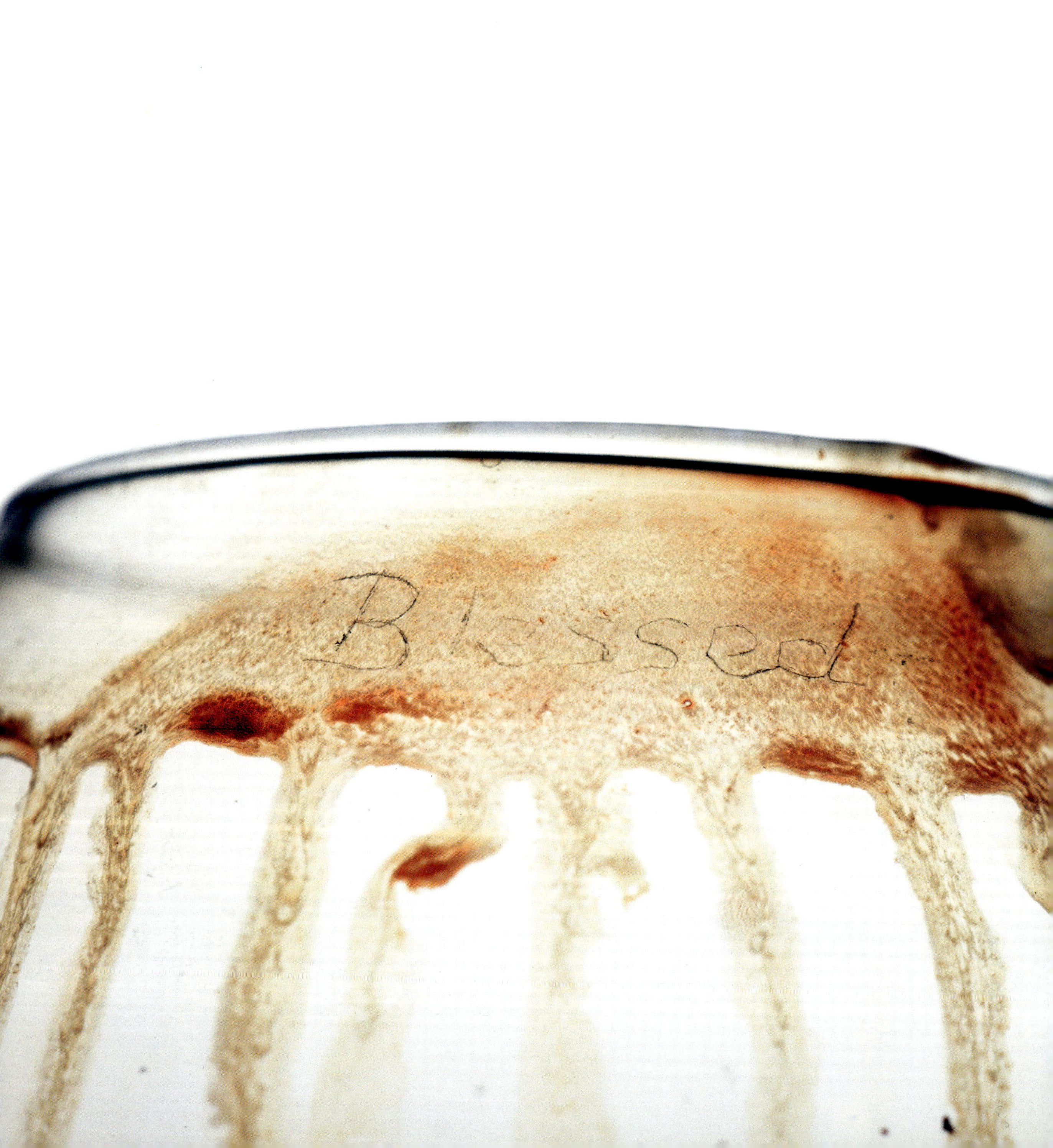
Blessed

on it, taken from my twelve earlier anonymous sources.

A toast was made and a nameless happy birthday was sung. I blew out the candles. This marked the transitional moment into the next section when the mark making would happen. Standing behind the cake, watching these people sing this happy birthday to me, stripped me of the safety of any kind of performance persona I might have tried to construct. This was my actual birthday and my actual birthday party. I think I smiled inanely, a little overcome. Unknowing.

The cake was removed from the table and I lay on it as the brandy glasses were collected.

The assistant pulled down my stockings and the back of my dress and one by one heated the brandy glasses creating suction in the glass so that they would stick to my body, sucking up the skin. Ten were applied to my back and two to my legs. These were left for ten minutes allowing blood to collect in these areas under the surface of the skin. They were then removed one at a time. A shallow cut was made and the glass reapplied. This time the suction acted to pull small amounts of blood through the slight opening in the skin. As each cut was made a sealed envelope containing one of the fragments of texts and a party popper was given to each guest.

As the blood leaked out gradually and slowly into the brandy glasses each guest was led around the table. I sought to catch their eye.

My body had become so heightened, the energies built inside me to such an extent, that I felt like my skin, that fragile membrane that separates my inside from the outside, would no longer contain me. Eventually the glasses were removed and the blood could spill; the relief was palpable and astounding to me. Blood and brandy running everywhere. I stank. I turned my head to see the guests and tried to make eye contact with each of them. Finally the white table-cloth underneath was wrapped around me and the guests led out of the room.

Documents and Remains
Photos
Scars
Memories
Stories
Advertisements in the local paper
Birthday cards
Cake order form
Paul's tape of party music
12 brandy glasses
Tablecloth
Candles from the cake
Buffet menu
Anonymous guest's response
This text

It was important to document the event, as the work was to have another life within this publication. Photographs were taken, carefully and discreetly during the course of the party and the action. I had not wanted a flash to be used as I

"It's miraculous that I'm still here, it's a real gift"

"Curious, indifferent to space and time but overjoyed at living"

"Gratitude"

"Halt and optimism"

"Blessed"

"I thrive with a lot of help from my friends"

"A fairground ride – an octopus"

"My father raped me and I said sorry"

"Hiroshima"

"Use it, don't use it. It's your choice"

"The knowledge I neither wanted nor expected to have but I'm glad I've got it"

"Passion"

Anonymous texts

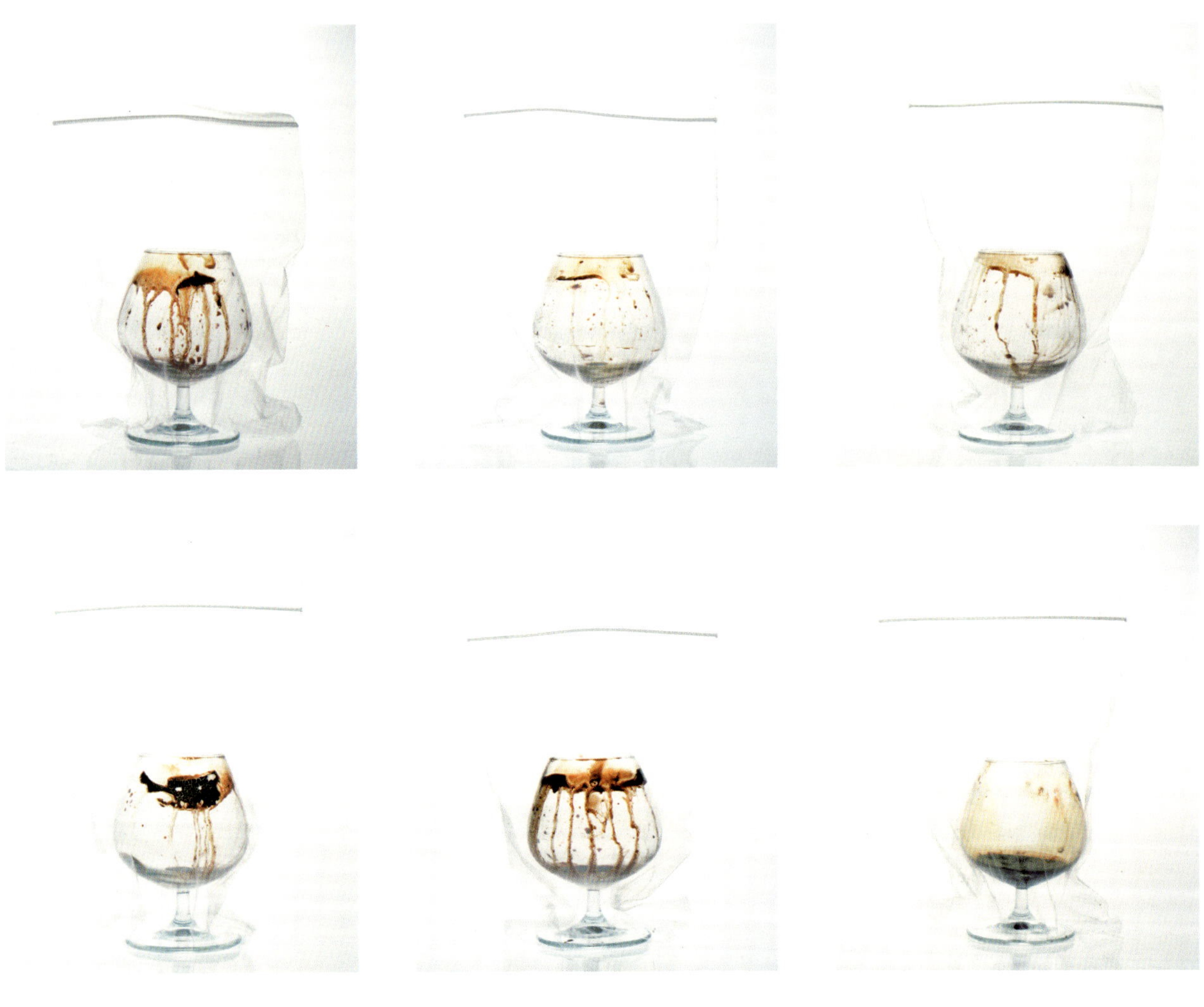

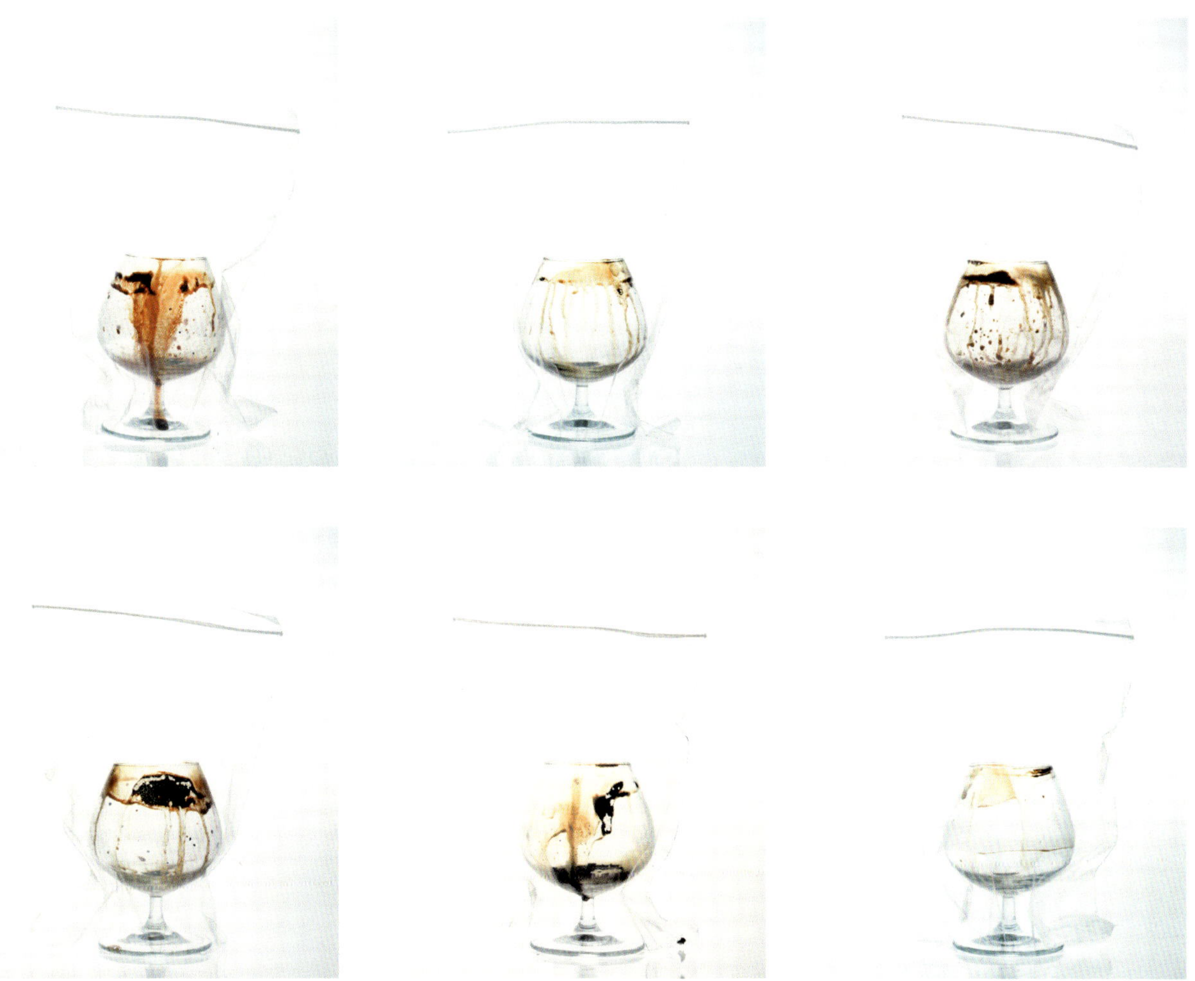

had felt it would intrude on the event and disrupt the sense of intimacy within the situation. The lighting conditions were so low that most of the images were lost. The work continues to exist in its remains, memories and objects. The bloodied brandy glasses and table cloth. The now fading scars on my body. The birthday cards. The stories individual guests may or may not have told after the event; private anecdotal accounts they might have felt moved to speak. Perhaps.

The body of this text is a residue, that which is left. An act of remembering and (re)writing, and of retracing myself, with all the inadvertent dislocations, slips and distortions that occur. As this has been written some three months after the occasion, the glasses and the table cloth have been revisited, re-photographed. The blood has dried and cracked on them. They smell faintly of brandy and of the passing of time, time drying out, fading the objects, the subtle drying-out of memory.

"I found it very cruel while at the same time peaceful almost like meditation but my mind kept thinking while the ceremony was on of the most terrible things that might take place and that more blood was going to come … although I can't stand the image of blood I had to remain silent in between of a group of strangers … thinking all the time the paranoia of the bits of skin in the glass exploding and eventually hurting you immensely … I found it shocking and extremely cruel … but I suppose you might have wanted it this way and these feelings … but it ended up too soon and also too sudden … another thing I wanted to add at this point: if I knew about the blood and the cruelty I would have drunk the whole of the brandy you gave us and even more of the wine … in order to get dizzy and a bit of drunk … and then play and rediscover my feelings and my phobias (fears) while the actual ceremony would take place … at the end my feelings was of a strange fear and also emptyness … but mainly fear of going out of the hotel … maybe fear towards the outside reality …"

Anonymous guest's response

Thank you

Katrina Horne, assistant no. 1 (cupper and cutter)

Rebecca French, assistant no. 2

Irina Padva, party photographer

The anonymous guests

The anonymous contributors of text

Paul Clarke

Liz O'Reilly for the flowers

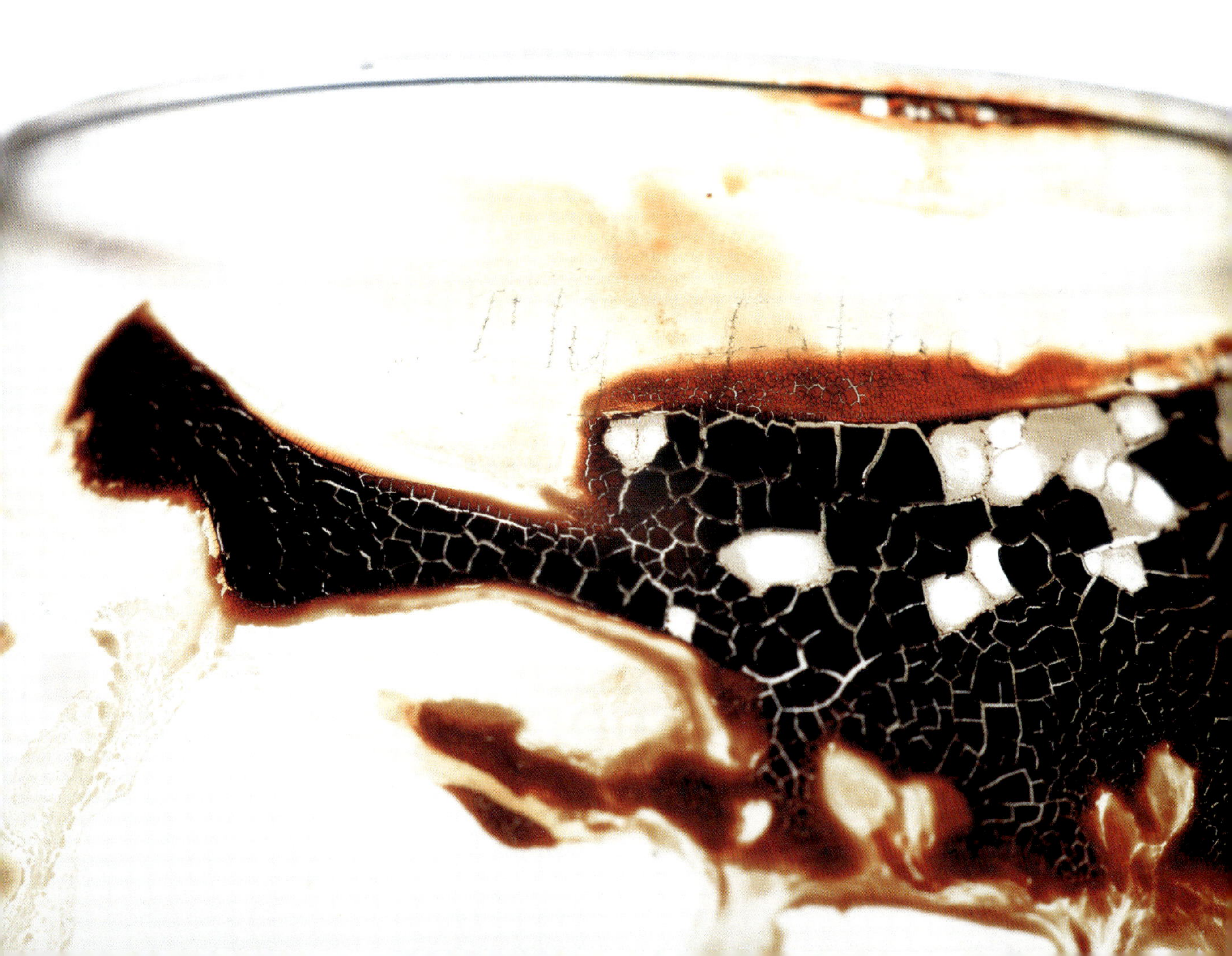

Deborah Levy

*six small acts
for big women
or six big acts for
small women*

1   Between 1994 and 1998 I wore blue mascara on my eyelashes. This seemed to me to be the opposite of femininity. No man ever said "Are you a natural blue?" To which I would have replied: "No, I am a writer."

2   In 2000 I gave birth to a baby daughter. This seemed to me to be the opposite of femininity – although it is supposed to be its centre. Milk. Flabby body. Love and tears. Is this it then? Is this the 'it' of it? Is this femininity in aces? Is this pure woman? Panic in the flesh because flesh is your place in the world as all the French theorists said in the 1980s. Yet the new century finds me not returning to Helene Cixous with her rhapsodies and exclamation marks and insistence that women should write in mother's milk, but scary-eyed Herff Applewhite known as DO to the millennarian disciples of the Heavens Gate Cult – all of them lost souls in their own skin who regarded their bodies as a vehicle, a mere container. As is the mind of course. It is possible that it is not putting my nipple into my baby's mouth, but writing books that is my purest expression of femininity. Language is a place where all the N's in femininity are up for grabs – femininity is not a virgin, never let anyone save it for themselves and tell you it belongs to them. Writing books was my way of walking into the centre of the world without anyone knowing I'm shy. Now I walk into the centre of my kitchen and deposit wet nappies into the bin. Which of the two are the more feminine actions?

3   Never forget that a daydream on a bus is sometimes a vision. And a vision is sometimes no more than a daydream on a bus.

4   If you are thinking about the future and what it holds for you – remember that the future is just a view. There are views to be had under the table and on top of a mountain. The view on top of a mountain has a grander place in the scheme of things. However, the view from under a table can be vast and might even earn you money if you can find people with power and funds interested in your point of view. But I don't want to eulogise the view from under the table – better to crawl out and stand on the table. A view is also:
a   an idea
b   wanting to do something and getting a glimmer of how to go about it
c   a place you want to be in and deciding what you have to do to get there
d   a new understanding of a situation (past, present, future)
e   believing that the present will change into something else
f   merely turning your gaze in another direction.

5   Between 1984 and 1994 I wanted to blow language apart. Now I just want coherence. I hope the above is coherent but inflected with some pleasurable difficulty? Difficulty should always be a pleasure. This is a new revelation so I might be a little shaky on this one. Regarding coherence, always remove brackets between words: for example when a forum becomes a (trans)forum or she and he become (s)he, you have not confidently claimed your enquiry into a grey area. There are of course many shades of grey, but brackets are a received shade and resemble the sort of crutches they give out in casualty when you break a leg. This might contradict what I wrote earlier about language not being a virgin – but really, cowering behind brackets is not the sort of activity you should waste your time on. Make yourself a gin m(art)ini and think again. The most recent bracket should have made you wince – if it didn't, wear beige lipstick: a fashion that seems to me to rub out lips and make them (lips), or consider alternative ways of presenting a broken bone.

6   Refugees from what was formerly known as Eastern Europe are now a common sight begging on the streets of London. Particularly women. Wearing brightly patterned long skirts, shawls and head scarves, often with gold in their ears and teeth, it is this splash of unfamiliar colour that apparently sticks in the throat of many citizens of this island. Britain's poor and dispossessed are dressed in the colours of the pavements; it's as if there is an unspoken understanding that the British poor must camouflage the gutters and climate. The Eastern European women beg with their children and tend to ask for money whilst on the move. Britain's dispossessed tend to beg with dogs and ask for money whilst sitting down. It's as if the British think that if you own a dog you are basically a good person, whereas if you own a child you are basically a bad person. The next time you meet a Romanian refugee with rosebuds on her skirt – and happen to be a linguist – offer to translate her first novel. Possibly a novel that will reflect her femininity in a way that feels more expressed to her than pushing out children to beg with.

Bobby Baker

Pull Yourself Together

text by Clare Allan

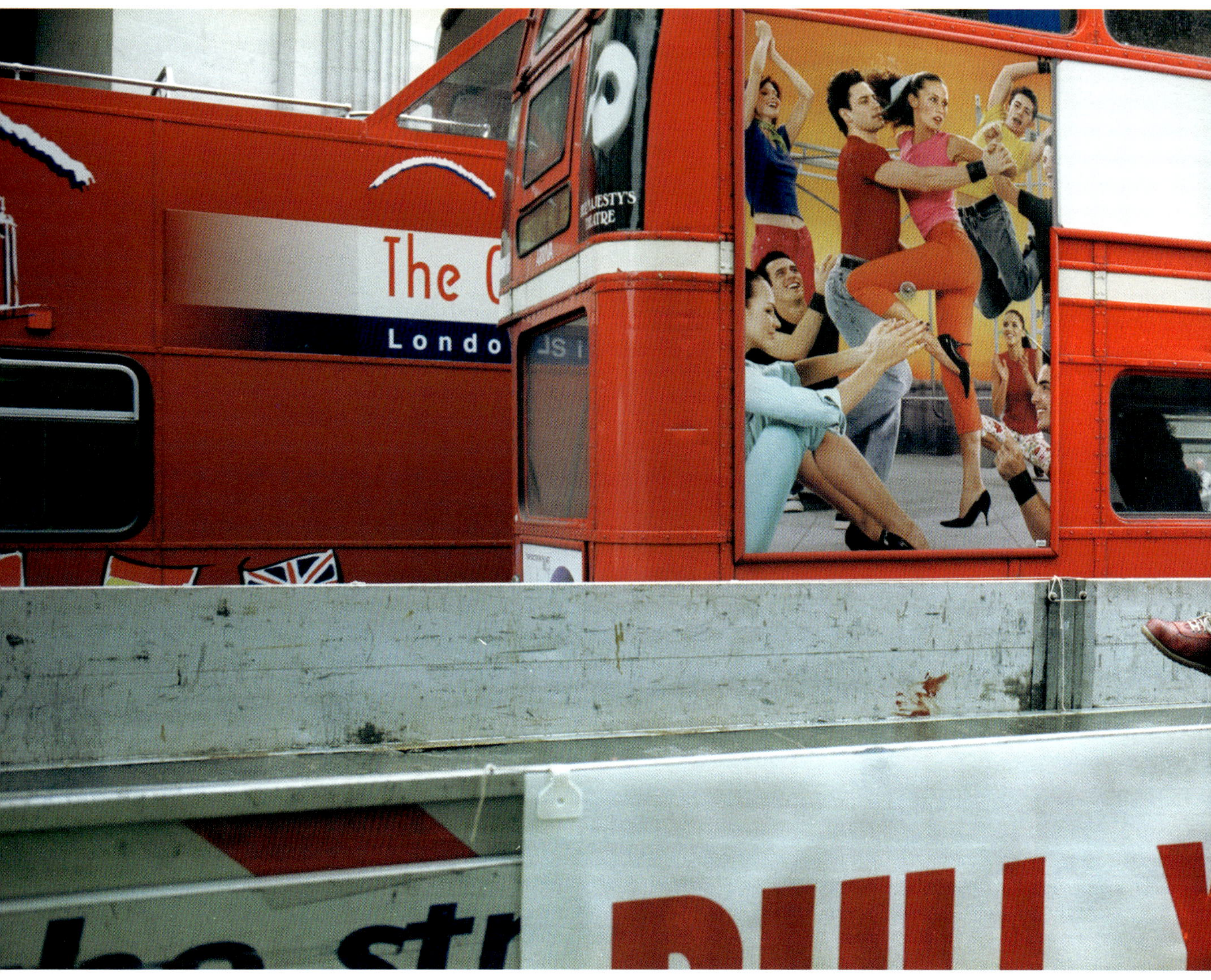
The C
London
HER MAJESTY'S THEATRE
the str
BULL

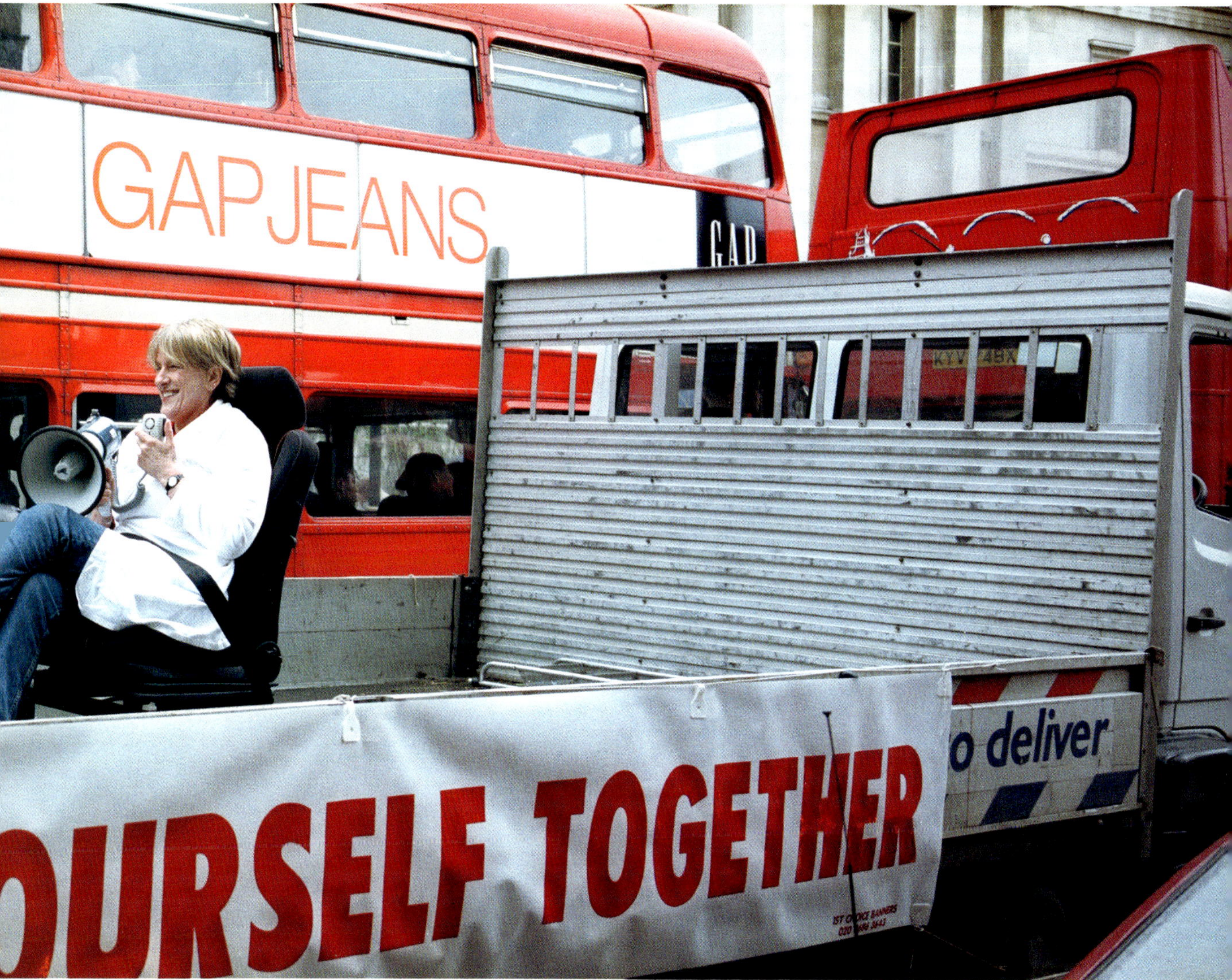
GAP JEANS
GAP
o deliver
OURSELF TOGETHER
1ST CHOICE BANNERS
020 7686 3643

Bobby's had me training for weeks. Water Aerobics, every Monday night at Archway pool. Protest is pointless. In vain I attempt to explain that, as my part in the day requires only the use of a hand, my right one, to be specific, jotting a few pertinent observations into a spiral bound notebook, such excessive physical preparation might be unnecessary, wasteful, potentially even dangerous. "Nonsense," says Bobby. "Mens sana in corpore sano." Which is bollocks anyway because I've known some lunatics with very nice bodies and I've known doctors who looked as though they lived on treacle pudding, and not the 95% fat free sort either.

The night before. Bobby and I attend our final session. She follows the instructor's movements with rigorous exactitude, tongue stuck out slightly in the effort of concentration. My feet slip and slide in every direction, every direction except that taken by the choreographed limbs of the other thirty or so participants. "Don't you just love her?" whispers Bobby, nodding towards our demonic instructor. "She's got such a sweet expression when she does that backwards leg thing." Fortunately, I don't have the breath to reply. But mere physical discomfort is as nothing to what comes next. Because it's now that the mad bit kicks in. The pool is overlooked by the first floor gym. Some fifty figures panting away in garish lycra with the spectacle of us for entertainment. The spectacle of ME for entertainment, I should say, for paranoia is a very selfish thing. It starts as a joke, a little harmless teasing from the voice in my head, grows in second long stages first into a suspicion, then into a firm suspicion, then into a concrete suspicion, and by the end of a single leg flip it has become a monstrous certainty. My psychiatrist is up there watching.

Bobby and I share a psychiatrist. With lots of other people as well, I mean. I don't suppose we are his only patients, though certainly we take up a good deal of his time. That's how we met in the first place, in fact, in the psychiatrist's waiting room, surrounded by leaflets and posters, brightly optimistic against the general drabness of the setting (the posters, that is, not us. It would never do to visit a psychiatrist in an optimistic frame of mind. To do so would be pointless, even obscurely offensive). Drugs counselling, alcohol counselling, Depression Alliance, self-harm support groups, Mind crisis telephone lines, the Samaritans, groups for people who hear voices, groups for the relatives of people who hear voices, groups for survivors of child sexual abuse, groups for survivors of groups (well no, but I am merely correcting an omission).

Bobby didn't seem very mad. Sane as a sandwich was my first impression.

I even remember a slight suspicion that she wasn't a patient at all, but rather some sort of spy, posted there to keep an eye on the likes of ME. Of course at that stage I hadn't seen any of her shows, knew nothing about her penchant for wrapping herself in food-painted sheets or firing mouthfuls of tomato ketchup across the room. Had I known all that then, I might have revised my diagnosis.

"Bobby," I whisper. "Bobby!"

She pauses, woggle poised above her head like a foam halo.

"I'm sure he's up there." I gesture to the glass-walled balcony, the lean figures pounding the treadmills like hamsters possessed.

"Who?"

"Dr X" (Forgive the pseudonym. I am a liar and a coward.) Bobby grins, delighted.

"He is!" I insist.

"Not at this time. He always comes at five-thirty."

"You mean he *does* come!"

"Of course," she nods. "Blue lycra shorts." She grins. "Gorgeous."

"So maybe he is up there then. That's it. I'm going." But Bobby just bursts out laughing. "Get a grip, Clare," she says.

And only now do I realise what Bobby meant by training. Only now do I realise that Bobby's been training on me.

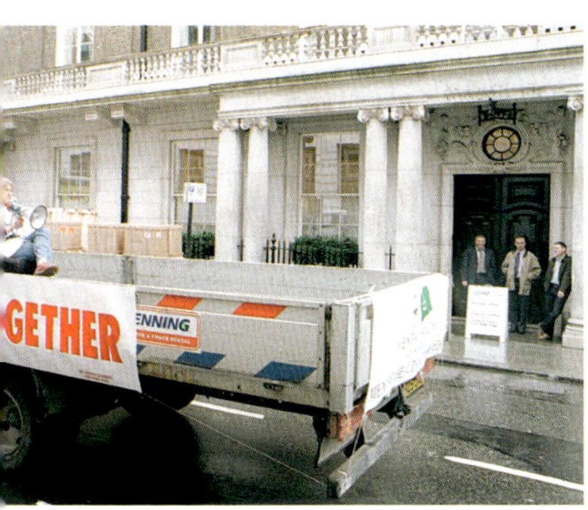

9.30 Thursday morning, and I step from the mini cab, limbs aching, outside Bobby's house. Unmissable, the huge flatbed truck parked outside, with its oddly incongruous car seat welded on the back. Bobby and Steve, the production manager, are attempting to attach the banners. Huge red letters shout from the sides. 'PULL YOURSELF TOGETHER' and a slightly more sober ensign across the back reminds passers-by that this is Mental Health Action Week. Bobby disappears into the house, to return a minute later clad in the familiar white coat which, along with footwear befitting each show, forms her standard performance costume. I glance at her feet, bright red Campers, and am quietly attempting to puzzle out their significance when Bobby catches my gaze and grins. "I thought I'd wear red this time," she explains. "For anger." She climbs up the ladder onto the back of the truck, and the angry red shoes disappear behind the sides as she straps herself into the car seat and picks up her megaphone.

Mad, crazy, insane, berserk, bonkers, barmy, round the bend. It is no coincidence that madness and anger share a vocabulary. Madness is anger hidden from view. Anger which doesn't want to hurt anyone, anger with no-one to hurt, anger rebounding out of indifferent silence, anger dismissed as anger, anger dismissed as madness.

We leave Tufnell Park and head down through Camden Town towards Trafalgar Square. Steve drives and I sit up front with him in the cab. I can see Bobby through the windows behind my head and I can't help feeling how incredibly exposed she is out there, far more so than in front of the largest theatre audience. "I just hope they'll get it," she confided beforehand. "I just hope they get the fact that I'm being ironic." The megaphone is very directional. It is possible to pick people out individually simply by pointing it at them. We stop at a red light. Beside us, two men are loading equipment onto a lorry, bent over,

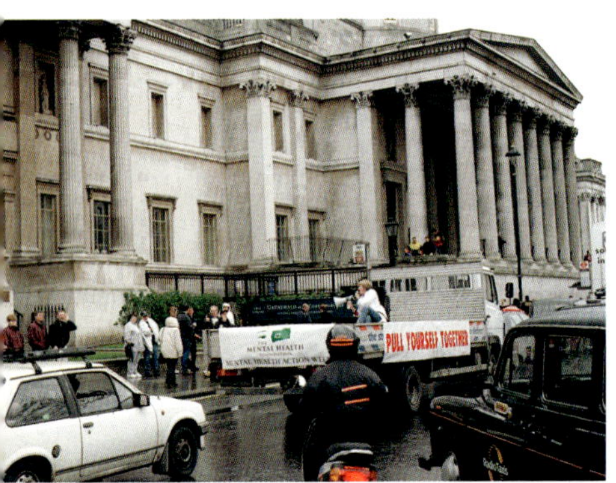

backs facing the road. Suddenly, seemingly out of nowhere, a voice booms down from above their heads. "PULL YOURSELVES TOGETHER!" They turn to find a middle-aged woman in a white coat, strapped into a car seat on the back of a lorry, aiming a megaphone at them. "What do you want?" asks one, but he's smiling now. "I want you to pull yourself together," says Bobby. "I'll try," he promises, laughing. And off we go.

Laughter is the most common reaction. Good-humoured, good will. "Have you noticed the general jollity?" asks Bobby, and indeed it's impossible not to. She's warming to her theme now, drawing confidence from the reactions of her targets. "GET A GRIP! PULL YOURSELF TOGETHER NOW!" On a jammed-up Thursday morning in the pouring rain, with the streets a mess of road works and litter, and cigarettes gone up to over four pounds a packet, the level of friendliness is enormously impressive. It occurs to me that, as therapies go, it might be rather more effective to spend a day like this, on a tour of rain-drenched London in a truck with Bobby, than to sit in a room with ten other depressives and listen to their stories of abuse. But then I'm no psychologist.

Not everybody laughs, of course, but very few are openly abusive. I could replicate the entire day's V-signs without having to employ a single finger twice. Two women standing on Regent Street, brassy and bored, clutching their latest purchases, scarcely look up as they fire back an automatic "Ayo fak awwff!", before hailing a cab. A man waiting at a crossing taps his head at Bobby in that universal gesture, so casual and yet so desperately unnerving for anyone for whom mental illness is a daily reality and not merely a term of abuse or a bad joke. I remember sitting on Hampstead Heath with a couple of (sane) friends. Nearby a father screamed at his high-spirited young kids. "For God's sake, you two! Just calm down! You're behaving like a couple of lunatics." My friends burst out laughing. "It's true," they agreed. "They are!" I couldn't think of anything to say. Nothing, at least, that wouldn't alienate, that wouldn't unleash the monster anger into a pleasant North London afternoon. Perhaps that's one reason why Bobby's piece is so effective. The red shoes are hidden from view. Her humour, ironic without being cutting, acts as a unifying rather than a divisive medium. Twisted round in the cab to capture people's responses, what I witness is a sequence of intimate and individual connections. "Why?" ask two women, beaming, arm in arm outside the National Gallery. "Why should we pull ourselves together!"

We drive round and round Trafalgar Square. Volunteers from the Mental Health Foundation are handing out leaflets. Tourists photographing each other beside huge lions turn and stare as Bobby glides past. "Get a grip! That's no way to get the baby bathed." A group of lads start heckling. "Are you on day release? What is this, care in the community?" What strikes me is their utter lack of malice, their certainty that Bobby is in on the joke, that she's one of them, as opposed to one of *them*, the nutters, the loons, the dribblers, the ones who foam at the mouth, or howl at the moon, or run around knifing people or whatever else we mad people are supposed to get up to if we're let out of our padded cells for more than five minutes at a time. An elderly man, crossing behind the truck in St James's Square, pauses to look up at Bobby, "Don't they give you an umbrella?" before disappearing into the London Library.

My favourites, though, are the panickers. The ones who, caught in the blare of the megaphone, try to pretend that the voice isn't meant for them. Heads down, arms straight by their sides. Is it really possible not to notice a lorry pull up alongside you with a woman strapped on the back, yelling advice through a megaphone? And yet the pretence. Transparent, hiding nothing, heroic almost in its hopelessness. That's what's so funny. At least to an observer. Less funny, the fact that I know it's what I would do. And indeed, the ostrich effect is far more common amongst women, while men are more likely to react with a quick joke or a bit of banter. Disappointing, but undeniably true. I haven't noticed before how nervous a great many women are when out on the streets of the capital. Even in the middle of Trafalgar Square, surrounded by pigeons and policemen, the men stand back, arms crossed, enjoying the bizarre spectacle of a white-coated Bobby, megaphone in hand, circling her herd of potential prey, while the women hurry past, heads down. The men spread outwards, hoping to be picked, the women shrink inwards, hoping to become invisible. I exaggerate of course.

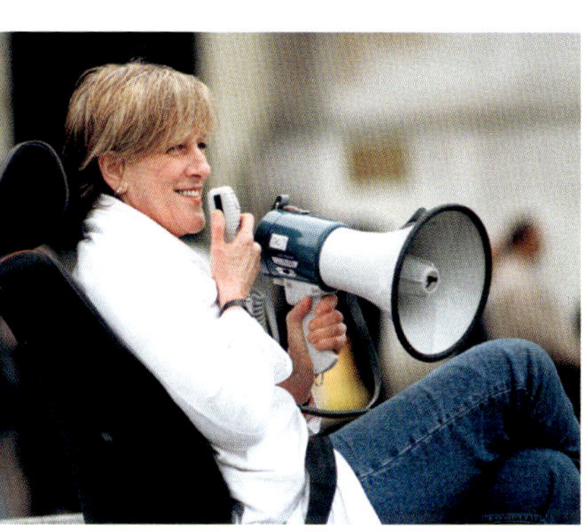

It's lunchtime and we head south over Waterloo Bridge driving past a small group of friends. "Pull yourselves together," shouts Bobby, and they do, literally, pulling themselves together in a jovial group hug. "Did you see that!" cries Bobby, just making sure her writer's paying proper attention. It hasn't stopped raining all morning and Bobby is soaked to the skin and freezing. The megaphone, on the other hand, has got itself overheated and emits a sound like a dying mouse. We get them both in the cab and Steve works on the megaphone while Bobby, wrapped in my fleece, drapes herself across all four heaters simultaneously. "Feel that" she complains, holding out a dripping arm for my inspection. "Well thank heavens you did all that training," I tell her. "I mean after all you're used to being wet."

In the afternoon we tackle Regent Street, Soho, Covent Garden, St Pancras. A flood of reactions and images. The waiter dancing in the doorway of his cafe, the small crowd cheering from a pedestrian crossing. "We will!" "We'll try!" A man drawing up alongside us in the back of a cab. "Don't I look together?" he asks. "Not enough," Bobby tells him. "You're mad", says the man. "No I'm not." "Well you look it." But what does madness look like? Hannibal Lecter or Princess Diana? Or Bobby Baker? Or me? Or you? "The second sign of madness is hairs on the palm of your hand … The first sign is looking for them." So ran the joke at school. "The little white van's going to come and take you away," I would tell people, never dreaming that one day it would come for me. Because that is the thought that cannot be tolerated, that is the thought that must not ever be thought. Madness is other, and the jokes and the gestures and the hurrying past are all, more or less, attempts at keeping it so. Only mad people go mad.

But why is madness so high in the stigma charts? Two reasons, I think. Firstly, a lack of physical evidence. Madness is an opinion, not a fact, and just as there's no proof that you've 'got it', there's also no proof that you've not. And secondly because of its peculiar reflective quality. Madness, like a mirror, resembles nothing so closely as the person looking into it. There is no us and them. It's all just a matter of degree, and the slope is slippery. Look long enough, and it's easy to become convinced that the only thing keeping you sane is your own insistence that that is what you are. Lose that and you've had it.

No wonder then that most people don't stay long enough to look. No wonder that for the vast majority of people, in our culture at least, mental illness is still, at the dawn of the twenty-first century, the most unnerving, embarrassing, humiliating condition of them all. And I'm not referring to the sufferer's experience, but rather to that of the spectator, if such distinctions can be drawn in what is essentially an act of self-recognition.

In Camden Town a drunk lurches out into the road and hangs for a moment off the side of the truck. "What's all this in aid of then?" "Mental Health Action Week." "Right on!" He gives her a double thumbs up, "Right on!" but in doing so loses his hold and lands neatly back on the pavement. We squeeze through the bottleneck of Kentish Town. "No! You pull *yourself* together" and on up to Archway, my special request, where Bobby addresses the spectacularly ugly Waterlow Unit on Highgate Hill, where I have spent a number of unsuccessful vacations. The car park is empty. Usually a small huddle of patients, regulars, sit perched on the front wall drinking cans from the offy over the road, but the rain has driven everyone inside and the windows are so tiny (whether through fear of escape or invasion it is difficult to tell) that it is impossible to make out anyone inside. "Pull yourself together!" shouts Bobby to the empty forecourt. And all I can hear is the faintest hint of an echo resounding back.

The training has paid off. A hot bath, a glass or two of wine, and Bobby is restored. As always at Bobby's house, there seems to be a constant supply of people drifting in and out. Friends, kids, kids' friends, some living here, some staying and some just dropping by. Just as I'm starting to think I've got them sussed, a completely new face appears, hovers a moment, then floats off again, forever unaccounted for. We squeeze ourselves round the table and demolish a mountain of Indian take-away. Later, when the crowd has dispersed, Bobby and I sit pecking up what's left of the poppadoms and discussing the day. Bobby is pleased. Doubly so. For people laughed, but they also listened. Perhaps the former enabled the latter. And as we talk through the day, sifting together our various impressions, what emerges more than anything is an overriding sense of people's warm good will. That, in the end, is what we're left with.

But not only that. "So I'll see you next Monday," says Bobby as she shows me to the door (note please the lack of a question mark).

"Monday?" For a moment I am genuinely confused. For a moment more I cling to the pretence.

"Water aerobics," says Bobby.

Somehow I didn't think I'd be getting off that lightly.

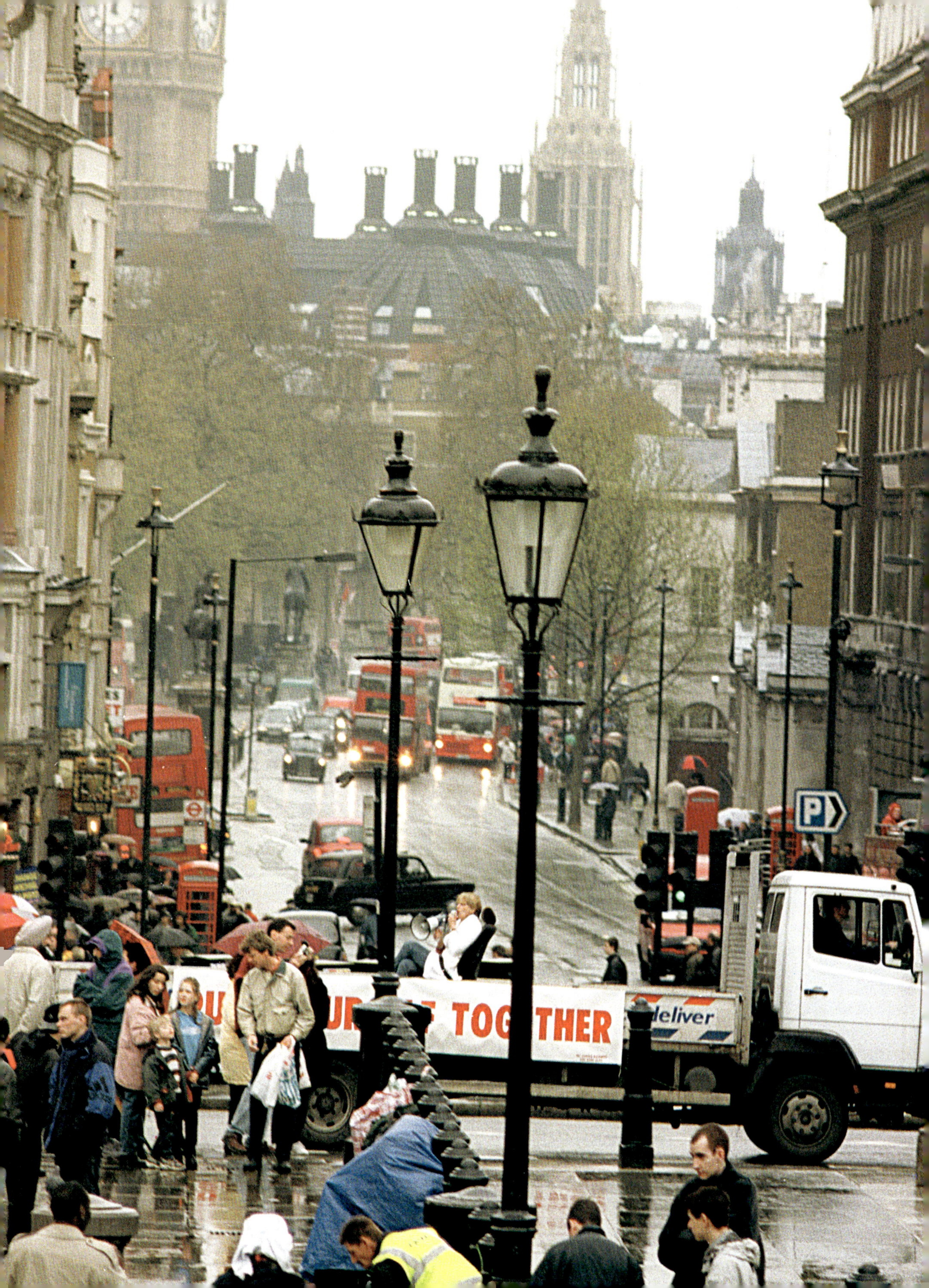
TOGETHER
deliver

Chris Dorley-Brown

Staying In

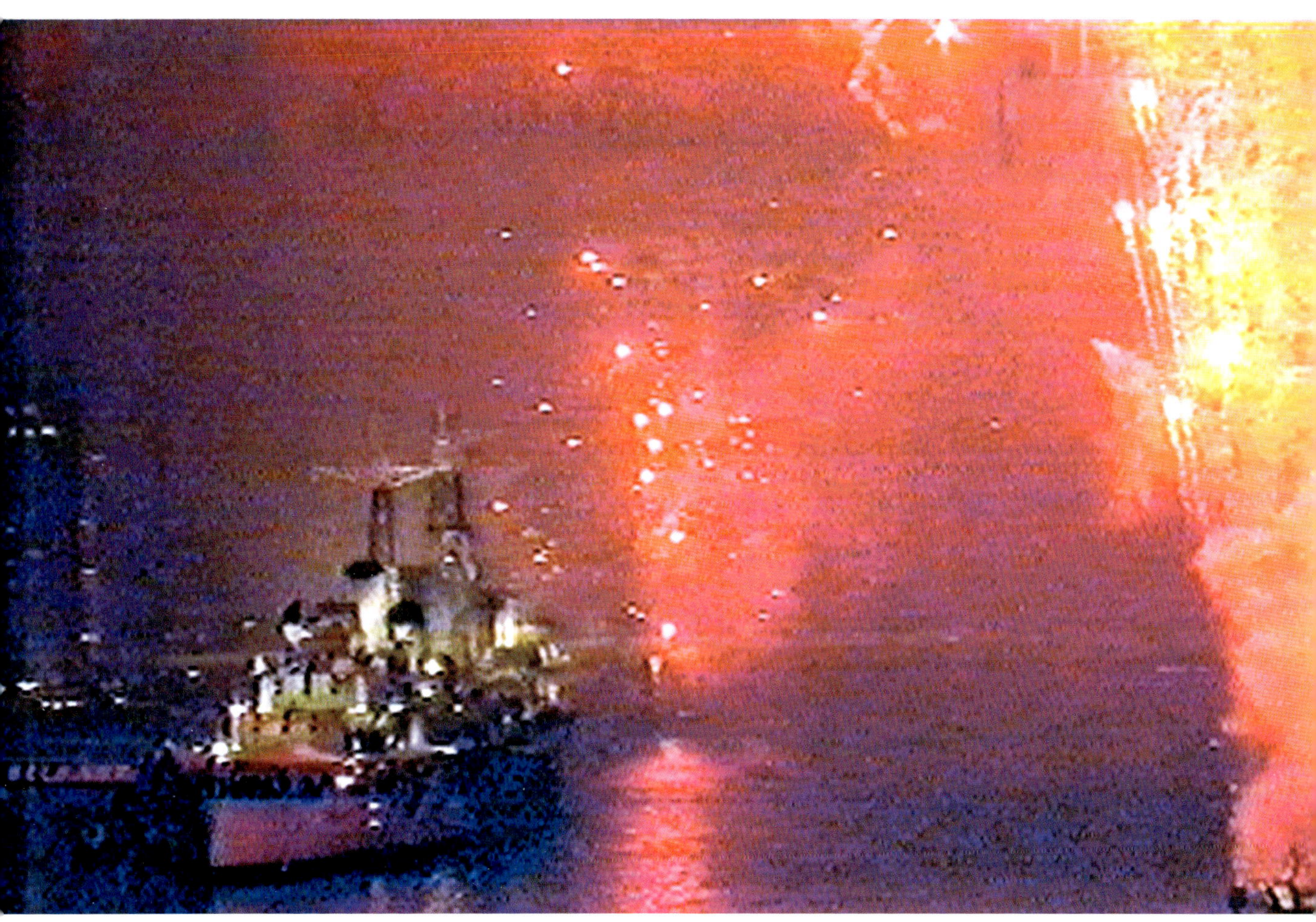

London

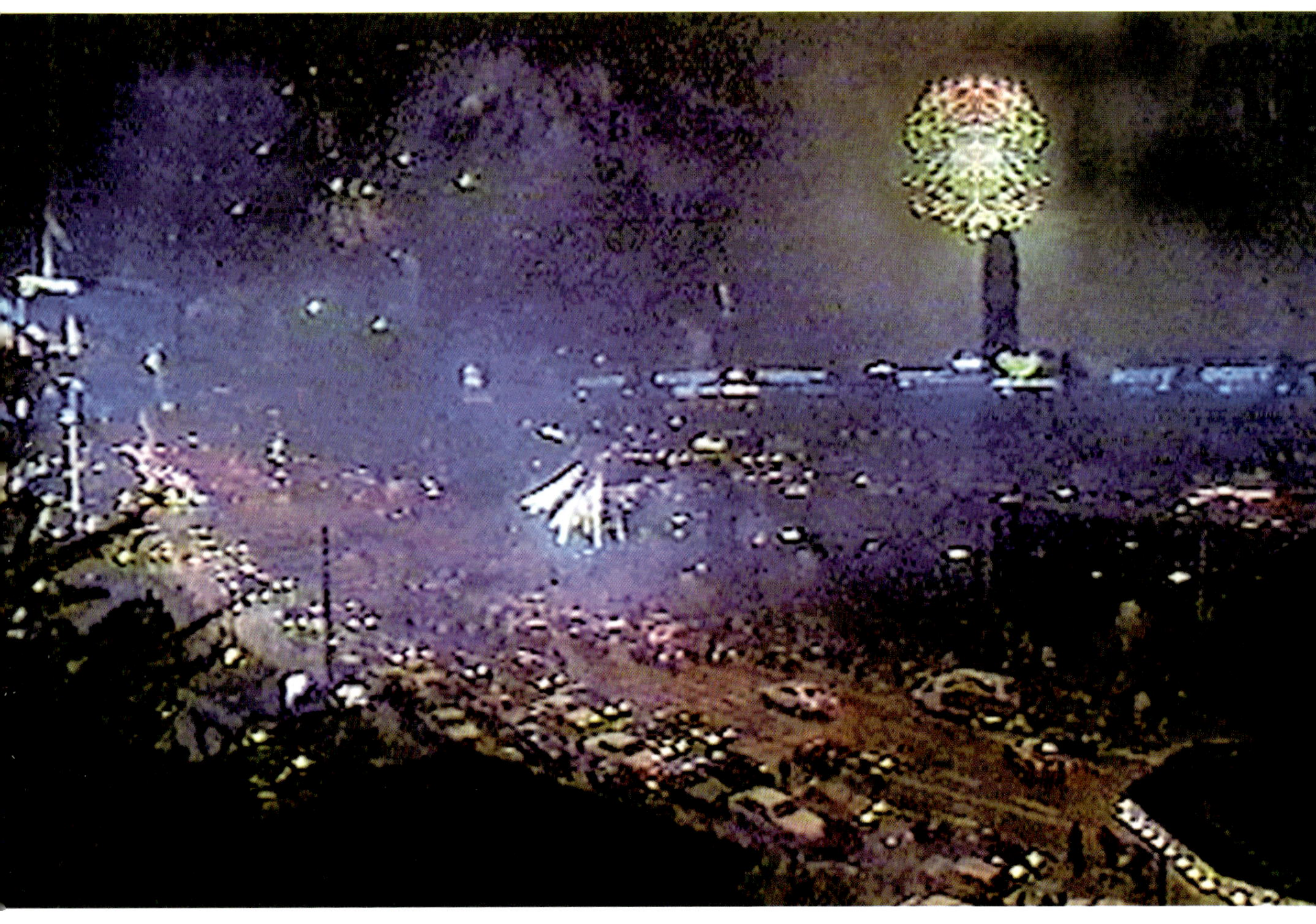

Oslo

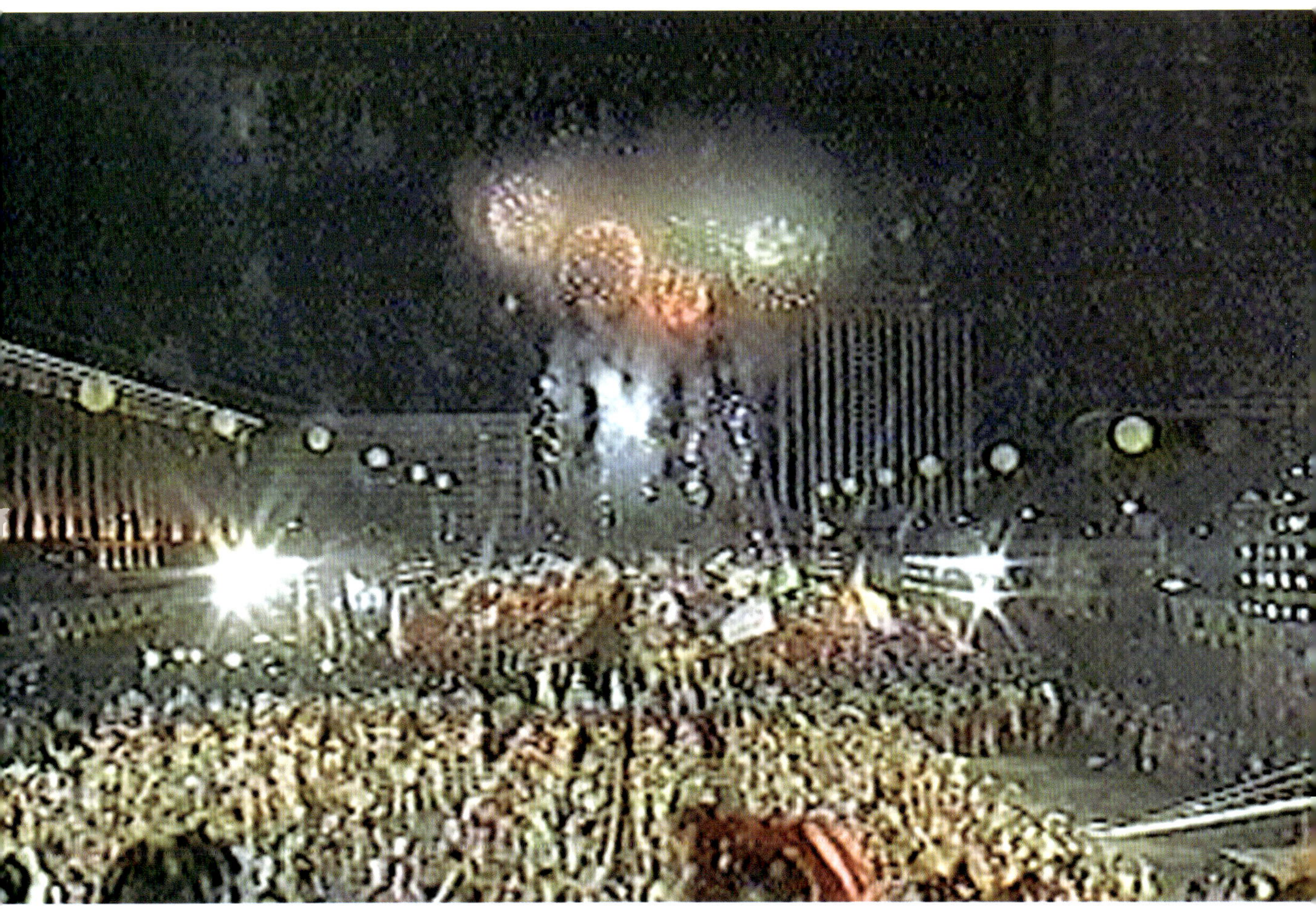

Beijing

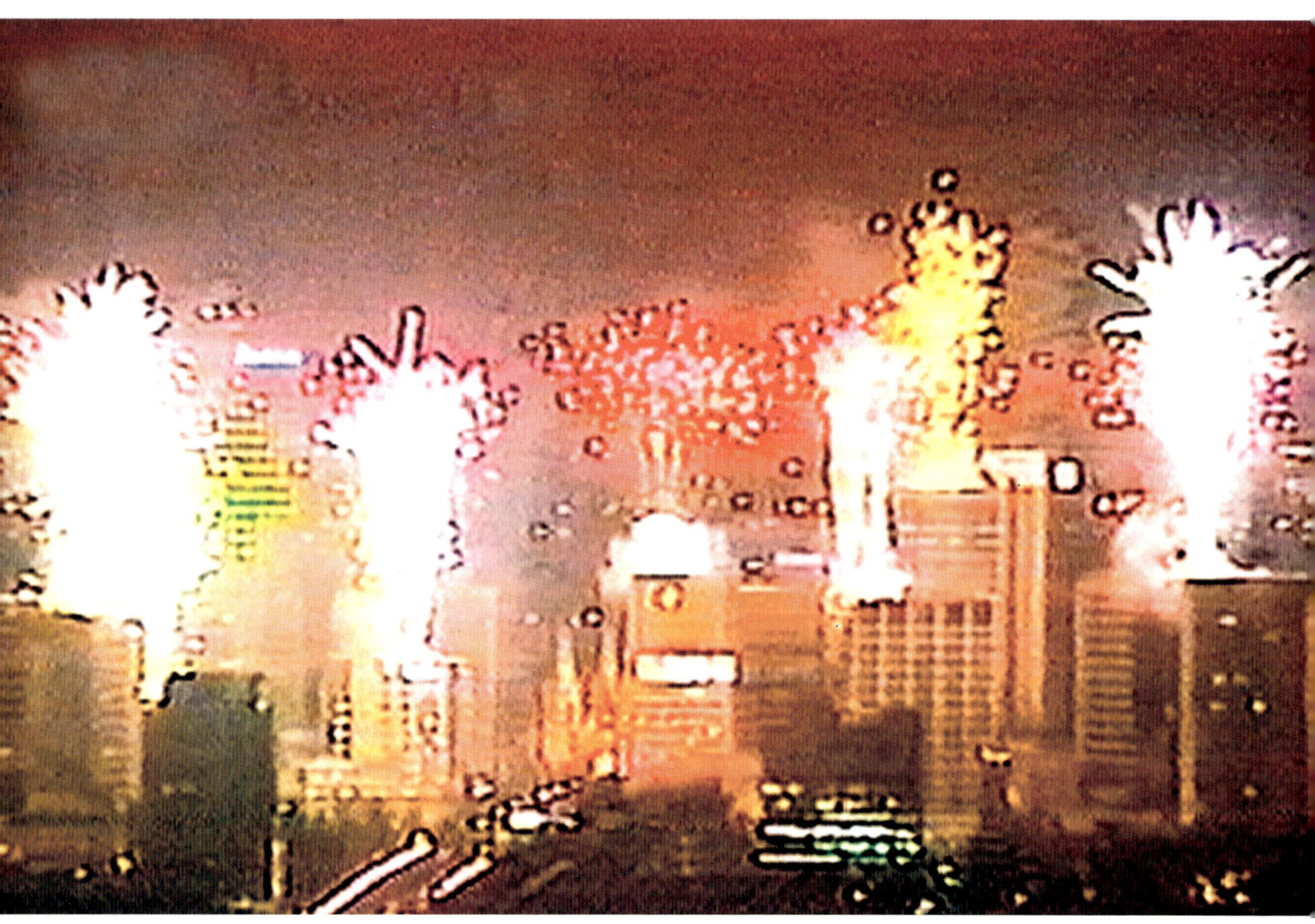

Auckland

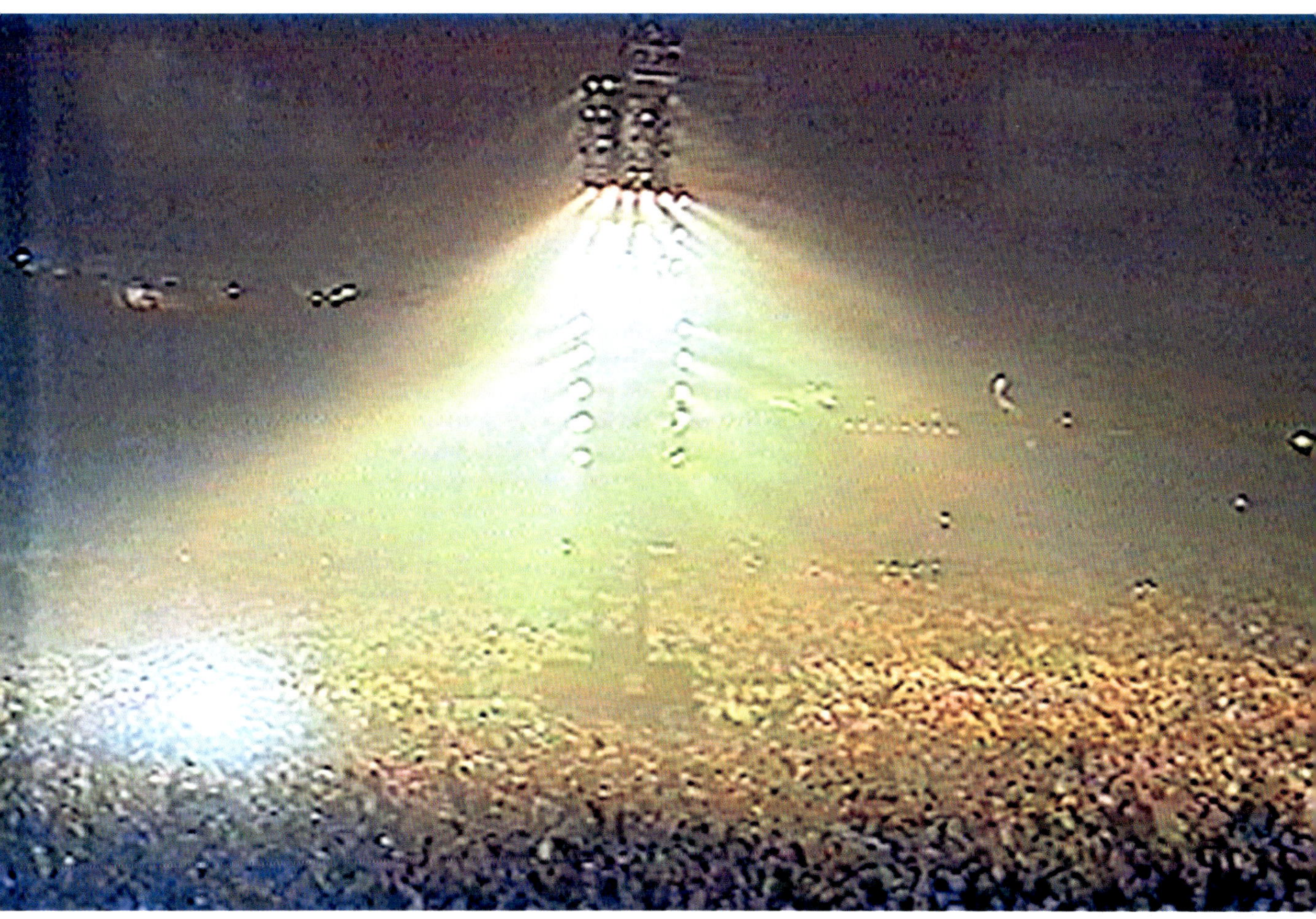

Cairo

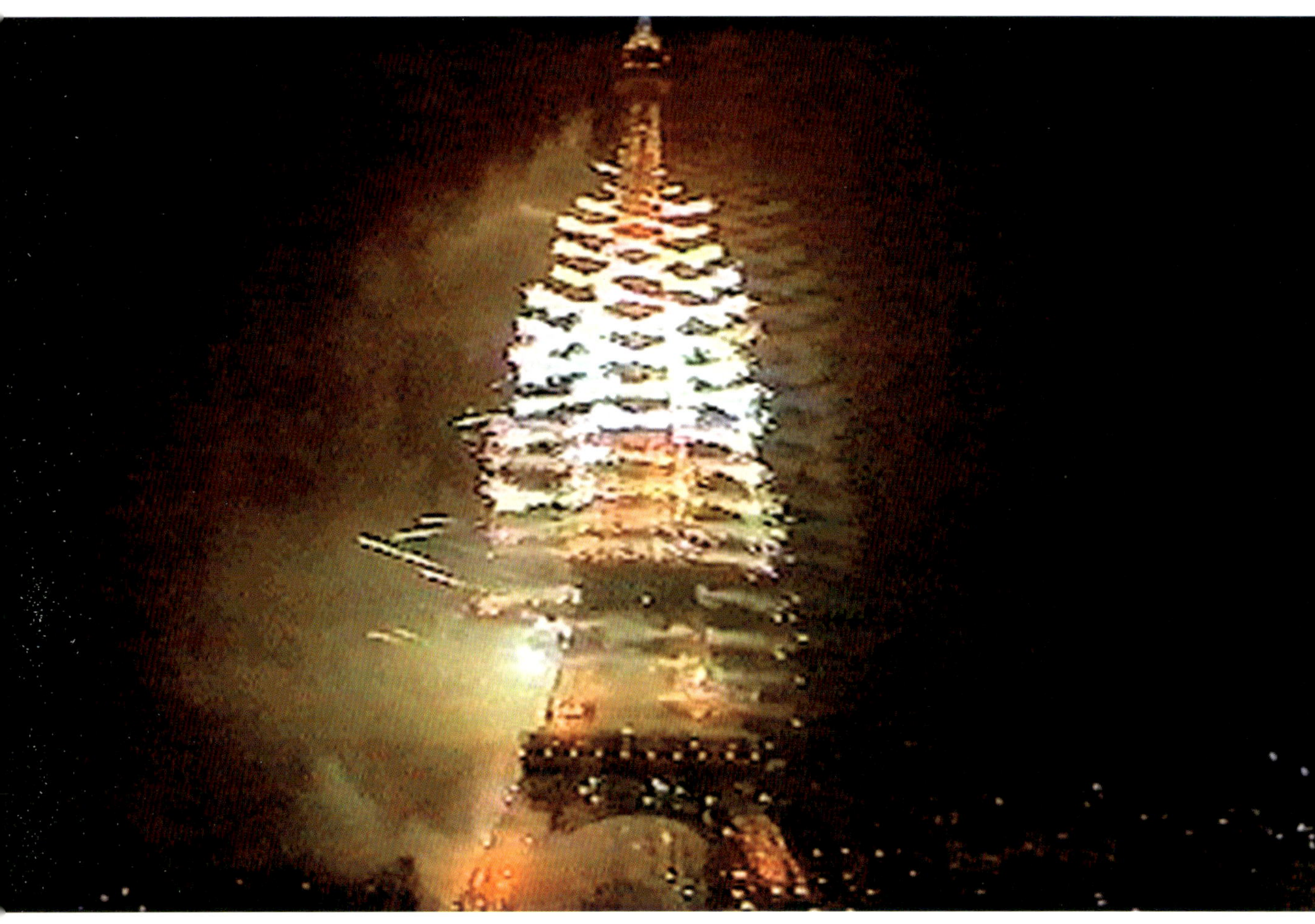

Paris

Robert Pacitti

Suspended Sentence

A second chance, a probationary period, or language caught on a breeze ...

Eyes and ears are bad witnesses for men having barbaric souls

Heraclitus

Suspended Sentence came out of a desire to explore notions of authenticity, truth, and its absence, within contemporary culture, particularly in oral and text-based communication. My early intentions for the work were structured around disrupting notions of information comfort in order to challenge what I see as the presence in society of a prevalent sensibility built around different levels of faux trust. Whilst this is not necessarily a wholly bad trait for a society to display I believe that it often lulls us into a false sense of security; as if information we receive has been somehow ratified by an unseen 'other' and is therefore bound to be trustworthy. The implications of this are potentially horrific. If indeed information is power, then taking an apathetic approach to one's own sifting of truth within the maelstrom of contemporary information exchange is to play into the hands of those with advantage. I have long been interested in rumours, their cultural status, their subversive potential to undermine received wisdom, and their ability to affect cultural change. So, as a counter to the apathy that the information age instills, I set about spreading my own deceits.

At the start of the year 2000 I began to make a number of texts which were utterly fabricated yet were written in such a manner as hopefully to appear factual. This was achieved by various means: assimilating scientific jargon, using 'confessions', constructing short slogans set firmly within the languages of product advertising or religious statement. I have now succeeded in placing a series of manipulated, confusing and often contradictory 'truths' in public spaces. Sometimes explicit, always far-fetched, these truths are currently floating about free-form, somewhere in the public domain, way outside of my control.

A primary working method for the project was the construction of a series of filled boxes. The prompt for this form came from the archive of the Mass Observation project, an ongoing nationwide survey of social mores and behaviour housed in the library of the University of Sussex. The contents of the archive are delivered to readers in flat brown boxes. My own boxes contained a variety of different items: 'false' texts printed on thin tissue paper; bold statements emblazoned across yellow card; birds nests constructed from found twigs and containing nestling 'eggs' of screwed-up pages filled with my lies; vague images of people in social situations pilfered from the internet and made to look like surveillance photography. I made numbered multiples of some of the boxes whilst others were one-offs. Each contained a sticker giving a phone number to ring for further information. In fact these were the numbers of live phone-in programmes on local radio stations close to the vicinity of the item's planned deposit site; my hope being that country-wide people would ring for more details only to find themselves being broadcast on air. When completed each box was then left in a public place – on a street, in a garden, by a tower block, on a train – to be found, ignored, treasured or trashed.

Some of the constructed texts I made for the project began to reference the historical literature of sado-masochistic practices and distorted retellings of sexual power play informed by my own experiences. When this area of the work began to emerge I realised that, like Pandora, I found the boxes containing these tracts to be seemingly far more expansive in their potential readings than those outlining faux scientific developments or quick fix slogans. Like a recipient of the locked puzzle box from Barker's *Hellraiser* the content felt as if it could shift drastically and dangerously at any moment. As I continued to write these particular pieces the realisation dawned that I could not really shake off the essential grain of initial truth underpinning my sought-after lie; that because I somehow owned a percentage of the text in a real way I was unable completely to fake it. At this point the making process of the project seemed to have turned full circle. In search of a critique of authenticity I seemed only to have ended up embroiled in a struggle to locate its presence. And whilst I feel that these more sexual texts are in many ways the most successful in terms of form, they also seem ironically to represent the least fulfilling result in relation to my initial intentions for the work. This I feel owes much to the fact that they are not about the future altered body within scientific or species development as much as the altered experience of the contemporary body, and as such they remain inherently plausible.

I am interested in how they may have travelled throughout the country: what distance did they go, how did their contents distort through retelling, what elaboration has been added, or indeed removed? I am glad to have made work that is 'shared' in this way, work which is outside of a theatre or gallery space and is inherently about organic change. The possibility of extreme response which work of this nature could perpetrate has also been exciting for me, although I have tried to be ethical throughout every aspect of the project. For example I used great caution when depositing the boxes as I didn't want people to think that they were bombs. However, I have to acknowledge an element of glee at the potential disruptions the work could generate. To what extent, if any, have the box contents infiltrated the realities of their finders? And what consequences may this have in the psyche of those people over time? The project has been wholly ephemeral in its distribution and so trying to gauge what levels of impact it may have had is a difficult task. But I feel that there is an intrinsic validity in the very notion of trying to infiltrate cultural communication by means of dishonesty and deceit.

During the course of this work I have made 300 boxes and over 100 'false information' email communications. To the best of my knowledge they are all still out there, just quietly waiting. And that is why I have not outlined any of the lies within these pages, or provided you the reader with any sample texts or images of the work. If you find it you do, and if you don't then someone else will. In fact maybe they already have.

Hugo Glendinning

Snow Portraits

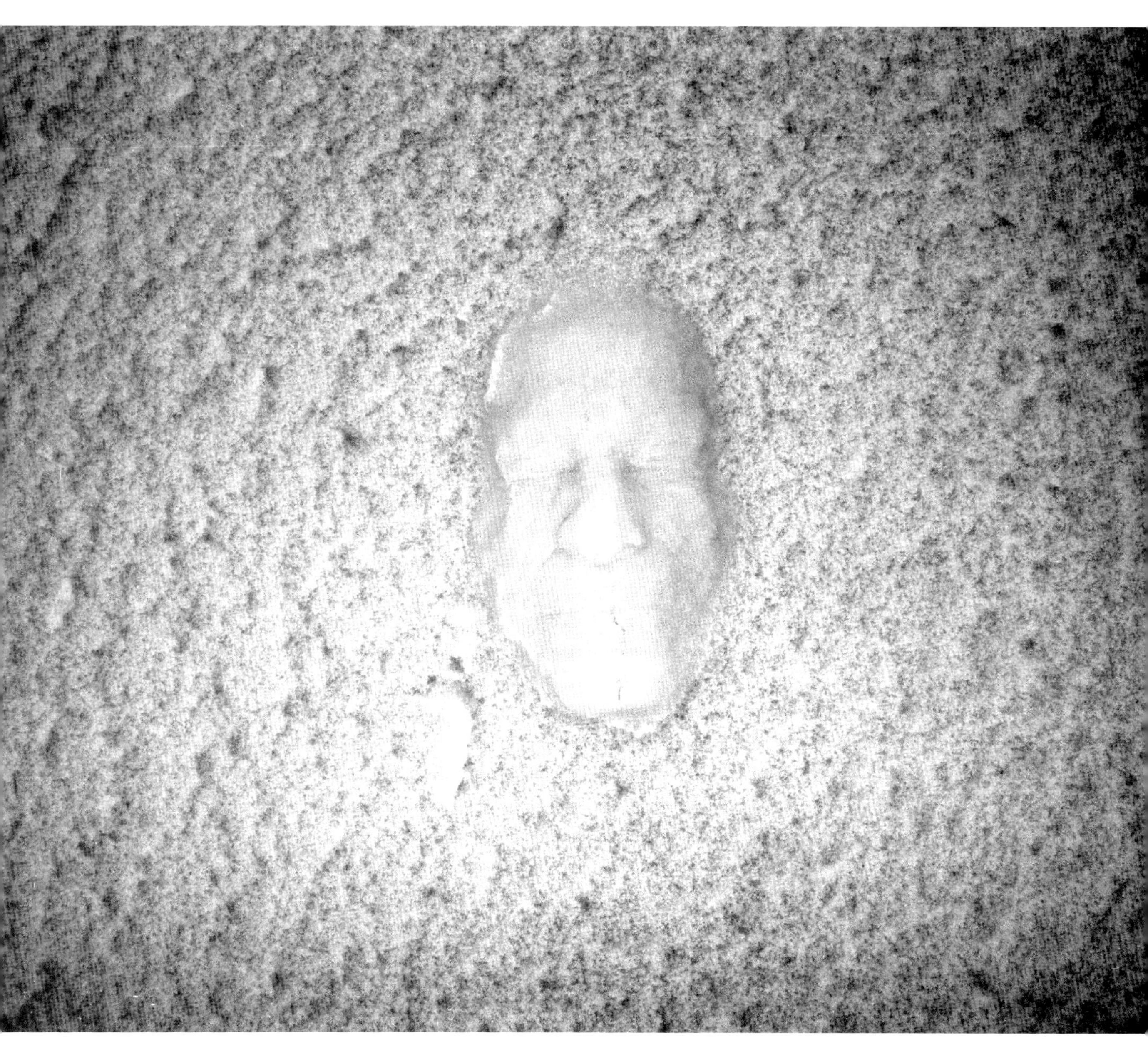

04.02.2000 at 20.30 hrs
Self-portrait

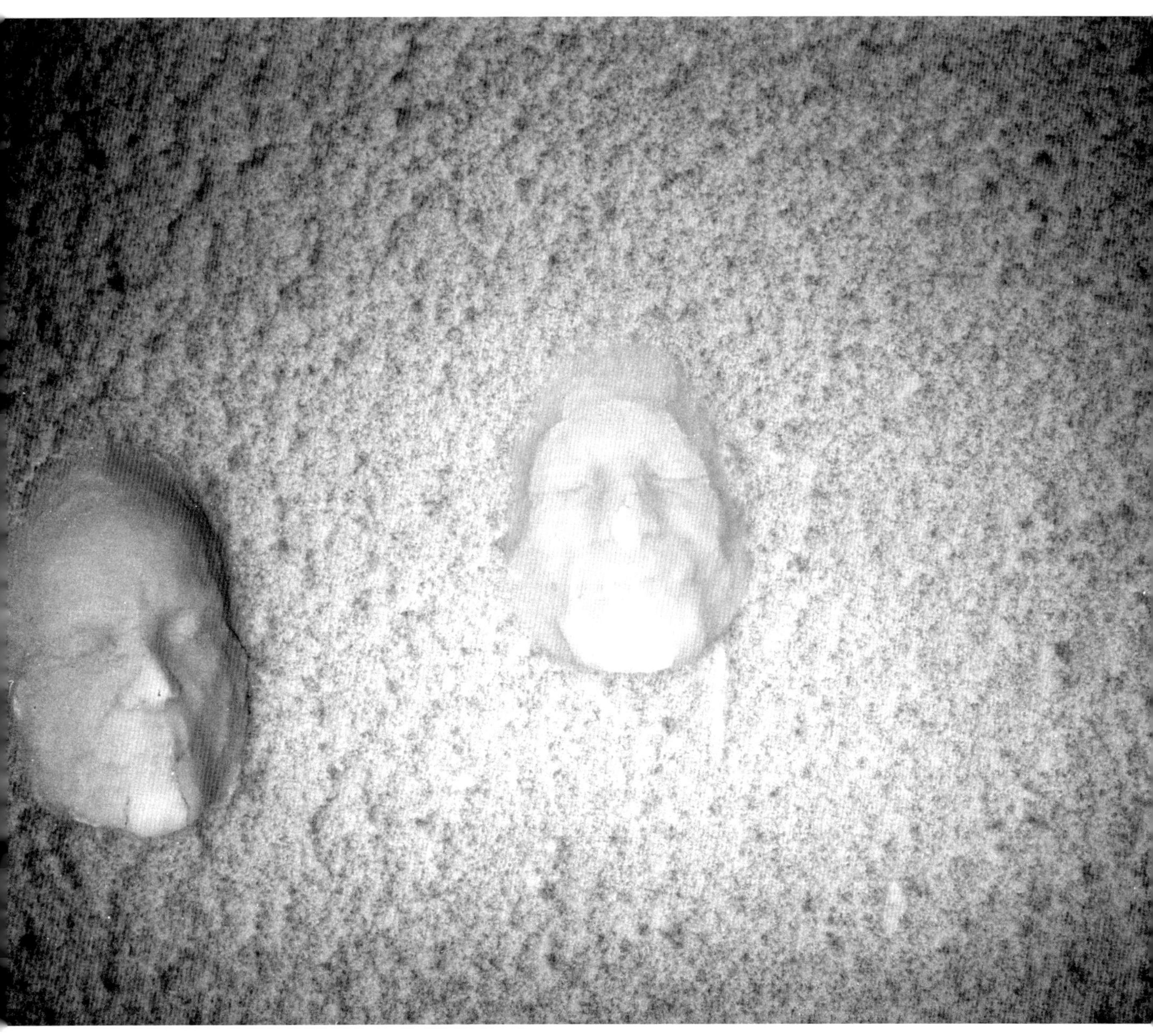

24.02.2000 at 20.30 hrs
Ebba Matz and Siobhan Hapaska

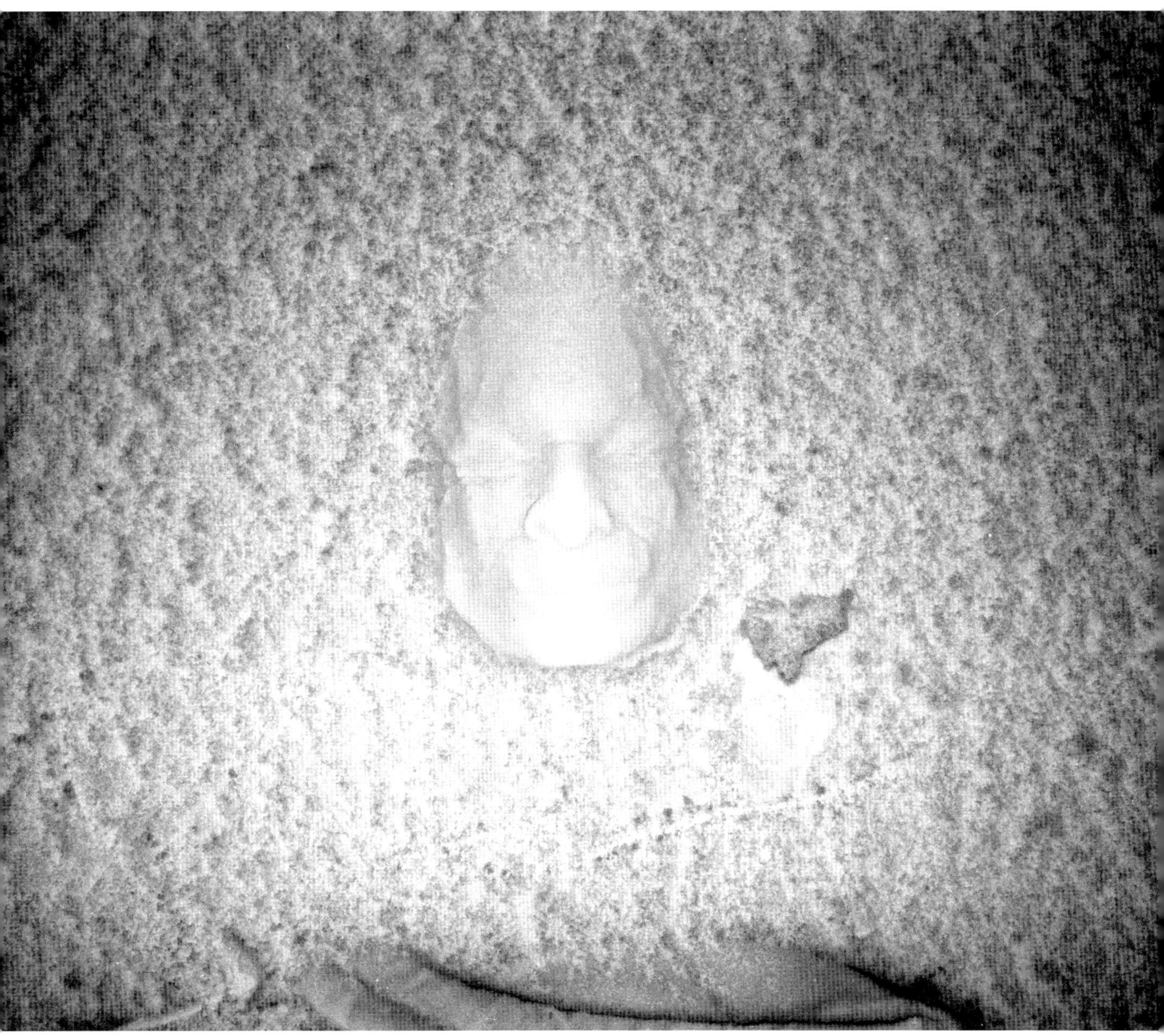

24.02.2000 at 20.34 hrs
Charles Long

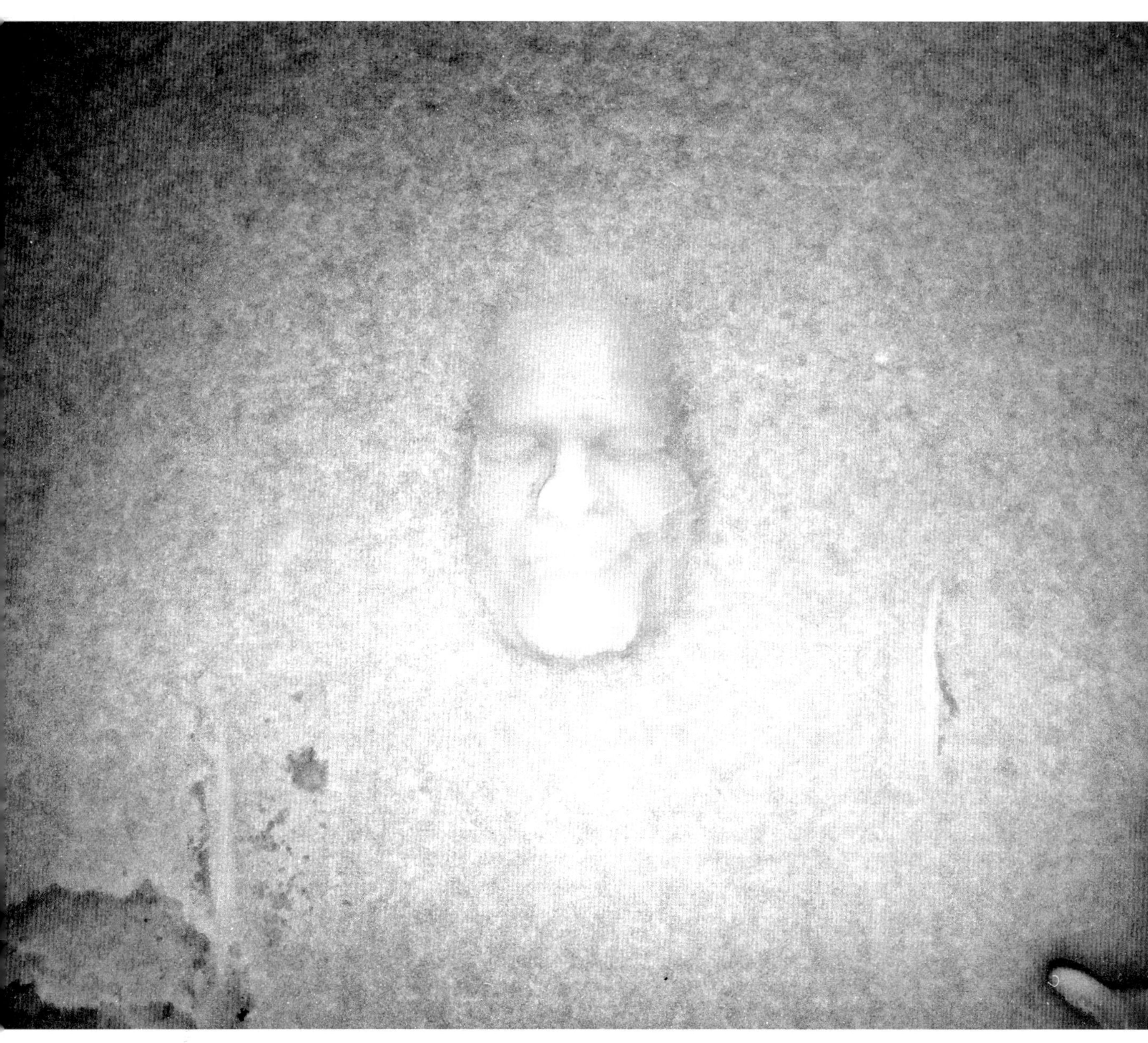

25.02.2000 at 01.30 hrs
Stephen McQuincy

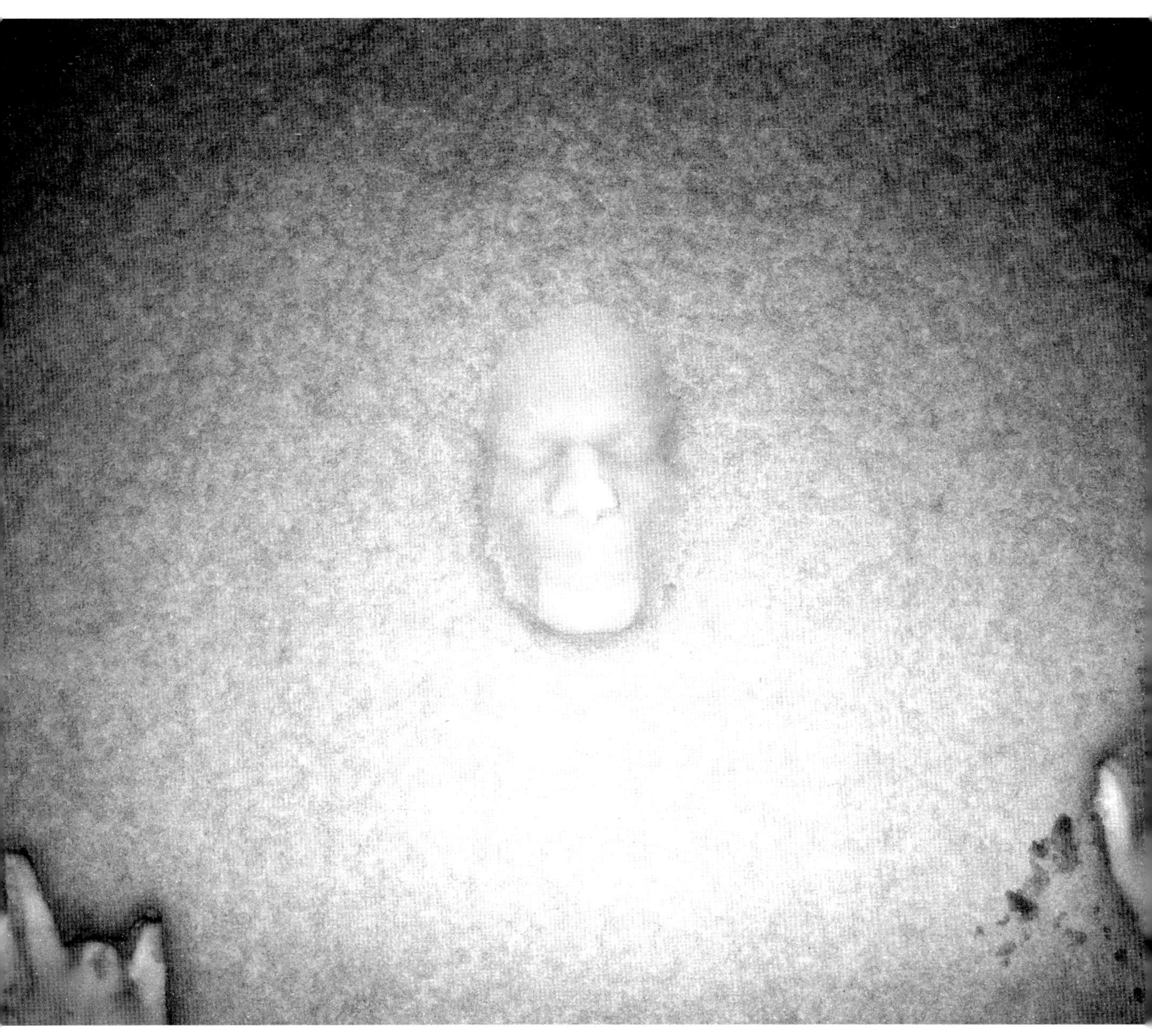

25.02.2000 at 01.38 hrs
Arik Levy

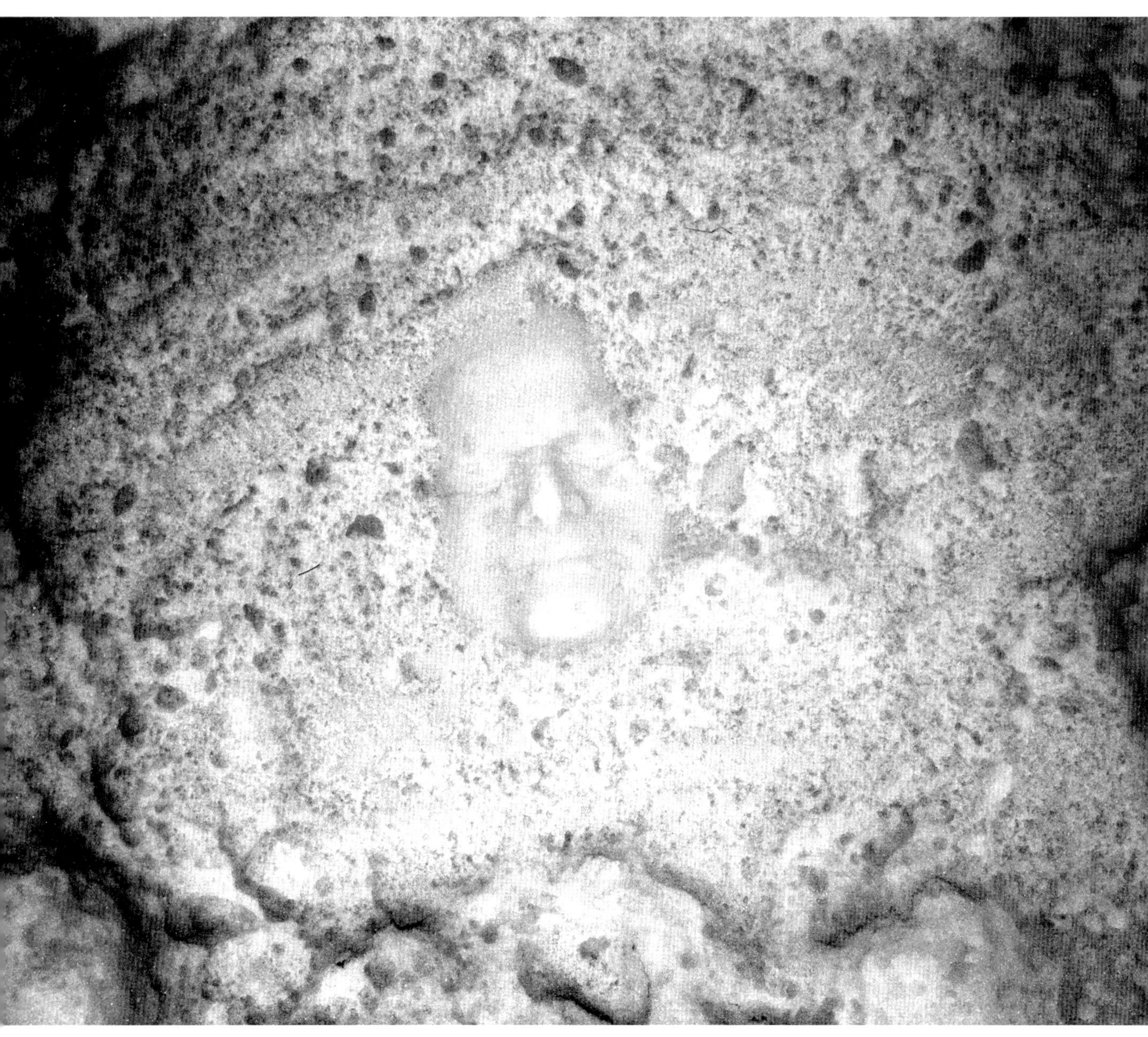

25.02.2000 at 23.15 hrs
Gunnar Söder

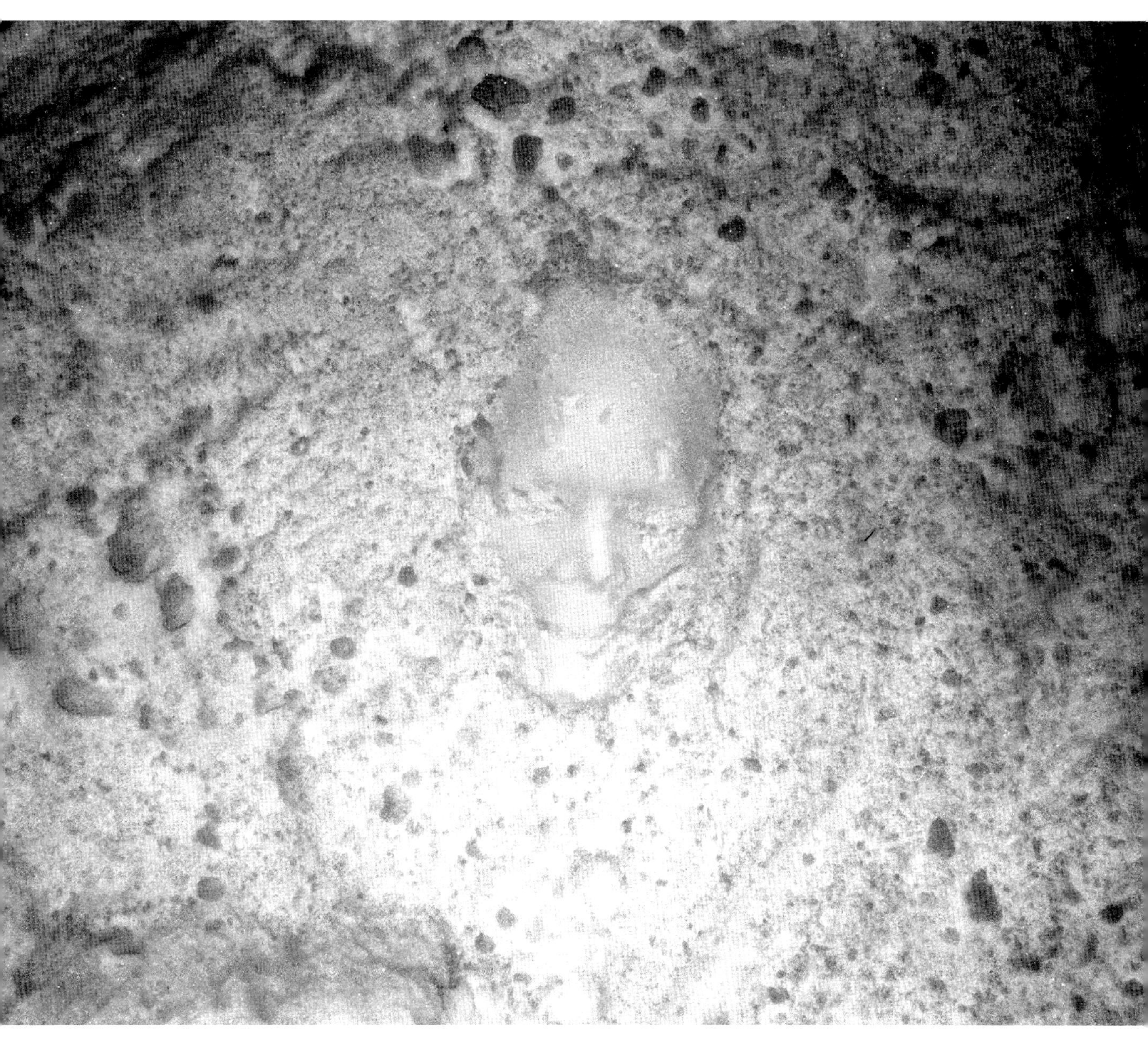

25.02.2000 at 23.20 hrs
Tia Johansson

Alexander García Düttmann

A Short Diary of the New

For Jared

24 *April* **There is a common answer** to the question of the new, an answer which is almost never preceded or held in suspense by a hesitation. It stresses the impossibility of understanding the new without reference to the old. Only in so far as it stands out against the old can the new be what it claims to be, only in so far as it is mediated by the knowledge of the old can the new be recognized. It is because this answer is so frequent that the new is more a longing for the new than the new itself, as Adorno once put it. The new which is related to the old is an extension of the old, a force of reproduction or feedback by means of which the old survives. It is like a mirror in which the old glimpses itself in a rejuvenated form, even if the old never simply or completely recognizes itself.

25 *April* Can there be a diary of the new? Can one note down which signs or indications herald the new, capture the new before it becomes recognisable, grasp what is new about the new, keep a diary of what has not yet occurred? Or note down day after day the new thoughts which the new generates, letting the entries be dictated by the new without denying the discontinuity which belongs to it? The continuity of a diary does more justice to the new than the discursive continuity of a paper which analyses the concept of the new and develops an argument with the necessary rigour.[1] The gentle compulsion of a diary punishes you as little for ellipses as for the inclusion of platitudes. You can skip a day, or a step in the argumentation. Conversely, though, the form of a diary threatens to relinquish the new to the everyday, reducing it to a matter of routine. A diary threatens to abandon the new to the impotence which results from a lack of effort: to a more or less orderly succession of arbitrary insights which remains indifferent to these insights and robs them of their force. Or are there various experiences of the new for which various forms of presentation must be found and invented? Is the new always new in and to itself? Is longing the expression of such an irreducible diversity rather than the symptom of a lack or a deficiency? Is it the longing of the new rather than a longing for it? In his essay on Goethe's *Elective Affinities*, Walter Benjamin warns against the "danger of a diary". A diary can expose "the germ of memory" which lies in the soul too soon, thus spoiling "the ripening of its fruits."[2] This danger is said to increase when the "life of the mind" expresses itself in a diary alone. Must not the new pass utterly into oblivion in order for it to impress itself all the more forcefully upon memory and thus effect a transformation? Does not habit, conversely, forget the new with such swiftness that it seems almost inconceivable how something which

yesterday would have been considered to be completely impossible is today taken for granted, as if it were a fact, and not something merely intended by way of anticipation?

Like the regular accumulation of unregulated ideas in a diary, the form of an inquiry, whether it be critical and preparatory or experimental and invocatory, proves to be ambiguous. It can establish a clearing for the new in the thicket of the familiar ('clear for landing'), but it can also serve as a perpetuation of the old which prevents the new from breaking through. Although it escapes its own wilful appropriation, the new exerts the pressure to make an effort, to say or to do something new, especially when one speaks about it. One is subject to the compulsion of the new to the extent that in every repetition, in every repeated utterance or act, a transformation is at work which makes repetition what it is in the first place. The new is a paradoxical fact. As a fact, as a 'that', an abyss separates it from intention, from the 'what', from the will to newness. There is no doubt that the pressure or the compulsion of the new – the inexorability of a fact which is paradoxical in so far as a fact can never be new and newness can never be essential to a fact – is something which is felt or experienced. It communicates itself to intention, it communicates as intention, it bridges the abyss and immediately blows up the bridge, because it is precisely intention, a careful approximation or a tentative inquiry which must miss the paradoxical fact of the new. Like all facts, the new does not tolerate being questioned, and precedes any possible questioning. One cannot negotiate or deal with the new. This is why fashion scintillates and shimmers, why it has an ambivalent character, why it is captivated by the ambiguity of the always-already and the never-before. But does not such dealing with the new, the ambiguous vacillation between the always-already and the never-before, respond to the paradox of its factuality?

26 April At the end of the third part of *In Search of Lost Time* the Duchesse de Guermantes learns that her upper-middle-class friend Swann, whom she has invited to travel to Italy with her husband and herself, is critically ill. She is in a hurry because she does not want to arrive late at a dinner party, and finds herself caught in a dilemma because of the unexpected news. Proust's description of this dilemma is clearly ironic: "Placed for the first time in her life between two duties as incompatible as getting into her carriage to go out to dinner and showing compassion for a man who was about to die, she could find nothing in the code of conventions that indicated the right line to follow; not knowing which to choose, she felt obliged not to believe that the latter alternative need be seriously considered in order to comply with the first, which at the moment demanded less effort, and thought that the best way of settling the conflict would be to deny that any existed."[3] Convention does not have to come into conflict with the new, as humane clichés would have it do. Irony is well aware of their compatibility. In Proust's novel the world of the Guermantes distinguishes itself from the equally elegant world of the Courvoisier precisely by the fact that the Guermantes continually alter the fixed rules of conduct of the aristocracy and so enlarge the scope of their freedom. If, in the eyes of the Courvoisier, venturing into such freedom cannot be regarded as enlivening but amounts to an almost scandalous transgression, this rejection of a cultivated eccentricity probably results from the knowledge that ultimately their very eccentricity denotes the superiority of the Guermantes. Indeed, cannot the institution of a habitual structure and a familiar framework even create conditions under which the possibility for a new experience to suspend the familiar and the habitual is given? Wittgenstein's visits to the cinema; Heidegger's regular and ideologically overdetermined retreats to his hut; Deleuze's unwillingness to travel to conferences or give papers; Barthes' pleasure in creating a daily routine and choosing the instruments required for his intellectual activities; Fassbinder's incessant productivity, far ahead of the finished or the unfinished work; Derrida's journeys, the journeys of an alert sleep-walker – perhaps all describe a circle limiting and restricting the influence of everything that disturbs and diverts the new: the new proper to a thought or an activity, the new arising in a thought or in an activity. One cannot deal with a fact, or rather: how one deals with a fact, and how one behaves with regard to it, cannot affect its being a fact. If, therefore, the way one deals with the forces of the new determines whether the new turns into an enemy or whether it becomes an ally, it is for this reason, too, that the new reveals itself to be a paradoxical fact.

27 April Seven years ago, on the way home, the truth suddenly appeared to me. In a single moment everything fell into place in a transparent and coherent picture. I experienced the euphoria of the new, which consisted of an unexpected insight, in an insight so clear that after a short while it seemed almost trivial. Now I wanted to set down the truth, just as it had established itself for me, for in doing so I hoped to effect the transformation I sought. But my euphoria had become rigid and taken on a form: the form of arrogance. The will to newness, which was a will to truth, was my undoing. I was struck blind, and no longer capable of remaining blindly within the truth. In possession of a concept of truth, my lucidity had become my blindness. The new is similar to truth in that, if it is to become an ally, one should not attempt to appropriate its forces, to seize hold of them or to usurp them.

29 April For X, the new becomes an ally in the 'life of the mind' through its recurrence. Dazzled and dazed, his mind in a condition of excitement which puts understanding last, X pursues the new without being able to behave freely. Once the new has ceased to provoke him, once the question of understanding and interpreting the new has replaced the excitement, X forgets the new and turns his back on it. X tries to look at things from another angle, viewing the world differently. In this way the new can return to X: as mobility. For X, the difference between the breakthrough and the recurrence of the new is the difference between liberation and freedom. Whether the new becomes an ally or not is decided in the space opened up by this difference. The new is not a matter of evaluation, X says, for as such it is neither good nor bad. Y objects that the new must already have a value for X. Why would X otherwise relate to the new as he does? X replies: "This value is only the value of a certain immediacy. As the poet James Schuyler says in an article about a friend's paintings, one will find no meaning in them because they do nothing but tell the viewer: 'Look *now*. It will never be more fascinating'."[4]

30 April   In the dialectic of the old and the new, the new emerges from within the old, while the old emerges from within the new. Thus the new and the old determine each other, rather than maintaining themselves in an abstract opposition. The day the narrator in Proust's novel unexpectedly returns to Paris and surprises his grandmother reading and unaware of his arrival, his intrusion has the effect of stiffening her face and turning it into a photographic likeness. It is as if her face had been deprived of the time it needed to insert itself back into a habitual framework and transform itself into something familiar. The stiffening leads to a revelation, as it does in the passage where the narrator recalls the devastation of Pompeii, and accords nature the power of objective photographic immobilisation: in the course of time, nature inscribes individual gestures into a face, turning them into the face's lines and features. As a photographic likeness reveals an expression captured by the camera's cold lens in the midst of the anonymous objectivity of that which exists independently of our recognising gaze, the face reveals the real to the mute witness or observer who has triggered the stiffening and who is himself brought into being by it. The narrator recognises that his grandmother will die soon: "Sitting on the sofa beneath the lamp, I saw a red-faced, heavy and vulgar woman, a sick and day-dreaming woman who let her slightly crazed eyes wander over a book, an overburdened old woman whom I did not know."[5] The old reveals itself as what is new to knowledge, laid bare by the visionary destruction of the idea, the figure, or the appearance, by the downfall of the image to which we have become habituated. This revelation is possible only because of the new context or configuration which an intrusion always brings about. Conversely, the new reveals itself as the old, as the reality which refuses to be summoned by the recognising gaze's necromancy. The narrator understands: in this moment of comprehension, in which the dialectic of the new and the old unfolds as if in a flash, the old and the new become indifferent, they are dissimulated, removed or sublated by what is comprehended, by the comprehension which the narrator has achieved, by the concept of life and death which he has attained. But can there not be a different experience of the new, an experience in which the new does not merely serve as a dialectical means of recognition or as a dialectical medium of knowledge?

1 May   The girls whom the Proustian narrator encounters in Balbec on the dyke are perceived by him initially as a group which does not consist of individuals with distinguishing characteristics and features. He encounters a cloud which constantly changes its shape because the characteristics and features of those who form the group are continuously interchanging. This shifting and drifting interchange dissolves every condensation, erases every demarcation, blurs every definition, and yields a "harmonious floating" which is not (yet) subject to the principle of individualisation, a "fluid, collective and mobile beauty".[6] The new approaches like this group of girls whose separation, isolation and individualisation has not taken place, a preindividual, impersonal, indeterminate community of elements which only fleetingly stand out from each other, which cannot be unambiguously assigned, and which have no consistency of their own that would be independent of the fluidity and vagueness of their appearance. Lyotard states that it is not the persuasive power of final arguments that establishes the community of those who practise the art of reflective judgment. The consensus which such a community promises on the horizon is always evasive, something to which one can only allude. The question of its 'real existence' remains an open question. This is a *"nuage de communauté"*, a community which exists only as a cloud and which is neither real nor unreal.[7] The new does not describe the unbroken line of a horizon from which it approaches the old and attracts it towards itself, it does not promise something which has to be fulfilled, it is not a longing for something which awaits its realisation. Rather, in the new, promise and fulfilment, longing and realisation coincide. The longing for the new is a longing for such a coincidence.

2 May   Perhaps the paradoxical factuality of the new can never be sensed more clearly than at the point where an event or a disclosure has prompted a sudden and irrevocable transformation. A bomb has exploded without warning, and has killed people or horribly mutilated them. A physician has established that I am suffering from an incurable disease which now, having invaded my consciousness, will determine what is left of my life. Past and future are violently torn apart by such events or disclosures. The factuality of what has occurred or of what has been disclosed forces us to look at the past in a new light. The old past becomes a past past and is replaced by a new one. But the newness of what has occurred or what has been disclosed keeps the old past and the anticipated future alive, spellbound in an unchanging present. Thus, it is possible to gauge the paradoxical factuality of the new from a certain anarchy of time. The conservative and the revolutionary, who perceive in the new a paradoxical factuality, the simultaneity of a position and a negation, or a moment of irreconcilability, which enjoins them to militant struggle, resemble each other in that they both fight against the new, against the anarchic violence of its paradoxical factuality. However, whereas the conservative wagers on the preservation of what is supposedly well-established to provide shelter from the violence of the new, and thereby tends to prolong this violence through counter-violence, the revolutionary seeks refuge from the new in the new itself, in its institution or establishment, and runs the risk of perpetuating violence through the abolition of violence. But neither the conservative nor the revolutionary are the true enemies of the new. They struggle against something which has communicated itself to their experience. The true enemies of the new are historicism and cultural relativism, the well-informed who know all about it, who won't have the wool pulled over their eyes, and who in the end equate the idea of the new with a simple historical construction in the evolution of a culture. The true enemy of the new is the equanimity which can never be impressed, the composure which bides its time until it becomes apparent whether the new is indeed something new and not a song and dance that was bent on merely being flashy. Adorno could reflect on the aging of 'new' or 'modern' music because he had spoken uncompromisingly on its behalf and because within such music he had militantly distinguished between progress and reaction.

(No date)   He dreams that he is waiting for a demon, a spirit, a messiah in the midst of a crowd. Suddenly the demon, the spirit, the messiah seems to have arrived. He

does not perceive anything, yet he behaves the way all the others do; they are carried away by their enthusiasm. He is not disappointed, he does not feel deceived, and he is not pretending or making it up.

3 May   Pierre Ménard, the author who in Borges' 'fiction' writes the *Quijote* anew as if the book were being written for the first time – that is without simply copying it, quoting it from memory or relying on emphatic assimilation – puts the paradoxical factuality of the new to the test. For in so far as they are facts, both texts remain indistinguishable. "The text by Cervantes and the one by Ménard are identical in their wording", the narrator tells us. At the same time, however, the second text is said to be "almost infinitely richer" than the first text – and thus proves to be a new one.[8] If the world of pure facts is tautological and can be grasped only by means of analytic judgments, one must not confuse the new with a negation of this world, with a denial of objectivity, with an impotent and subjectivistic arbitrariness or rebellion which would be as tautological as that which it negates or denies. Rather, the new is the tautological under the transforming aspect of something other that leaves it untouched, since as something other it cannot be apprehended the way facts can. The "almost infinite" richness which distinguishes the two identical books is concealed by the mere factuality of the literal. There is no factual proof for this richness, especially since Ménard seems to have burnt all the drafts, all the preliminary studies and stages leading up to the final version of his book. The narrator comprehends the richness as the effect of a dependence on context to which the understanding of a text is always indebted. He quotes two verbally identical sentences and interprets them as if they were almost opposed to each other. This double interpretation, and the opposition which results from it, corresponds exactly to the difference between an understanding of the factual, of what is the case historically, and an understanding of the intended, which offers a particular view of events. Does this mean that the perception of the stipulated richness is itself dependent on a context – on the context in which the factual and the intended, the textual and the contextual can be distinguished? If one reads the narrator's statement literally, it turns out that it is impossible to agree on what he actually states without an understanding which presupposes the possibility of a dependence on contexts. In the Spanish text (*"casi infinitamente más rico"*) and in its literal English translation ("almost infinitely richer") the restricting adverb can be related to both the infinity of the richness and the infinite richness itself. According to the first option, there is virtually no doubt as to the fact that Ménard's work is infinitely richer than the one Cervantes wrote. According to the second option, however, it is only virtually the case that the book written by Ménard reveals itself to be infinitely richer. The paradox of the fact cannot be dissolved; the new cannot be identified and determined.

Translated from German by Humphrey Bower (in collaboration with the author).

[1] *A Short Diary of the New* was first delivered at a conference organised by Michael Newman at the Institute for Contemporary Arts in London (May 1999), then again at Deutsches Haus, New York University (September 1999).
[2] Benjamin, Walter, 'Goethe's *Elective Affinities*', *Selected Writings*, Vol. 1, Harvard University Press 1998, p. 338
[3] Proust, Marcel, 'The Guermantes Way', *In Search of Lost Time*, Vol.III, Vintage 1996, p. 688
[4] Schuyler, James, *Selected Art Writings*, ed. Simon Pettet, Black Sparrow Press 1998, p. 16
[5] Proust, Marcel, 'The Guermantes Way', *In Search of Lost Time*, Vol.III, Vintage 1996, p. 157 (translation modified)
[6] Proust, Marcel, 'Within a Budding Grove', *In Search of Lost Time*, Vol.III, Vintage 1996, p. 688
[7] Lyotard, Jean-François, *Pérégrinations: Loi, forme, événement*, Transcrit de l'américan par Jean-François Lyotard, Galilée 1990, p. 78 (*Peregrinations: Law, Form, Event*, Columbia University Press 1988)
[8] Borges, Jorge Luis, 'Fictions', *Collected Fictions*, The Penguin Press 1998, p.94

Emma Kay

The World from Memory

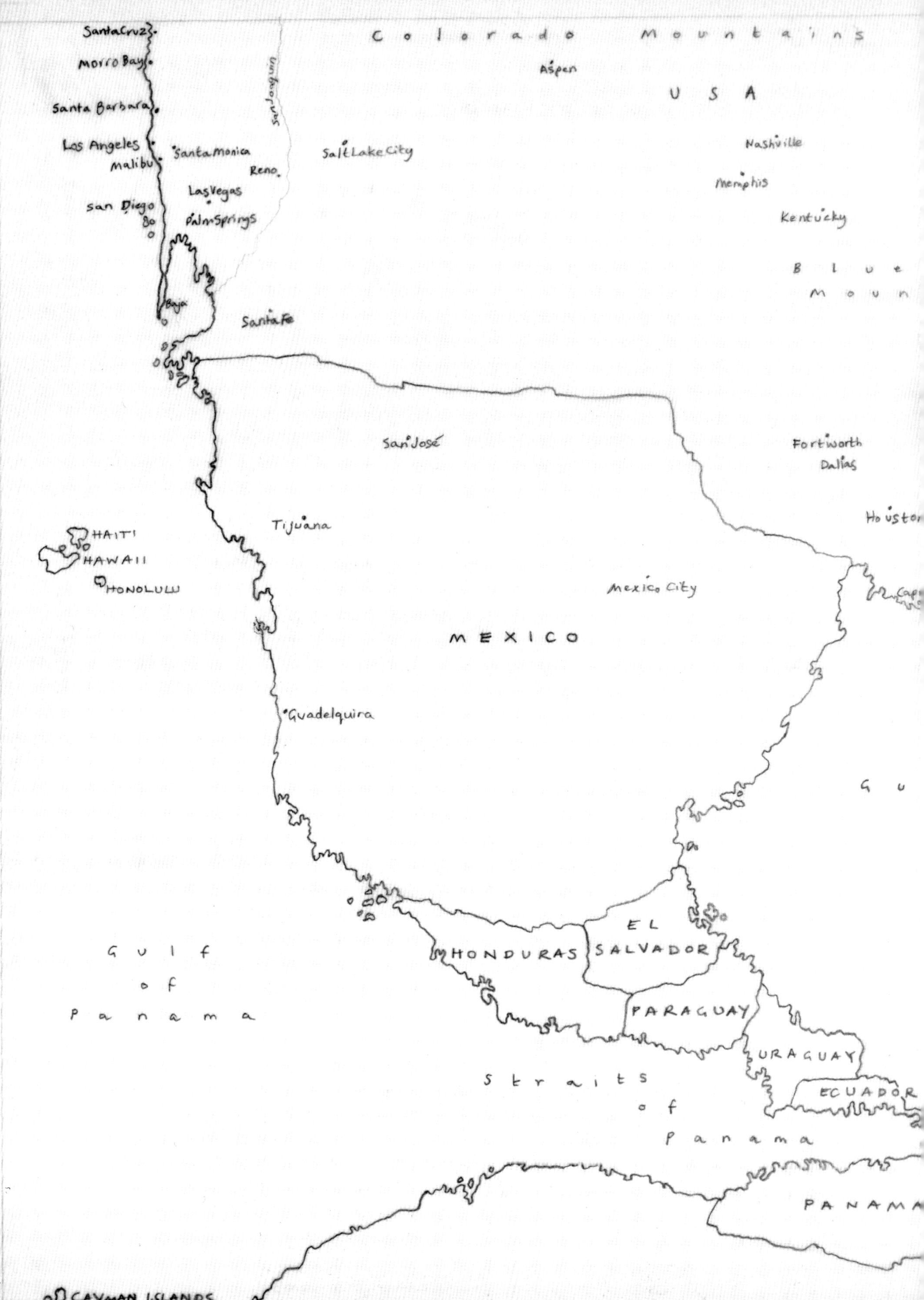

Santa Cruz
Morro Bay
Santa Barbara
Los Angeles
Malibu
Santa Monica
Reno
San Diego
Las Vegas
Palm Springs
Baja
Santa Fe
San Joaquin
Salt Lake City
Colorado Mountains
Aspen
USA
Nashville
Memphis
Kentucky
Blue Moun
Fort Worth
Dallas
Houston
San José
HAITI
HAWAII
HONOLULU
Tijuana
Mexico City
Cap
MEXICO
Guadelquira
G u
GULF
of
Panama
HONDURAS
EL SALVADOR
PARAGUAY
URAGUAY
ECUADOR
Straits
of
Panama
CAYMAN ISLANDS
PANAMA

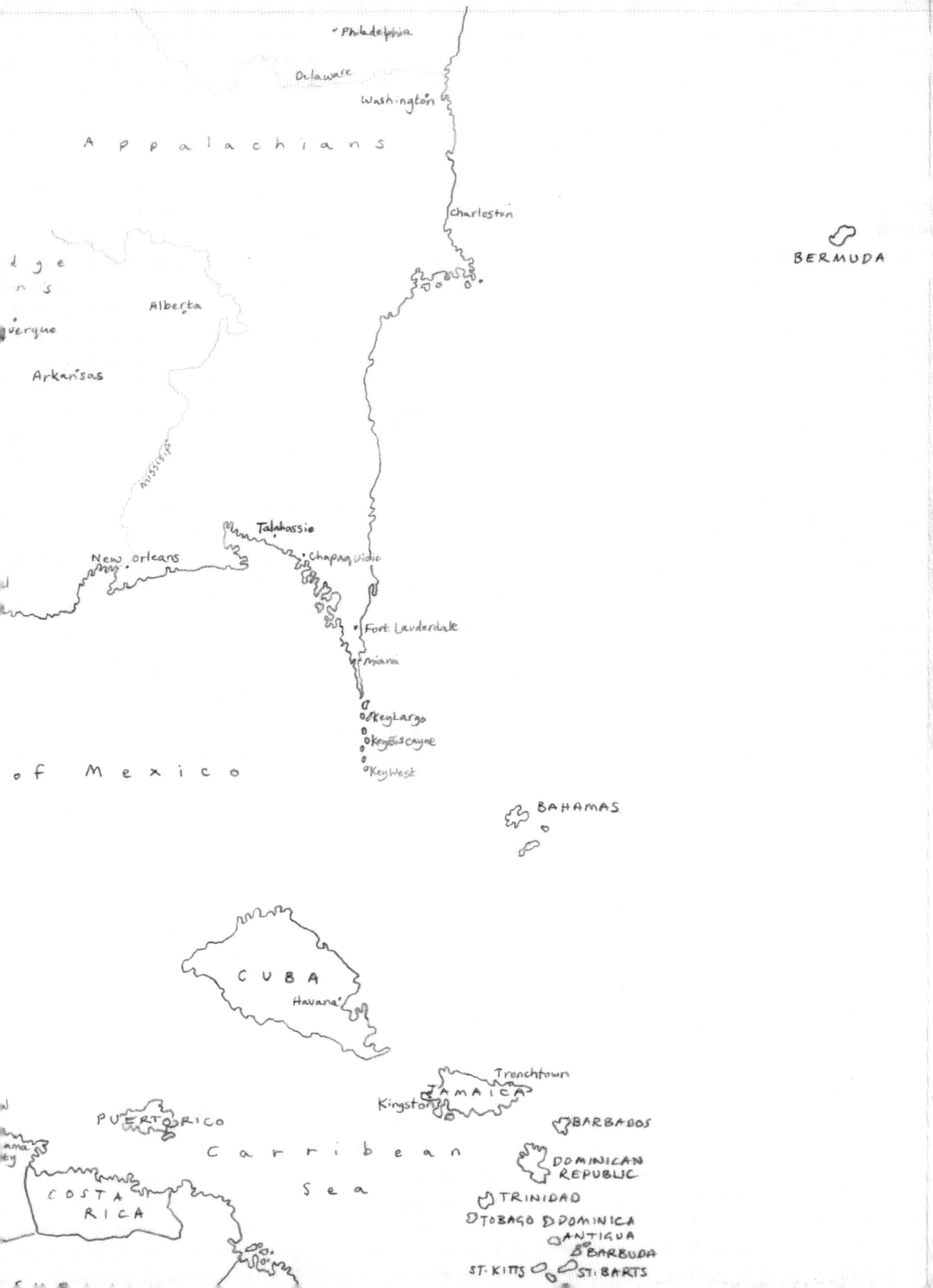

Philadelphia
Delaware
Washington
Appalachians
Charleston
BERMUDA
dge
ns
Alberta
uerque
Arkansas
Mississipi
Talahassie
New Orleans
Chapaquidic
Fort Lauderdale
Miami
Key Largo
Key Biscayne
Key West
of Mexico
BAHAMAS
CUBA
Havana
Trenchtown
JAMAICA
Kingston
PUERTO RICO
Carribean
Sea
BARBADOS
DOMINICAN
REPUBLIC
TRINIDAD
TOBAGO DOMINICA
ANTIGUA
BARBUDA
ST. KITTS ST. BARTS
COSTA
RICA

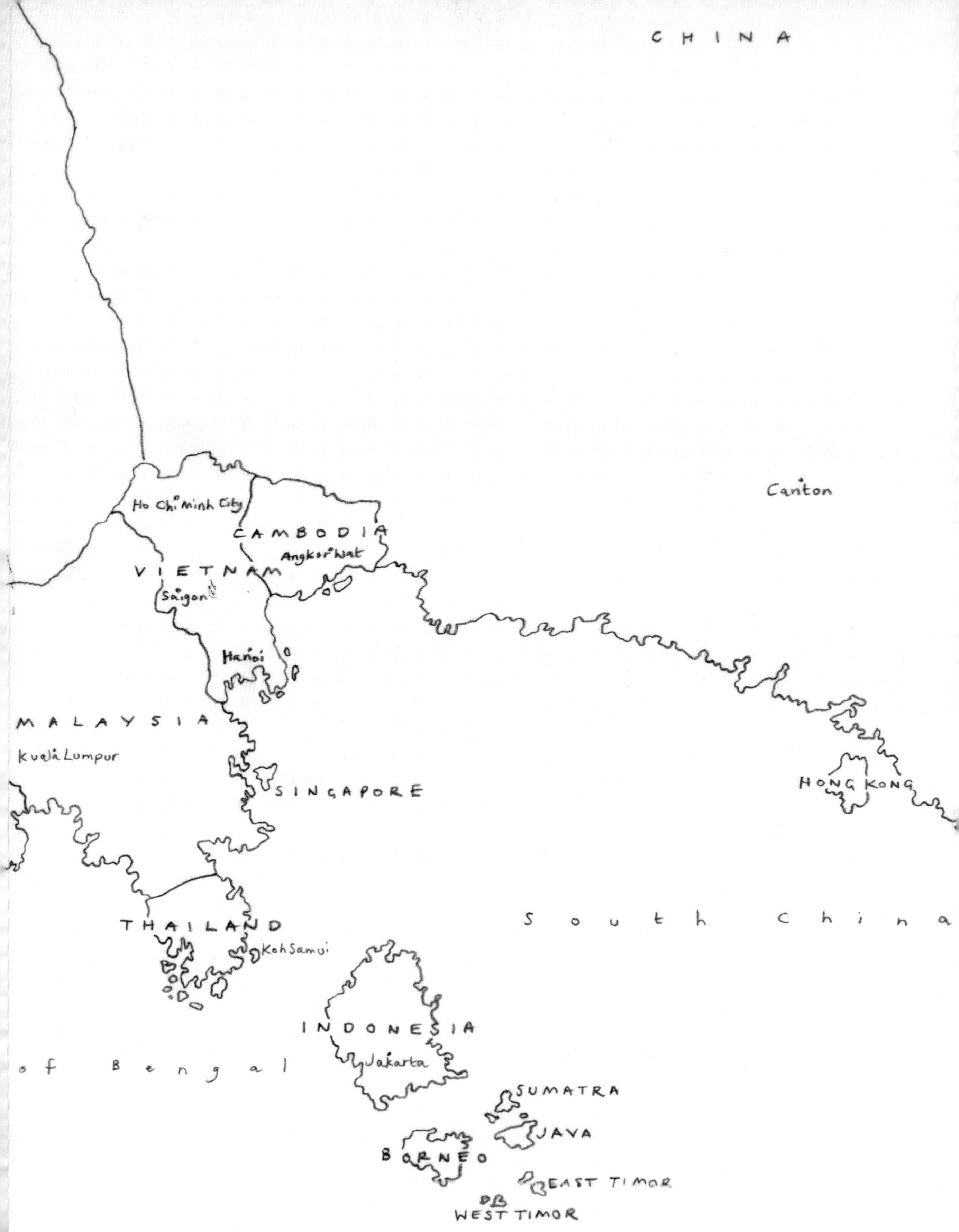

CHINA
Canton
Ho Chi Minh City
CAMBODIA
Angkor Wat
VIETNAM
Saigon
Hanoi
MALAYSIA
Kuala Lumpur
SINGAPORE
HONG KONG
South China
THAILAND
Koh Samui
of Bengal
INDONESIA
Jakarta
SUMATRA
JAVA
BORNEO
EAST TIMOR
WEST TIMOR

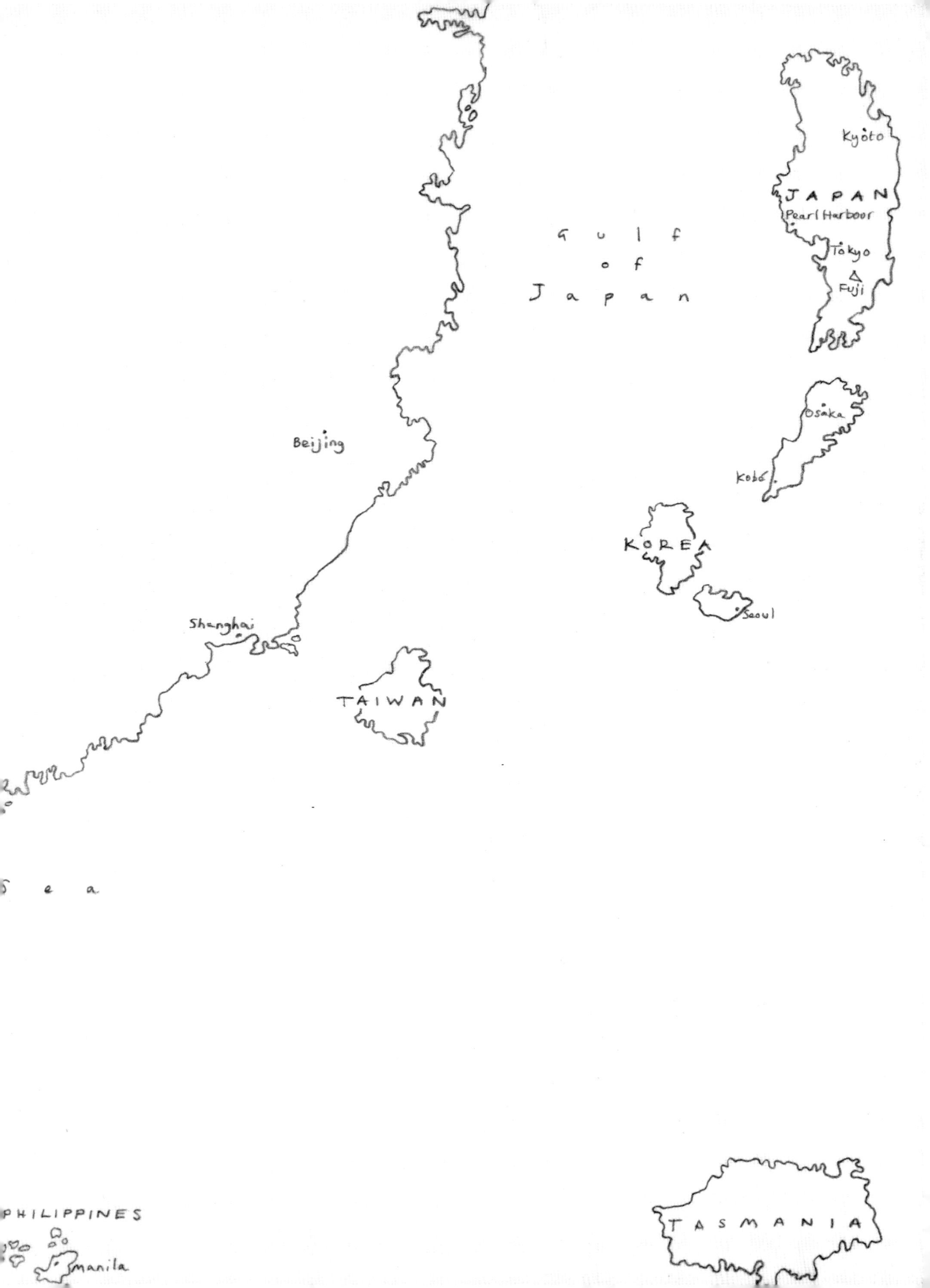

Kyoto
JAPAN
Pearl Harbour
Tokyo
Fuji
Gulf
of
Japan
Osaka
Beijing
Kobé
KOREA
Shanghai
Seoul
TAIWAN
Sea
PHILIPPINES
Manila
TASMANIA

FAEROE ISLANDS
Bergen
SWEDEN
FINLAND
Gothenburg
Oslo
Turku
LA
Stockholm
Helsinki
ESTO
Baltic Sea
Harris Arran
OUTER HEBRIDES
Lewis
SHETLANDS
North
Aberdeen
Falkirk
Dundee
Obap
Kilmarnock
Ben Nevis
Tiree
Edinburgh
Glasgow
Sea
Copenhagen
DENMARK
Hamburg
Kiel
Gdansk
Gretna
Carlisle
Marienbad
Donegal
Isle of Man
Kendal
Newcastle
Texel
Utrecht
Ruhr
Belfast
Enniskillen
Ballymurphy
UNITED
Coventry
Kings Lynn
Rotterdam
Eindhoven
Essen
Hildesheim
EIRE
Dublin
Holyhead
Den Haag
dies
Hanover
Cork
Dun Laoghire
Caernarvon
Manchester
Birmingham
NETHERLANDS
Amsterdam
Köln
Rhine
Danube
Kinsale
KINGDOM
Chester
Vlissingen
Maastricht
Aberystwyth
Ipswich
Oxford
Harwich
Cardiff
Milton Keynes
Ostende
Ghent
Wolfsburg
Berlin
Bristol
Thames
London
Dover
Antwerp
GERMANY
Exeter
Canterbury
Bruges
Brussels
Truro
Taunton
Southampton
Ramsgate
BELGIUM
Penzance
Falmouth
Portsmouth
Isle of Wight
Brighton
Calais
SCILLY ISLES
Dieppe
English
Bonn
Channel
Deauville
Trouville
Fécamp
Karlsruhe
Le Havre
Omaha
Paris
Épernay
Roscoff
Cherbourg
Loire
Kassel
Jersey
Alderney
Sark
Stuttgart
Guernsey
St Malo
Seine
Munich
CHANNEL ISLANDS
Alencon
Le Mans
Bergen
Tours
Anvers
FRANCE
Bay of
Dijon
Gstaad
Oberammergau
Biscay
Mont Blanc
Bâsle
Matterhorn
Berne
Zurich
Lille
massif
St Moritz
SWITZERLAND
Courchevel
Les Arcs
Méribel
Geneva
Beaumont
Central
Courmayeur
St Foy la Grande
LUXEMBOURG
Turin
Bordeaux
Dordogne
Bergerac
LICHTENSTEIN
Rhone
Milan
Nîmes
Draguignan
Grasse
Aups
Marseilles
Genova
Auvergne
Arles
Nice
Antibes
Biarritz
Toulouse
Orange
Marseilles
MonteCarlo
Cremona
St Juan Les Pins
Cap Ferrat
Cannes
Bolo
Pisa
ANDORRA
Pyrennees
Alicante
Grosseto
Santander
La Coruña
PICOS de EUROPA
Rocca mare
IT
Oporto
Santiago de Compostela
CORSICA
Guimares
Barcelona
Aveiro
SARDINIA
Coimbra
Figuera da Foz
SPAIN
Segovia
PORTUGAL
Madrid
MALLORCA
Solder
Pollença
Toledo
Tagus
criptana
LIPA
ISL
Cuidad Real
Palma
IBIZA

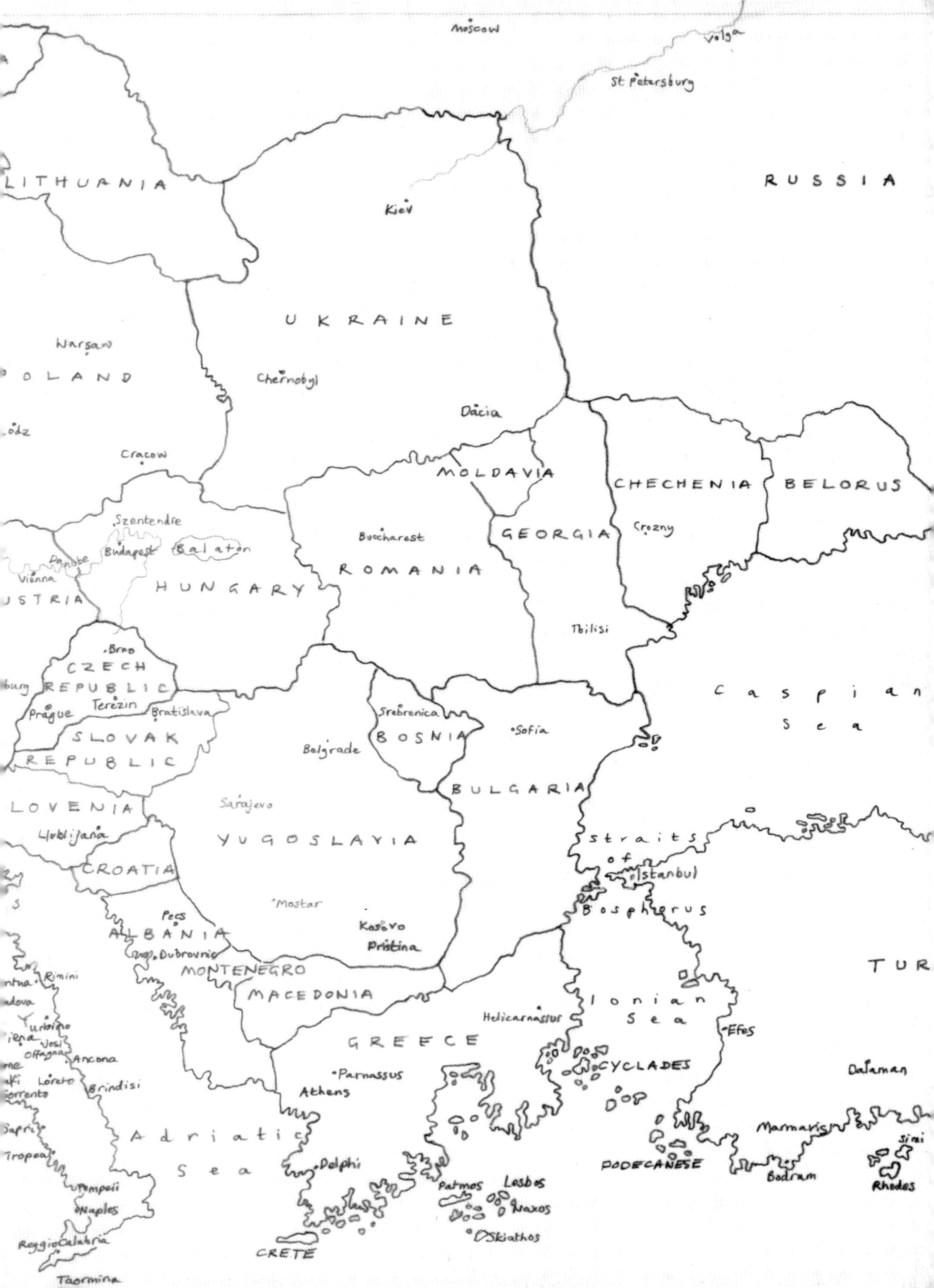

LITHUANIA
RUSSIA
Moscow
Volga
St Petersburg
Kiev
UKRAINE
Warsaw
POLAND
Chernobyl
Łódz
Dacia
Cracow
MOLDAVIA
CHECHENIA
BELORUS
Szentendre
Buccharest
GEORGIA
Crozny
Danube Budapest Balaton
ROMANIA
Vienna
HUNGARY
USTRIA
Tbilisi
CASPIAN
Sea
Brno
CZECH
REPUBLIC
Srebrenica
burg
Sofia
Prague Terezin Bratislava
BOSNIA
SLOVAK
Belgrade
REPUBLIC
BULGARIA
LOVENIA
Sarajevo
Straits
Ljubljana
YUGOSLAVIA
of
Istanbul
CROATIA
Bosphorus
S
Mostar
Pecs
Kosovo
ALBANIA
Pristina
TUR
Dubrovnic
MONTENEGRO
Rimini
ntna
MACEDONIA
Ionian
dova
Sea
Turbino
Helicarnassus
Efes
iena
Jesi
GREECE
Offagna
me
Ancona
CYCLADES
Dalaman
fi Loreto Brindisi
Parnassus
orrento
Athens
Adriatic
Marmaris
Japri
Sini
Tropea
Sea
Delphi
DODECANESE
Bodrum
Pompeii
Rhodes
Naples
Patmos Lesbos
ReggioCalabria
Naxos
CRETE
Skiathos
Taormina

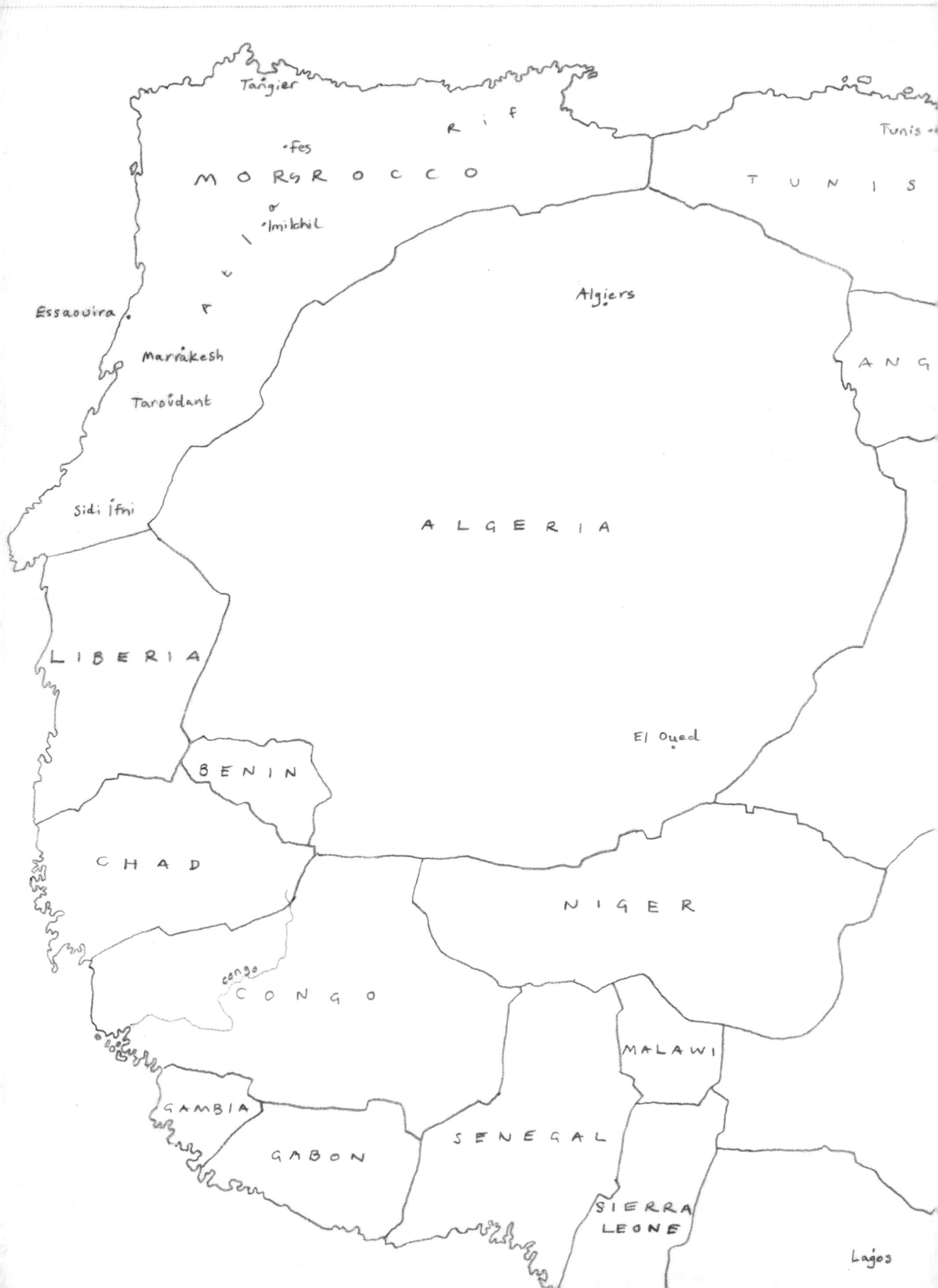

Tangier
Fes
RIF
Tunis
MOROCCO
Imilchil
Algiers
TUNIS
Essaouira
ANG
Marrakesh
Taroudant
ALGERIA
Sidi Ifni
El Oued
LIBERIA
BENIN
CHAD
NIGER
congo
CONGO
MALAWI
GAMBIA
SENEGAL
GABON
SIERRA
LEONE
Lagos

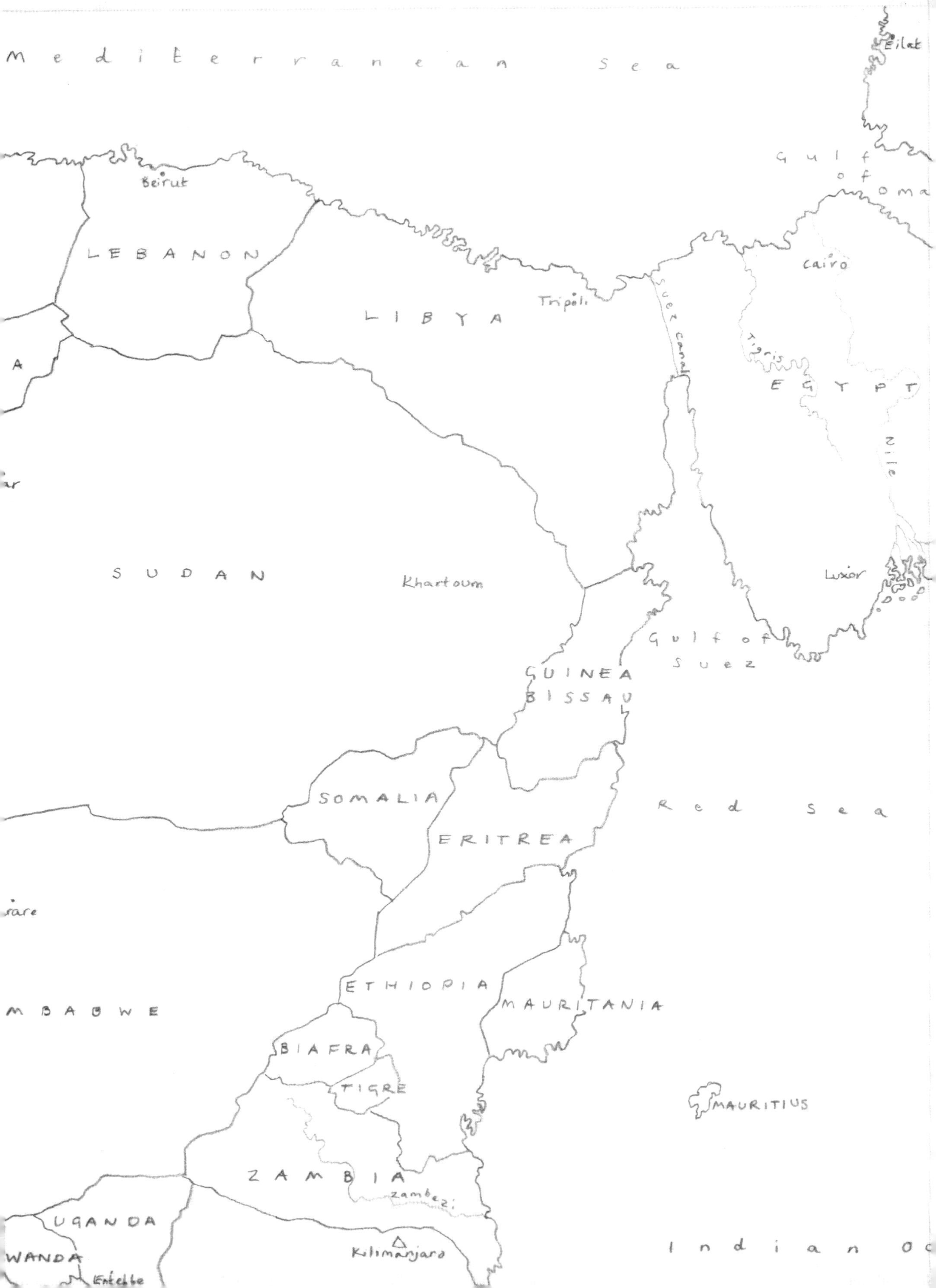

Eilat
Mediterranean Sea
Beirut
Gulf of Oma
LEBANON
Cairo
LIBYA
Tripoli
Suez Canal
Tigris
EGYPT
A
Nile
ar
SUDAN
Khartoum
Luxor
Gulf of Suez
GUINEA BISSAU
SOMALIA
Red Sea
ERITREA
iare
ETHIOPIA
MBABWE
MAURITANIA
BIAFRA
TIGRE
MAURITIUS
ZAMBIA
Zambezi
UGANDA
Kilimanjaro
WANDA
Entebbe
Indian Oc

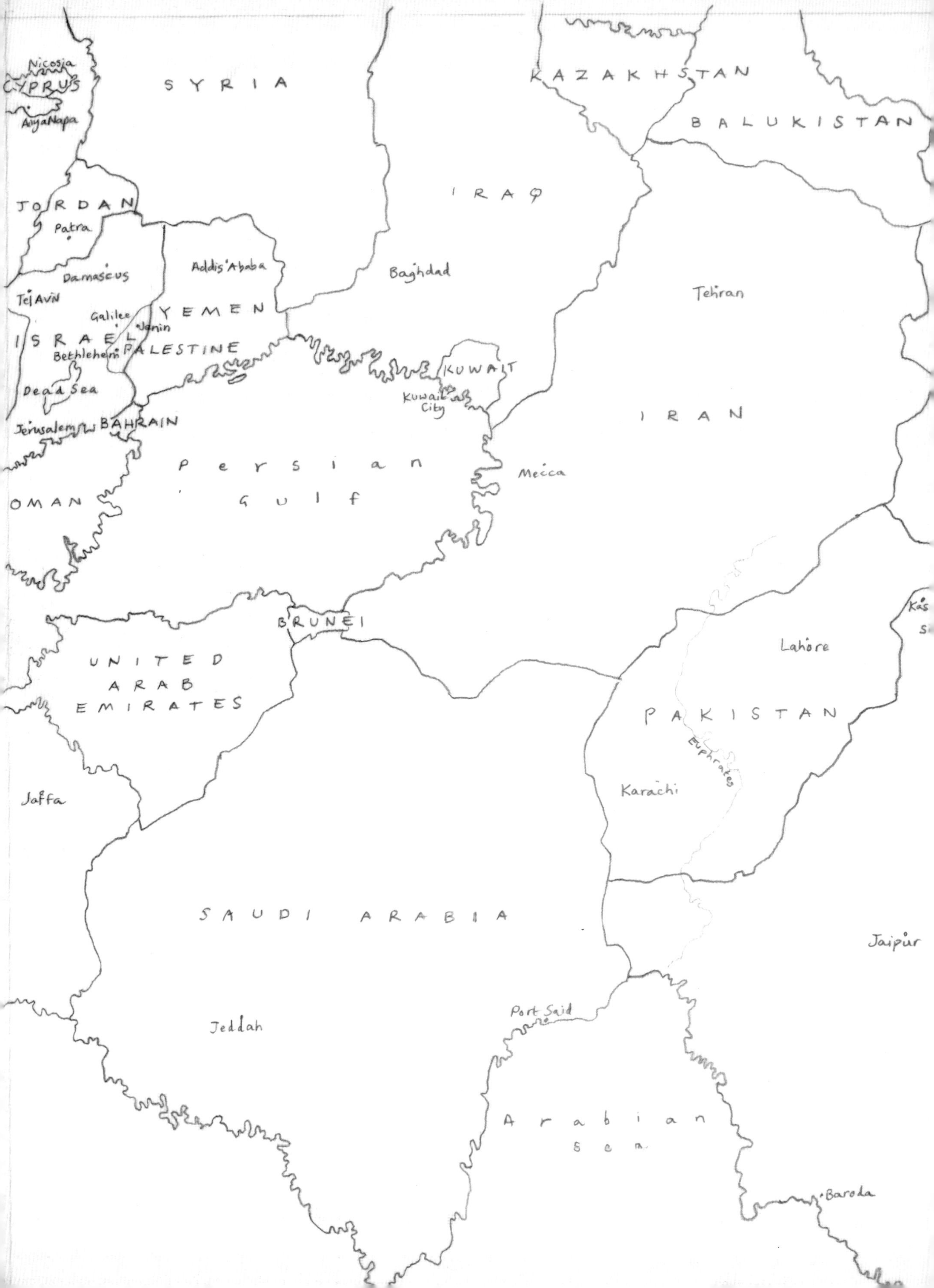

Nicosia
CYPRUS
Aiya Napa
SYRIA
KAZAKHSTAN
BALUKISTAN
IRAQ
JORDAN
Patra
Damascus
Addis Ababa
Baghdad
Tehran
Tel Aviv
Galilee
YEMEN
ISRAEL
Jenin
Bethlehem
PALESTINE
KUWAIT
Kuwait City
IRAN
Dead Sea
Jerusalem
BAHRAIN
Persian
Gulf
Mecca
OMAN
BRUNEI
Lahore
UNITED
ARAB
EMIRATES
PAKISTAN
Euphrates
Jaffa
Karachi
SAUDI ARABIA
Kas
Si
Jaipur
Jeddah
Port Said
Arabian
Sea
Baroda

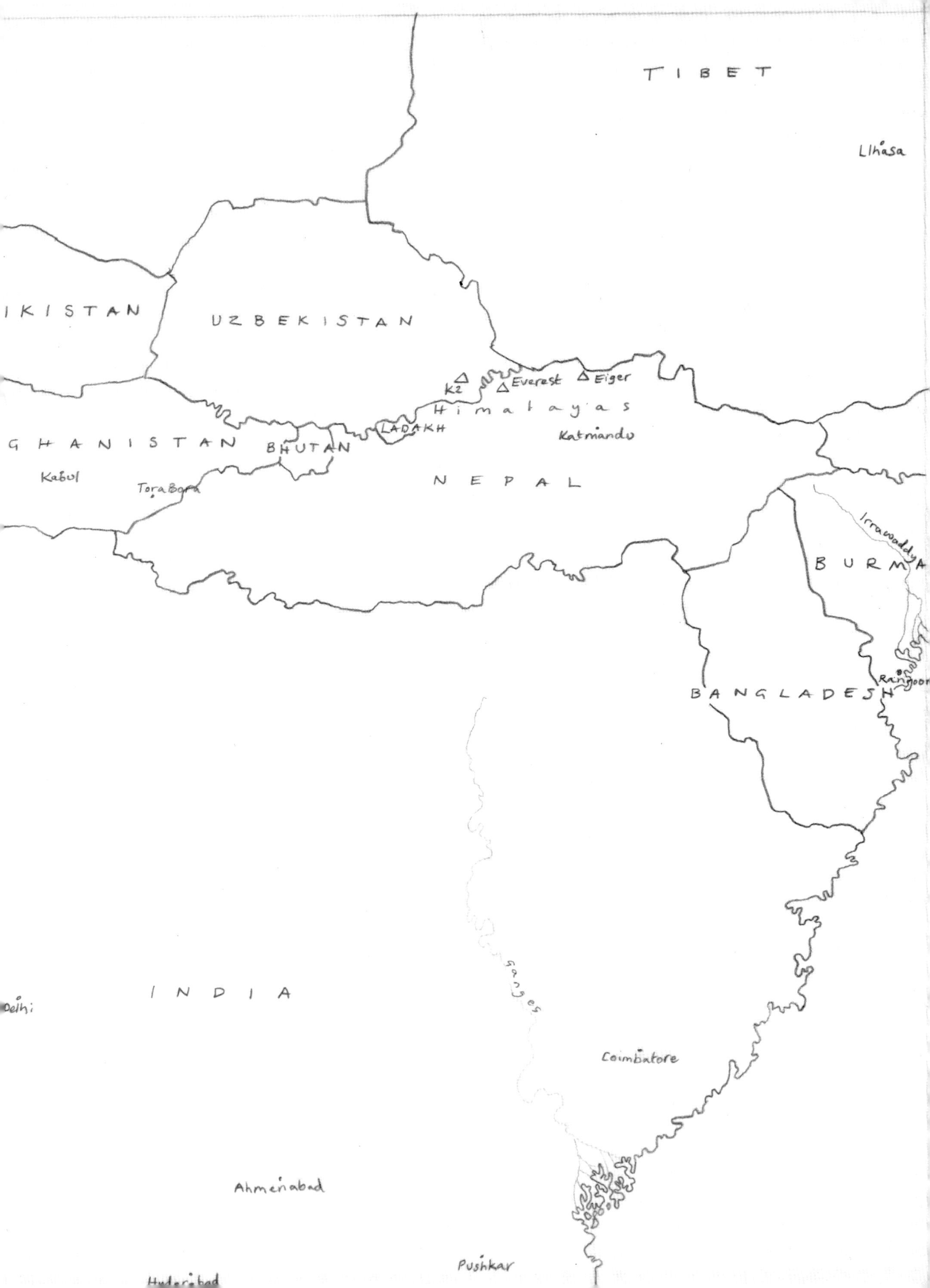

TIBET
Llhasa
IKISTAN
UZBEKISTAN
K2
Everest
Eiger
Himalayas
GHANISTAN
BHUTAN
LADAKH
Katmandu
Kabul
Tora Bora
NEPAL
Irrawaddy
BURMA
BANGLADESH
Rangoon
INDIA
Delhi
Ganges
Coimbatore
Ahmenabad
Pushkar
Hyderabad

Mike Pearson

Bubbling Tom

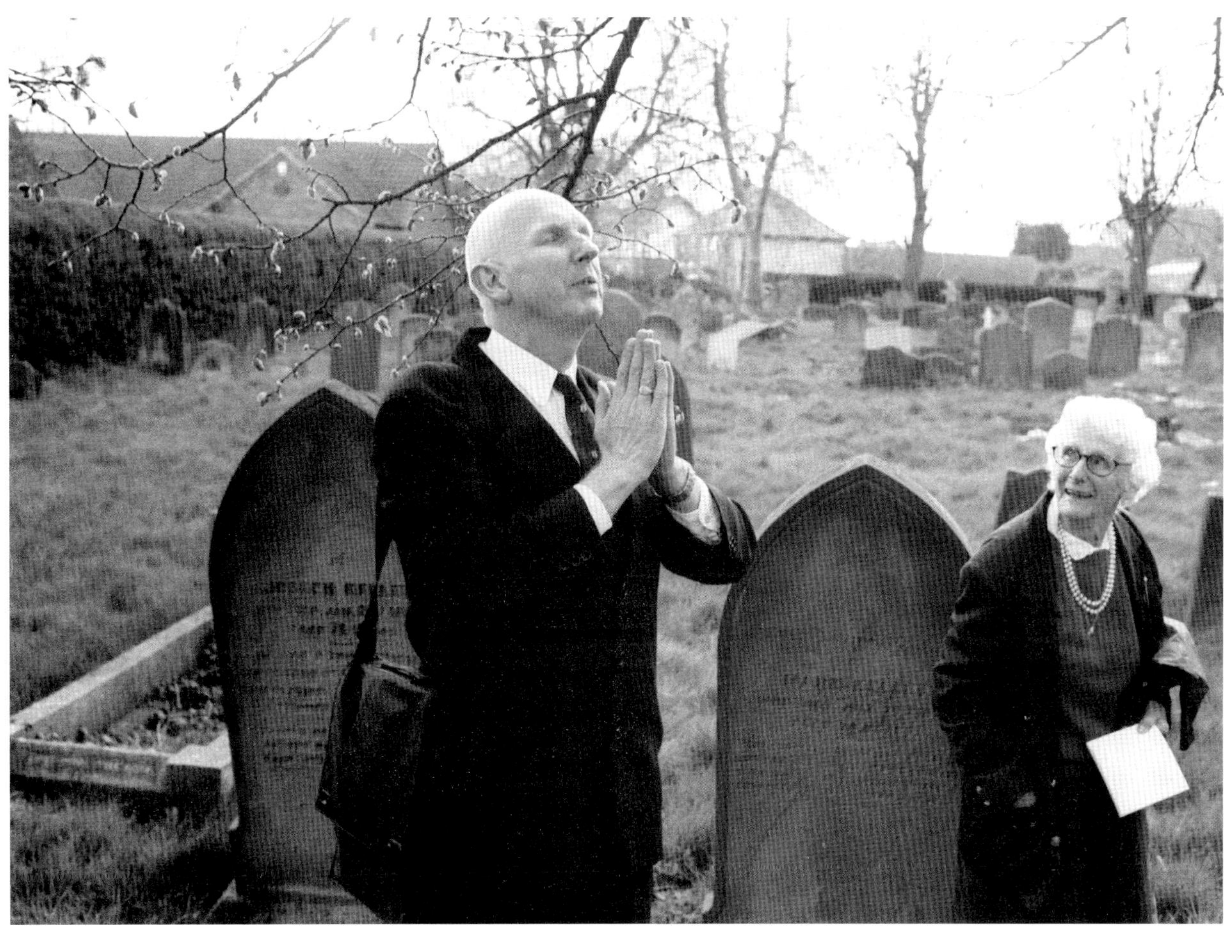

Walking in Hibaldstow 24/25 April 2000

In the year of the Millennium, I am fifty years old.

I was born in a terraced house in Scunthorpe, a trick of fate as my father was working there as a mechanic at the time, but before my first birthday we returned to the nearby village of Hibaldstow where most of our family lived. On my father's side the Pearsons and the Toynes were Lincolnshire farm workers. My mother's family was more exotic, drawn from Eire, the Falkland Islands, Australia ... When I was eight, we moved the four miles to Kirton Lindsey. For me then, the time in Hibaldstow constitutes the arena and landscape of my earliest experiences, sealed in a very particular envelope of memory.

The early Fifties were a period of aspiration and change: the mechanisation of agriculture, the intrusion of mass media, the onset of conspicuous consumerism ... a way of life expanding, warping, shattering ... But the old survived too, people and practices from the age of Victoria and before, now gone. And here face-to-face communication still had currency, here talk was an endless flow of truth and fiction, here – where my 'sense of place' was nurtured – my 'ways of telling' were simultaneously engendered. In Nan's kitchen, site of eulogy and elegy, I heard the approvals and disapprovals of family lore and communal tradition, stories told *sotto voce* in whispers, opinions expressed openly to an unforgiving world, incidents, genealogies, 'thoughts of the day' worked and reworked, endlessly. And here I learned the most sophisticated of intertextual procedures which could pass from pathology to geomorphology to psychology – instantaneously, effortlessly and seamlessly – with engagement, with opinion, with indifference and yet without ever having heard of any of them!

Eventually I walked off, walked out, walked away, in the great diaspora of the Sixties, lured by the candle flame of education, to be an archaeologist. I never went back: the great pilgrimage of the twentieth century has been the journey from the village to the city. My professional life has been in Wales, far off, and often in a different language, invisible and incomprehensible to the world I left. But I never truly abandoned Hibaldstow. Increasingly my performance work has involved matters of memory and identity, place and landscape. I have been concerned with the complex relationship between ourselves, our bodies and our environment; with our physical and sensual experience of place, and the impact a particular location can have on our lives. But these narrative performances have always been elsewhere, never 'on site'. It would feel strange, inappropriate, disturbing to make work 'at home'. Good enough reason then to try ... before I forget ... and whilst there are still those there who remember me.

In *Bubbling Tom* – the name of a stream in the village – I decided to create a site-work at my place of origin. Here, 'on my own doorstep' and 'in my own backyard', I would make a piece within, and concerning, the micro-landscape of my childhood, walking 'as if' in the couple of years either side of 1955.

It began with a work of archaeology: to reveal and record the memories of those who recall my actions up to the age of eight, particularly non-family members, and to record interviews relating to particular events. I set out to uncover records and photographs of me in this place, to discover physical marks I left in the landscape, in order to re-embody the traces the landscape has left in me: to relocate myself. This enquiry was informed and oriented by spatial notions which describe the Welsh 'sense of place'; a series of cognitive maps surrounding home and locality where diverse discourses – discrete 'ways of telling' – are engendered. And all of this, to work with fragments, with material traces, with evidence, in order to create something – a meaning, a narrative, a story – which stands for the past in the present. Leading to ...

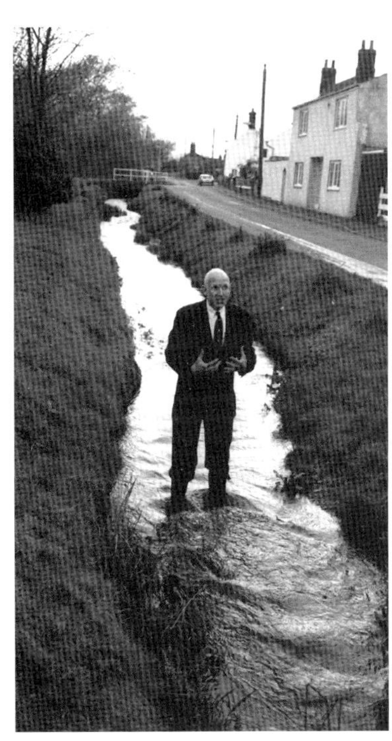

... a work of writing: to use the rediscovered landscape as a mnemonic, revisiting those places, those rooms, which were the location of dreams and day-dreams and which provide one with the cognitive maps for all other places. A way of seeing those maps from above, in colour; seeing me then, them now. And thinking of the pathology of my own body – physiognomy, posture, gesture, demeanour – the combination of heredity, habit and conditioning. Thinking of body scars, for the body bears the marks of its history and the skin is a map of accident and injury; thinking of objects bearing the patinas of their usage; and all those surrogate inciting incidents, those thresholds, those entrances and exits with which we measure the passing of our lives. I wanted to embrace memory in a contemporary project, as unafraid of critical romanticism as of nostalgia. Serving as the text for ...

... a work of performance in the form of a guided tour; a revisiting of the personal, though inevitably fictional and illusionary, landscape of my childhood; to find 'ways of telling' which are intimate and reflective, which mix useful information (about vernacular detail, people, events) with the pleasure of telling and which include anecdotes, secrets and fibs. Its point of attraction was intended to be the voice of the performer – chatting, lecturing, reciting, orating, seducing – in modulations and intensifications of speed, tone, volume, rhythm, emphasis. Here in the 'grain of the voice' is where the story comes to life. The vocal practice of the teller then engages and re-engages the audience with material which is intimately familiar and infinitely other; as familiar as their own history, or as exotic as the strange sights and smells of the explorer's account.

My object was to devise a mode of performance which concentrated on manual rhetoric – to indicate, demonstrate, locate and shape the details of a 'writing' which was not separate from a 'telling' – intimate, informal, at the edge of performance itself. I can no longer muster much interest in the fate of fictional characters. For me, drama need no longer be restricted to their dialogue. The monologue of the storyteller can exhibit a different form of 'dialogue': a high order of intertextuality, of dialogue between texts. It can encompass truth and fiction: the fragmentary, the digressive, the ambiguous, the appropriated, in juxtaposition and in contradiction; weaving together history, geography, genealogy, memoir and autobiography and including anecdotes, traveller's tales, poetry, forensic data, quotations, lies, jokes, improvised asides, physical re-enactments, impersonations and intimate reflections, in its attempt to hold the interest of the listener. Constituting ...

... a personal archaeology, which placed me at the centre of events, as both narrator and the subject of narration, and which dramatised 'the familiar past'. What I hope such work elicits is other stories, and stories about stories. It catalyses personal reflection and the desire on the part of the listener to reveal her own experiences, the minutiae of genealogy. It works with memory: raking up enduring ones, stirring half-suppressed ones.

Bubbling Tom is in the form of a leisurely stroll around the village, pausing at ten key points to remember significant events and people in a sequence of performed texts and informal chat. It is intended for an audience who need know nothing of the niceties and conventions of contemporary theatre and art practice. A specially prepared guidebook included photographs of these locations and related happenings in the mid-Fifties.

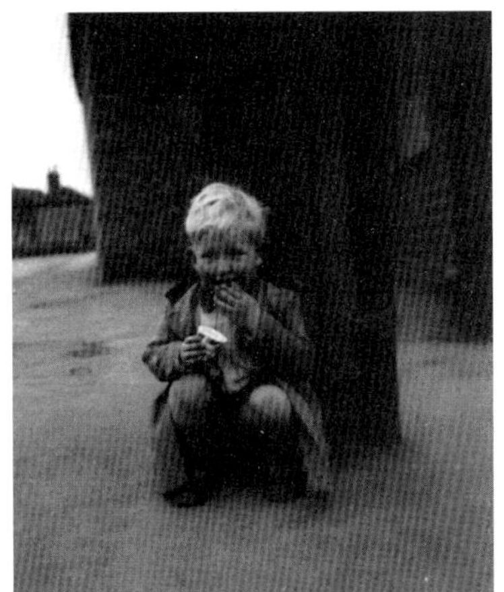

The following documentation includes some images and fragments of the text for each station. But there is no attempt at completeness here. The document is as fragmentary and partial as the memories which inspired the work, and the memories of the performance work itself, after a couple of days have passed. What's missing from the document, I realise, are my accounts of people, from Great-uncle Fred who as a child contracted polio and thereafter wore a metal caliper and a special platform boot, to Michael Holt, next to me in the school photo of 1955, who 'wasn't quite all there'. For my telling about them, I realise, is always the most intimate and involves acts of impersonation and embodiment, of making them present in performance, in a way that text never can. They are simply absent here, not forgotten.

1 Top corner SE 97760251 *"You don't want to get it mucky, duck"*

> *I have long been of the opinion myself that a child's observation and memory of what goes on around him in his very early days are very much deeper and more intense than people in general have believed them to be.* [1]

It's 1953 and I'm squatting ... here. I seem ... happy. It must be the ice-cream ... not the usual yellowing lump in a cardboardy cornet, retrieved by Norman from the bottom of Kendall's fridge, but a grown-up 'tub', its wooden spoon lodged in the corner of my mouth, yet to be manipulated efficiently by small fingers. And in my left hand too!

Wilf must be out there, in the road, also squatting, with his Kershaw 'Raven' folding camera – Zeiss copy, the camera of choice for de-mobbed tank crews – eight pictures on a roll of 120 film – black spool, red backing paper, sticky seal ('Just lick that duck'), each number appearing and disappearing in a small, circular window on the back: one two hundred and fiftieth of a second at f8. But he'll be alright, out there. He'll hear anything coming – grinding gears, blowing exhaust – long before he sees it and, by the look of my new coat, it's probably

Sunday anyway. That'll have to come off before we start washing the taxis: "You don't want to get it mucky, duck".

In this moment, this spot is the centre of my world: six feet from the step into Grandad's fish and chip shop – 'Alfred Melton Shaw, Fish Suppers' – on the home-made, hand-painted illuminated sign above my head. Of course, I can't read it yet but I already know the mantras of the customers: "One of each", "A fish and six", "Four pennyworth", "Some scraps", know the smell of melting fat ("They use oil now but you can't clarify it like beef dripping – just put it through a muslin" says me Mam), the spitting sizzle of battered haddock … The shop itself has turned through ninety degrees. Then there was a bench around the wall, a table in the corner, both scrubbed white, scrubbed so that the grain stood proud. And a counter shattered by the endless rapping of money. And if there was any trouble Grandad would soon sort it out, for though he was only five foot eight, he was an ex-Marine. "Ah'll sort 'em out! Get off home".

After a man has turned fifty he sees rather clearly
The people and surroundings that have made him what he is. [2]

2 Hibaldstow County School SE 97770246
"Pick that paper up, Michael"

When the many things I remember actually happened, whether early or late in the course of that six years, I haven't much of an idea. But I can locate most of them with a degree of certainty – where such and such a thing happened and where I was standing when I heard what I heard. [3]

It's 1955 and we're all present, against this wall, some smiling, some a little apprehensive, not knowing quite how we're supposed to look. There I am top centre, between Tony and Michael Holt. Gill Shadlock, Graham Coates, Nina Wynn, Patsy Bowers, Teresa Costello, my cousin Margaret, Karl Künzler in a splendid, exotic bow-tie, John North in purposeful pose ("Nice braces, John!"), Chud already practising his football team pose … And this photo goes with this book: Class 4 with Mrs. Andrews. And already I'm drawing cars, and boats and planes. And curiously, a cooker! "You haven't changed" said Janet Andrews a few weeks ago. "What do you mean?" I said. "Your mannerisms" she said. "What do you mean?" I said. "The way you laugh" she said. And she recognised her own handwriting.

What you can't see is the playground, stretching out there … country dancing with Miss Dawson, the 'Virginia Reel'; skirts tucked into blue or green flannel knickers, up-ended against this wall … and across there, the dreaded toilets … held it in until dinner I always did. The one thing you didn't want to do, whatever, was wee down your leg 'cos by, it chapped you in winter: blue knees, red thighs …

And what's going on here? Some sort of show we guess. There's Karl at twenty-five past six and Margaret Hughes at half-past. We seem to represent the services – me in Dad's RAF beret, Graham Coates in his dad's Navy cap and Geoff Bowers, with rifle, in full uniform. There's John Shaw on tambourine,

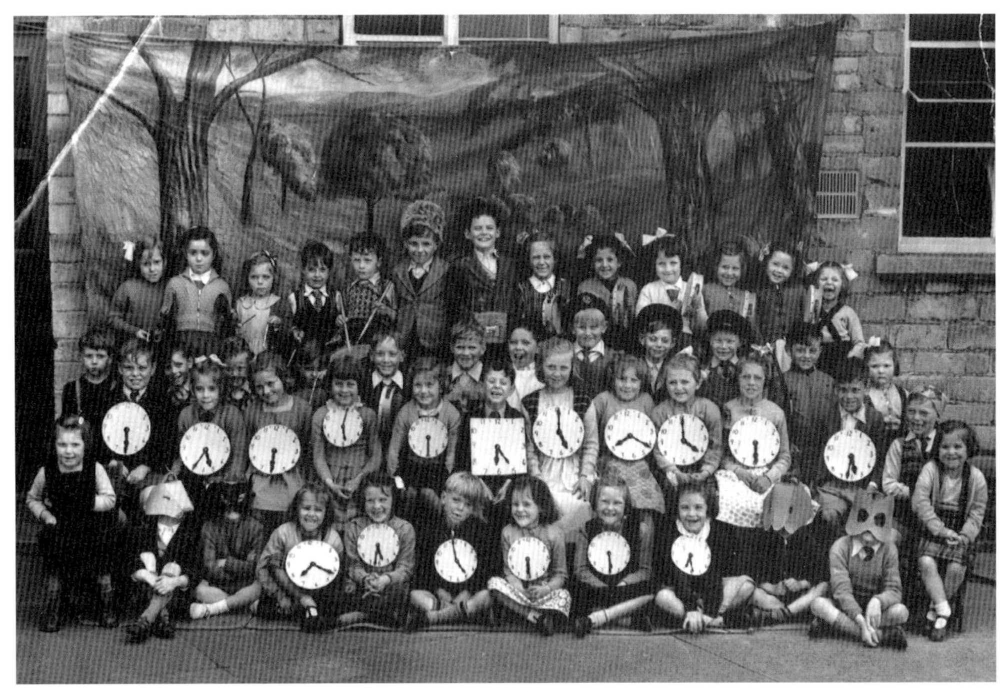

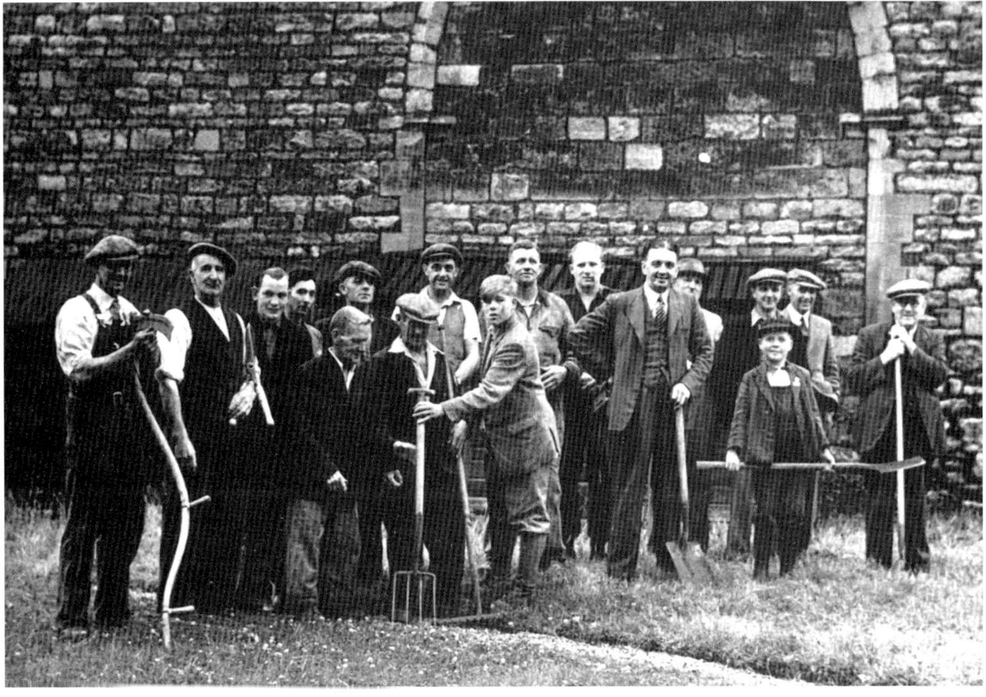

Marion Slack on cymbals and John North on drums. But what's Tony doing in his Davy Crockett hat? And Graham Maycock as a gypsy?

And Marion – Mrs. Michaelijw, Class 3 – recognised her own writing too! It's 1957 already and I now know that gardeners do not like Cabbage White butterflies, that our front teeth are sharp and used for cutting, that the heart is a pumping station, that snails have rows of teeth on their tongues...

3 East Street SE 97990257 *"... it was really something ..."*

"I learned to love it, I believe, before I learned to walk." [4]

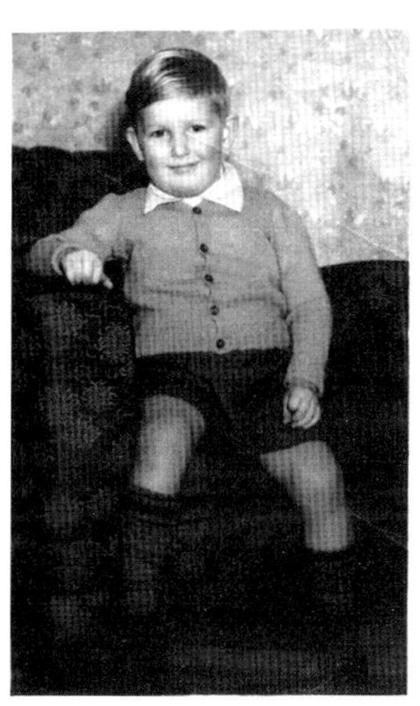

It's 1953 again and I'm on the move. We're whizzing down East Street and I'm clinging onto Dad's handlebars, perched on the small saddle fixed to his crossbar. He recently brought home a tortoise in his saddle-bag. Found it on Station Bridge where Grandad Pearson once met a red light swinging in the fog. Gingerly, he pedalled forward, to find that the lamp was tied to the tail of an elephant. Mind, he did like a drink ... and a bit of a gamble. He was "A quiet man. He didn't say a lot" and Grandma "So quiet, unassuming, wouldn't hurt anyone's feelings".

We're off to their house – 'Wheldale'. But to get here we have to move real quick: past Harold Cox the undertaker's yard where me Mam played in the coffins and used wood shavings as ringlets; past the cottages of people who are old and smell a bit: Tommy Goodbin, "scruffy, probably loaded"; Mr. Beadham, "hedge-cutter and dyker, clever at his work" who liked to spit. What's pulling me on is Sergeant's ice-cream cart, there – look – parked right outside Grandad's. Custardy Heaven!

I'm excited because Grandad shows me things: how he can make Denton's two dogs – strange, elongated wire-haired dachshunds – sit up and beg for cold meat; skylark's nests in Aggie Stothard's field, swallow's nests in her barn; how ash keys hang in bunches on that tree; how blackbirds peck strawberries; Geoff's shaft drive Sunbeam – "It was really something" – in the garage and the model aeroplanes hanging on black cotton threads in his bedroom. Lancaster, Blenheim, Spitfire ... all, after much beseeching, given to me to play with, to destroy ...

But I know I'll have to hold it in again, because their toilet is a plank, a circular hole, a bin, hard Izal toilet roll, air-freshener like a green wick in a bottle, some flies.

A man from Kelsey took the photo. And that impressed pattern, imperial chrysanthemum, on the armchair ... my fingers are creeping towards it even now, ready to trace it over and over.

4 Churchyard SE 97980261 *"... but did you hear the one about his false teeth ..."*

Like turning on a tap when the water is under high pressure, a flood of reminiscences comes to me, if I give it a chance ... [5]

At a guess it's 1954 and everyone turned out to cut the churchyard. Of course, the tower wasn't there then. The original fell down in the last century, when they

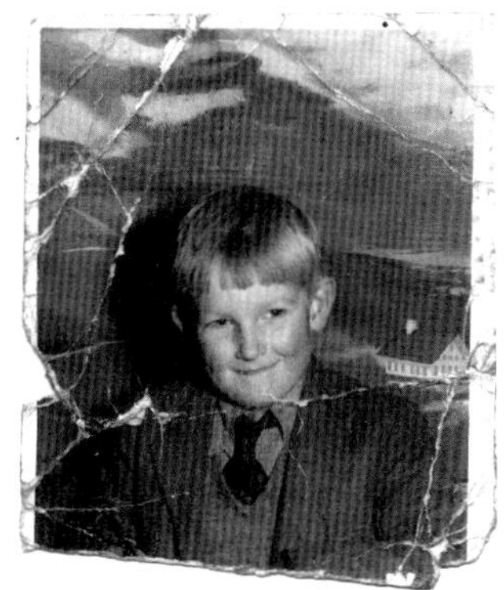

rebuilt the nave. And these men – Mr. Skipworth with his scythe, Charlie Tennant, 'Blackie', Pete Skip with a spade – are standing in front of the shed in which the bells hung ... well, all except the one that had fallen off. Our Pete says you used to be able to throw stones at them through the gaps; remembers them striking, "so many for a man's death, so many for a woman's", followed by the number of years. They were rung by pulling a handle and wire on the inside wall. This I saw when I joined the choir ...

On my first night Daisy Heath and Daisy Cox accused me of singing out of tune, made me sing it by myself, which I did ... perfectly. Hard to believe now! Mind, Daisy Heath's singing! No, I shouldn't ... oh why not, everybody knew it. Without fail she would start one note before everyone else, sounding off, getting in there first ... before the other Daisy.

And these things I remember here: the smell of incense and Jeff Cox lighting the charcoal ring, blowing on the glowing ember, in the censor; the Reverend Clay's scraggy neck in a hard white collar; Wilf kneeling, hands clasped angelically, at Bri's christening; asking Ron Coates if he would cut my hair in his wash house with his hand clippers – 'good for your muscles' – after the service; holding my breath to get from door to gate after choir practice.

Time to come clean! One group of mowers, not included here, shows Choco Glover. Choco was a dillyman. You always knew when they were in the village: emptying toilet buckets into the open vat on the back of their lorry. They wore leather armour to help lift and support the slopping pans. How did he get his name? Well one day he was lifting a pan, got it on his shoulder when the bottom fell out! "But did you hear the one about his false teeth?" me Mam said.

Meanwhile, I seem to be on a trip to a Swiss alpine village ...

5 'Tin Tab' SE 97880257 *"... I am the family face ..."*

Everyone in the community is joined to everyone else by a mesh of stories and incidents if not by family relationships.[6]

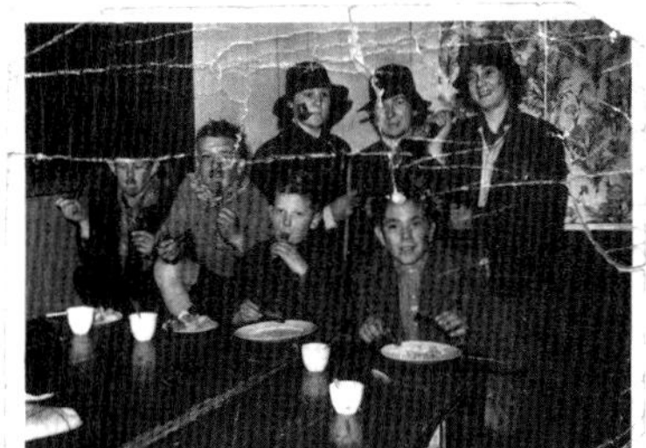

It's a beef pie supper in the 'Tin Tab', a reward for cutting the churchyard. Everyone scrubbed up well, even Charlie Tennant: men mostly, one 'body'. There's me Dad, left centre, just behind Plim Hall, 'Father Christmas'. I'd worked out that nobody can get round the world by himself on one night so there must be a lot of Father Christmases, maybe one in every village. And to bring all the presents he must have a lorry and Plim Hall's got a lorry. So Plim Hall must be Father Christmas! And there centre back, turned slightly, in the only photo I know of him, is Grandad Pearson. As Thomas Hardy writes in *Heredity*:[7]

I am the family face
Flesh perishes, I live on
Projecting trait and trace
Through time, to times anon,
And leaping from place to place
Over oblivion.

What strikes me is the size of everyone's ears. Country men used to have enormous ears. Every night me Mam would check if I was sleeping with my ears folded under, lest they stuck out in later life. Either she fought a losing battle with heredity or I fooled her for years!

And two more in the 'Tin Tab', already beginning to lurch precariously: a tramp's supper – Mrs. North with splendid dog-end – and something about which we all look a bit sceptical, a bit suspicious ... Margaret and John Shaw, Jill Shadlock, Val Raspin, Roger Wilk, Karl, me brother ... and the Mrs. Harpham, Chudley, Havercroft, Miller, Balchin and Nurse Harrison, who'd delivered half the village.

After a man has turned fifty, he wears the face he deserves ...

6 Beckside SE 97980274 *'... where the child first learns everything which is of real importance ...'*

'[Here] the child first learns everything which is of real importance [...] history and geography'. [8]

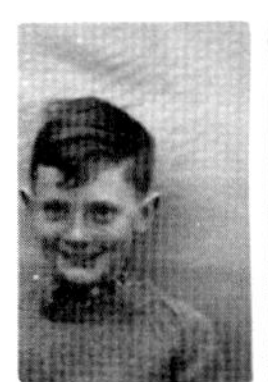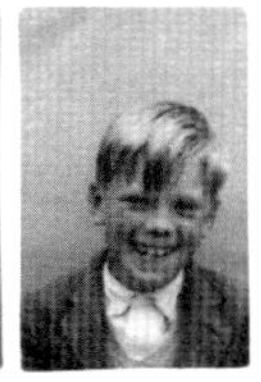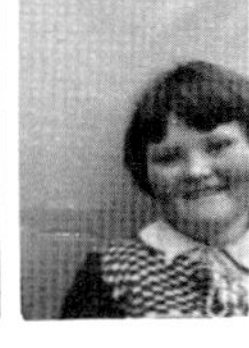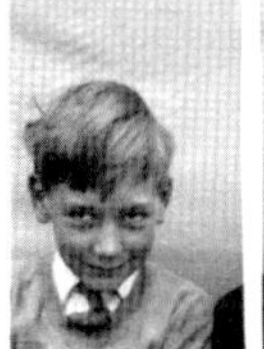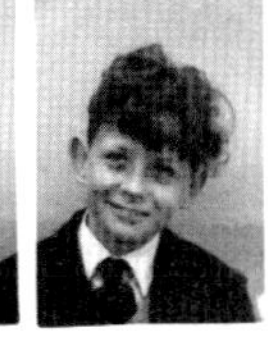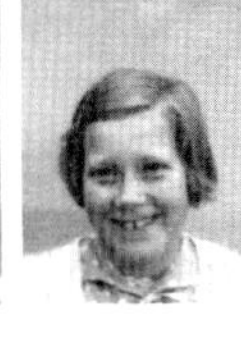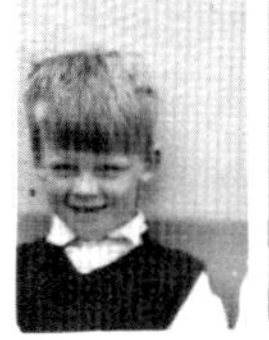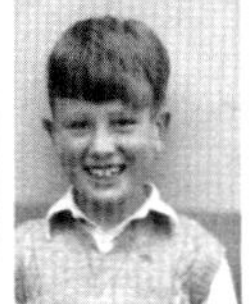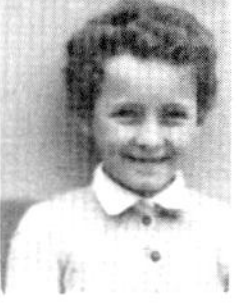

The world of our childhood is small. The Welsh call it 'y filltir sgwar', the square mile. But we know it intimately, in detail, in a detail we will never know anywhere again. The landscape of our earliest years ... Where to find pigeons' eggs, carrying them down from the nest in your mouth. Where to catch sticklebacks, the throats of the males blushed red in the breeding season. Or stone loaches camouflaged against the limey bottom of the stream. Or rats with the help of Mr. Skip's quivering, excited Jack Russells. Mind, his brother-in-law was a rat catcher ... Where to find the best fossils, whether in field or wall. Curling ammonites, bullet-shaped belemnites, gnarled and twisted gryphaea or 'devil's toe nails' as we called them. Which ponds were favoured by toads, which by newts. Where to find owl pellets, the regurgitated remains of voles, shrews, rats, mice, sparrows, beetles ... fur, bones, wing cases.

And at the village show each June there was a competition for the largest number of species of wild flowers in a jam-jar. And another for the largest number of dead Cabbage White butterflies, also in a jam-jar. You had to know your gardens for that! They weren't daft, Hibaldstow gardeners.

Sticklebacks in a nylon net from Mrs. Massey's were easy enough. Funny how she had them in, them and marbles, just on the day we needed them. But loaches, patiently tracking them from stone to stone and then surrounding one with jam-jar – minus their golliwogs – and lifting it carefully. Then tickling the surface. Worth it to see their whiskery faces through the glass. And through the small events of our life we learn the difference between 'do' and 'don't do' ... to kill or not to kill.

Meanwhile John seems to be slipping away quietly and Karl is muscling in on our John! And I've lost all my teeth! It'll be 'suck only' then, on that giant stick of Cleethorpes rock.

7 Pottage's Beck SE 97790266 *"... let's go and get some chips ..."*

*" ... how often an idea of the country is an idea of childhood: not only of
local memories, or the ideally shared communal memory, but the feel of
childhood: of delighted absorption in our own world, from which eventually,
in the course of growing up, we are distanced and separated, so that
it and the world become things we observe."* [9]

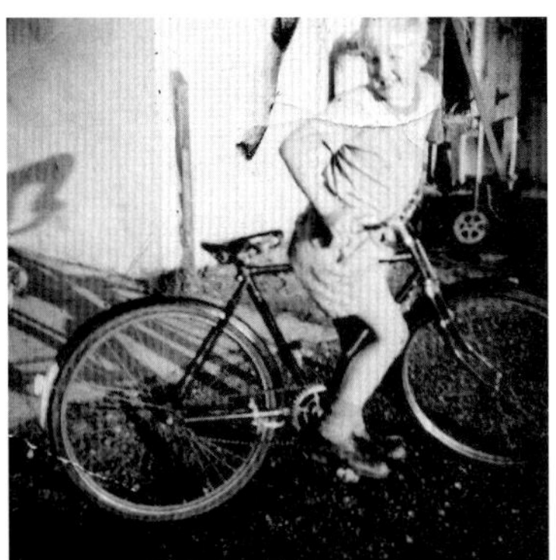

Yet this is slippery ground, a place without firm boundaries, where horizons are
ever expanding. Here is a way of life warping, shattering and splintering ... And
here new space is constantly conquered ... on a 'Hercules Jeep' bike by the look
of it, my first two-wheeler! We bought it second-hand from Pete Skip who was
already listening to Tennessee Ernie Ford while I was stuck with Uncle Mac and
Mandy Miller and 'Nellie the Elephant'. He was a big influence: 'Pete' was the
first word I ever said. "Come on", he said one night, "let's go and get some
chips" he on the Hercules, me on my fairy cycle. I didn't know, and me Mam
certainly didn't know, that he meant from Brigg! Seven, eight miles, me little legs
pumping. I was knackered! And you know, from the earliest, Pete's ambition was
always to be the dustman.

Here there are favourite places: places of light and dark, of heat and cold, of
textures and smells, of comfort and discomfort ... But also places to avoid:
Manton Lane bridge where somebody hanged himself; bottom drain 'cos it's full
of stretchy leeches; the churchyard, at night ... The square mile is a place of play,
imagination, experiment ... finding the best place for doing things ... creating
worlds under our own control ... fantasy landscapes ... secret places where we
can struggle to the North Pole, climb the mountains of Wales, dance a Navaho
dance on a wet afternoon ...

"I walk this way because this is a desert. And I wear this bucket on my head
because I am a Crusader." "I'm blowing out my cheeks and slowly waving my
arms because this is the bottom of the ocean."

8 Roadbeck SE 97650264 *"Yet another goldfish-in-a-bag ..."*

There are bits of me scattered all over that land. [10]

... here lorries cornered, lurched, wobbled and spilled their bounty. Usually it was
muddy, road-kill sugar beet that we never knew quite what to do with. Then
came the day one of them tipped over, shedding its load of oranges which were
doled out to us, under the stern eye of PC Creek, by the armful.

In this field, Franklin's Fair made its annual visit – hairy coconuts on their
sawdust plinths, village strongmen in action though I reckon Wilf always bought
one for us, piercing the eyes on the end with a metal meat skewer, drinking the
milk and then hitting it with a hammer; roll-a-penny for yet another bloody
goldfish-in-a-bag and stick three cards with darts for a plaster ornament which
would be chipped by the time you got it home. Mind, by this time we were already

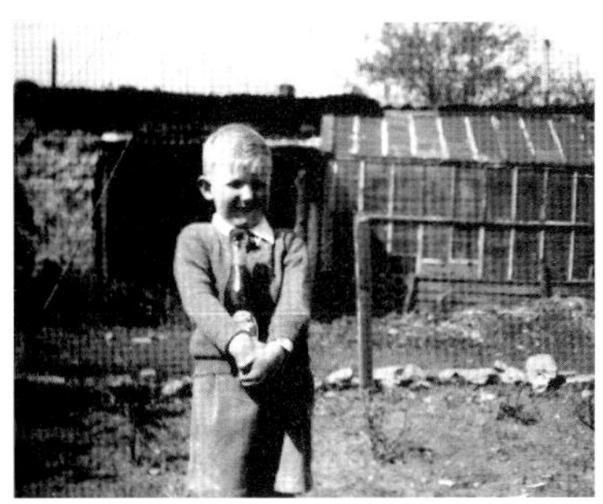

making our own in red rubber moulds – a frog; three swallows that flew across Grandma Pearson's wall up to the end; a kilted Scottish soldier whose head always came off however carefully we peeled back the mould. But we already have our eyes on something else, Airfix kits, sprigs of plastic parts – wheels, propellers, wings, fuselage, cockpit, pilot – tantalising in their clear polythene bags ...

A tiny circus once came to the village. I think they had a llama. They certainly had a clown with enormous shoes and a squirty button-hole: scared me witless.

The railings on this side have been altered, here you can see the remains of the fittings. On that side, they're still original. And we sat, like this, for hours ... plotting. We planned to build a submarine. We had a trolley – everybody had a trolley – four old pram wheels and some planks. We could build on that. If only we could persuade Grandad to give us one of the hinged chests that whole stalks of bananas came in. We could nail that on the trolley, I could lie in it and then Tony could push it down the bank. Of course, we couldn't because there was ten shillings deposit on the box : '10/- deposit' in black letters on the side. And we'd probably given away too much of our plan in the asking ...

9 Manchester House SE 97760254 *" ... we're the good guys, you're the bad ..."*

It was lying face-down on my bed that I read Twenty Years After, The Mysterious Island *and* Jerry on the Island. *The bed became a trapper's cabin, or a lifeboat on the raging ocean ... a tent erected in the desert ...* [11]

Desperadoes ... "Looking for trouble" as Marion said. We know them all: Hopalong Cassidy; the Cisco Kid and Pancho; The Lone Ranger and Tonto ('Hi ho Silver, away'), Champion the Wonder Horse and the Range Rider with Dick West, all American boy. Cousin Margaret complains bitterly that she always got lumbered with being 'the mother who stayed at the wagon', usually our coal-house. And things didn't improve much even after she got the Annie Oakley outfit.

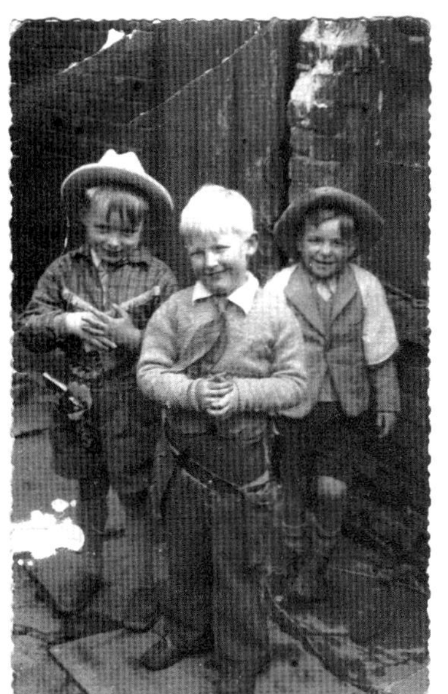

Plenty of points for style here: ducking and diving; drawing; shooting; sound effects ... And hanging off the side of the horse – Tony's wall – Dick West style. But we don't yet know quite how 'to be': hands and feet still a bit of a problem.

And on the days when Mr. Skip ran Kirkby's cattle through the village – from the 'ings' to the crew-yard to stand all winter long, up to their bellies in their shit – we were in ecstasy or Texas or ... We were dealers in fantasy, speculation, rumour ... "don't fib"; "stop telling tales". Beginning to mimic, to make, to dramatise the story of our lives and those of others, without need for plot or script. "We're the good guys, you're the bad."

Here I learned all the languages of play: exaggeration and irrelevance, fiction and lying ... Making rules and breaking rules, improvised responses, rules of thumb. Knowing that the next step will fill your Wellies with water and not caring. Because, after all, you have to cross the Rio Grande to reach Mexico.

We were often here or hereabouts: lying in wait behind the wall ready to cobble Roger Wilk. It was a case of getting in first! "Roger was a bit of a tough guy" says Marion. Or 'kicking about' in the old Home Guard rooms where me

Mam and Peggy, Tony's mum, had a fag … or the yard where Mr. Long drowned kittens … or his garden which was the best in the village for Cabbage Whites …

10 'Bubbling Tom' SE 97390258

"… and the stories I tell about them…"

And nothing remains today at the bottom of memory
But family and neighbourhood, man's sacrifice and pain. [12]

It's 1958 and it's here that I learned to tell the difference: to distinguish between Viper's Bugloss, Rose-bay Willow Herb, Lords and Ladies, Bulbous Buttercup, Ox-Eye Daisy, Ladies' Bedstraw, Spur Valerian, Cow Parsley, Self Heal, Hips, Haws, Sweet Chestnut, Horse Chestnut. Learned on nature walks with Mrs. Michaelijw, Mrs. Kitzul; learned from I-Spy books; from Brooke Bond picture cards, one card lodged between the inner and outer lining of each soft, green packet – "Illustrated and described by C.F. Tunnicliffe" who now has a museum dedicated to his work in Anglesey; from Observer's Books … learned to put names to people, to places and to things …

And some people seem everywhere here, women in particular … Grandma Pearson, who through some extraordinary process involving the visitation of family and neighbours, glimpses of the street from behind her curtains, the daily perusal of the obituary column in the local newspaper and some almost mystical divination, accumulated, processed and held together vast bodies of information: histories, geographies, genealogies. She knew who lived where, who was related to whom, what was happening over dozens of square miles, constantly up-dated and cross-referenced. A world picture, a world in which to live. Nana Shaw, who though a Protestant, born in Cork Harbour, kept plaster Madonnas and was popular with the Irish potato pickers who lived in huts on the aerodrome and who wore big suits, who had a gun belonging to her grandfather from the Falkland Islands and a gold nugget.

Me Mam, who once popped a bar of soap in my screaming mouth, though it doesn't seem to have done much good …

And now I've got the gun, and Nan's clock, and Fred's gold watch, and Wilf's trowel, and Dad's ring. These are things. Yet it's their other traces that still linger, in me: from the shape of my ears to the way I hold my knife, from the silences of my stubbornness to the stories I tell about them. They made me. And this place made me too.

After a man has turned fifty, he risks becoming the thing he most despised at twenty-five.

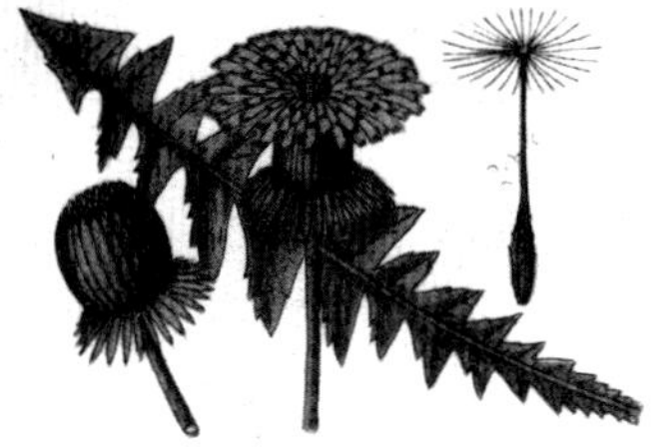

Dandelion (44)

One of the commonest of flowers—especially by the roadside and on waste places.

I-SPY yellow flower heads each at the end of a juicy stalk, and glossy leaves with pointed edges like the teeth of a lion. The seeds have a parachute-like top which helps them to spread about in the wind. Country people make dandelion wine from the flower heads.

I-SPYed (44) on…… *Friday* ……

at … *Near   Grandads   shed* …

and scored 15 points.

[1] Williams, D.J., *The Old Farmhouse*, trans. Williams, Waldo, George G. Harrap, 1961, p.11

[2] Gwenallt Jones, David 'The Dead' in *Twentieth Century Welsh Poems* ed. Joseph P. Clancy, Gomer, 1986

[3] Williams, D.J., op. cit., p.12

[4] Williams, D.J., op. cit., p.56

[5] Williams, D.J., op. cit., p.17

[6] Thomas, Ned, *The Welsh Extremist: Modern Welsh Politics, Literature and Society* , Y Lolfa, 1991, p.85

[7] Hardy, Thomas, 'Heredity', *Selected Poems*, Penguin, 1993, p.103

[8] Thomas, Ned, op. cit. p.86

[9] Williams, Raymond, *The Country and the City*, Chatto & Windus, 1973, p.297

[10] Parry-Williams, T.H., 'Bro', 'Locality' *Poetry of Wales 1930-1970*, ed. Jones R.G., Gwasg Gomer, 1974 pp.58-9

[11] Perec, Georges, *Species of Spaces and Other Places*, Penguin Books, 1977, p17

[12] Gwenallt Jones, David, op.cit. p.98

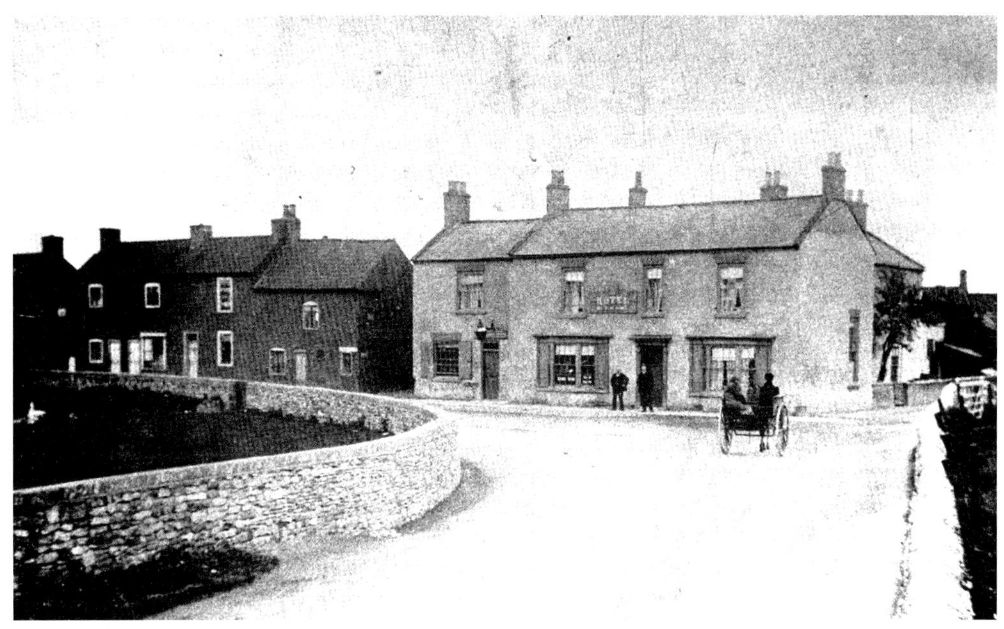

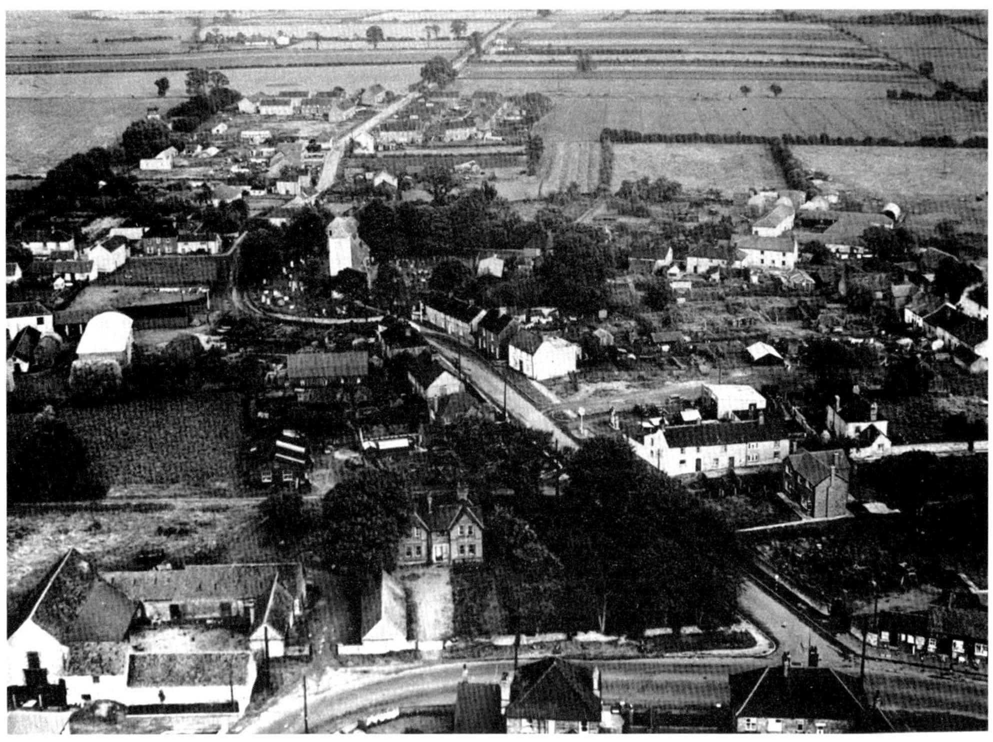

Contributors

things not worth keeping is a collaborative series by Kirsten Lavers and cris cheek. To date occurrences have included installations, works in video, bookart, live and web writing, performance and object events. Many of these involve conversation and exchange. *www.thingsnotworthkeeping.com*

Suzanne Moore began her journalistic career as film critic for the *New Statesman* in 1988 and was subsequently cultural editor of *Marxism Today*. In 1992 she joined *The Guardian* as a columnist and won the *What the Papers Say* Columnist of the Year award in 1994. She has written for everything from *The Big Issue* to *Tatler* over the years and is currently at the *Mail on Sunday*. She has published two books of collected journalism.

Robin Rimbaud, alias **Scanner**, has been at the forefront of new digital media for almost a decade, maintaining a uniquely public presence within a world of personal experimentation. His work has been heard and seen in exhibitions, time-based arts festivals, CDs, radio, documentary film, clubs, and even on London buses.

Tim Etchells is a writer and artist best known for his work directing the performance ensemble Forced Entertainment (*www.forced.co.uk*). He has published a collection of short fiction titled *Endland Stories* (Pulp Books 1999) and a collection of critical writing, performance theory and theatre texts titled *Certain Fragments* (Routledge 1999). The work on his essay *Permanent Midnight* arose during a Senior Research Scholarship at The Nottingham Trent University.

Brian Catling is a poet, sculptor and performance artist who shows work internationally. His works in the UK include *Were at Matt's Gallery* and *Were: The Chamber Works* at the ICA. He is currently obsessed with painting small egg-tempera pictures of his past performances, and preparing a new live work that will tour Northern Europe and Japan. His recent video collaborations with Tony Grisoni, which include *Vanished!*, *A Video Séance* and *Palermo*, continue to tour. Their new narrative work *The Cutting* will be made between 2000-2001.

Third Angel is a creative partnership between Rachael Walton and Alex Kelly. Working together in Sheffield since 1995, with a growing group of collaborators, they have made performance, film and installation work that has toured throughout Britain and into mainland Europe. *www.thirdangel.co.uk*

Peggy Phelan is the author of *Unmarked: The Politics of Performance* (Routledge 1993) and *Mourning Sex: Performing Public Memories* (Routledge 1997), and co-editor with Lynda Hart of *Acting Out: Feminist Performances* (UMP 1993), and with Jill Lane *The Ends of Performance* (NYUP 1998). She is Professor of Performance Studies at Tisch School of the Arts, New York University.

Graeme Miller is a composer of things that may not always be music. Alongside his work for the stage (Impact Theatre Co-operative, *A Girl Skipping*, *The Desire Paths*, *Country Dance*), he has made a series of works that reflect and take place in the imaginative landscape, (*The Sound Observatory* and *Feet of Memory, Boots of Nottingham* and with artist, Mary Lemley, *Listening Ground* and *Reconnaissance*). He also writes music for performance and broadcast.

Ann Whitehurst is an experimental artist and Paul Darke, her collaborator on *Conceiving Difference*, is a disability theorist and cultural critic who has broadcast and written wildly on disability, cinema and culture. Both work in a variety of media including film, digital media, sculpture and installation. They are founding members of Outside Centre, a leading innovative arts partnership, exploring difference and otherness across all academic disciplines. *www.outside-centre.org.uk*

Gilane Tawadros is the Director of the Institute of International Visual Arts (inIVA) in London. Responsible for the overall artistic direction of inIVA, Gilane has curated numerous exhibitions and edited several publications. She has written and lectured widely on contemporary visual art and theory and is author of *Sonia Boyce: Speaking in Tongues*.

Ronald Fraser-Munro is a London-based writer, director, producer, performer and graphics-video artist. His multi-media and cross platform work encompasses text, theatre, audio, photography, movement, video and the digital arts and is distributed throughout the United Kingdom, Europe and the United States. He is concerned with new models for contemporary arts practice, individual empowerment and the political aspects of creativity.

Lois Keidan is co-Director of the Live Art Development Agency, an independent organisation supporting the development and profile of artists, organisations and new performance practices in London. She also works with Catherine Ugwu as an independent curator and promoter of performance and time-based work. She regularly contributes papers and articles to a range of publications, events and conferences in Britain and internationally.

Daniel Gosling graduated from Dartington College of Arts in 1997. He produces in no specific medium, his practice being concerned with the articulation of context and the moment of encounter.

Brian Eno's career encompasses not only music, but also writing, lecturing, teaching and especially visual art. Eno has released a series of critically acclaimed albums, and is also one of the most significant record producers of our age. His audio/visual installations have been exhibited at galleries and spaces around the world.

Meloni Poole is an artist who has written and directed the films *This Charming Man, Sicknote for Michael, Straight Guide to Queer* and *Don't Put Your Shoes on the Table* for Channel 4 and the British Film Institute. She has also been commissioned to make work by the new Walsall Art Gallery, Site Gallery Sheffield and the National Review of Live Art. She is currently artist in residence at the National Coalmining Museum as part of Year of the Artist.

Adrian Heathfield writes on contemporary performance. He is the editor (with Fiona Templeton and Andrew Quick) of the box publication *Shattered Anatomies: Traces of the Body in Performance* (Arnolfini Live 1997) and co-editor with Andrew Quick of the forthcoming issue of *Performance Research, On Memory* (December 2000). He lectures in Theatre and Performance Studies at the University of Warwick.

Kira O'Reilly studied fine art at University of Wales Institute Cardiff, graduating in 1998. Since then she has shown throughout the UK and in Europe. Working mostly in performance, her works include *Wet Cup, 13* (in collaboration with Irina Padva), *A Woman to Dream About, Bad Humours/ Affected, Desiree.*

Deborah Levy's novels include: *Beautiful Mutants, Swallowing Geography, The Unloved* (Vintage), *Billy* and *Girl* (Bloomsbury). In November 2000, Methuen are publishing *Levy: Plays 1* – a collection of theatre texts written over the last fifteen years.

Bobby Baker is a performance artist based in London. During the last two decades she has produced an extensive repertoire of work, including *An Edible Family in a Mobile Home* (1976) and *Drawing on a Mother's Experience* (1988). In 1991 she began her *Daily Life* series, a domestic quintet of performances, which all toured extensively world-wide. In 1999 Bobby performed *Grown up School* which took place as part of LIFT. The last of the series, *Box Story*, will take place in 2001.

Clare Allan's first story was published in *London Magazine*. She graduated this year from the University of East Anglia with an MA in Creative Writing, and is working on a novel about madness.

Chris Dorley-Brown is a London-based artist whose recent works include *Blipverts* (new works for the cinema) (1995-7), *Iorkradio* (1998), *Livestream* (1999) and *hex, grammaphone & sit* (2000), a series of live webcasts and CD releases. He is currently working on *SixtySix NinetyNine*, a DVD adaptation of *Las babas del diablo* by Julio Cortázar.

Robert Pacitti is a London-based cultural activist working internationally in the area of performance. Combining a range of formal disciplines from film, sound and static visual arts practice, he creates group and solo works for theatre, gallery and site-specific spaces.

Emma Kay is an artist who lives and works in London. Her recent group exhibitions include *Orbis Terrarium – Ways of Worldmaking*, Antwerp Open 2000, British Art Show 5 2000, Istanbul Biennale 1999, *Abracadabra*, Tate Gallery London 1999. She will have a solo exhibition at the Chisenhale Gallery in 2001. Her book *Worldview* was published in 2000 by Bookworks.

Hugo Glendinning is a photographer and film-maker whose work has been shown and published internationally.

Alexander García Düttmann, born in Barcelona, is Professor of Modern European Philosophy at Middlesex University and lives in London. He has published the following books: *The Memory of Thought: An Essay on Heidegger and Adorno* (Suhrkamp 1991), *At Odds with Aids* (Stanford University Press 1996), *Friends and Enemies: The Absolute* (Turia und Kant 1999), *Between Cultures: Tensions in the Struggle for Recognition* (Verso 2000) and *The End of Art* (Suhrkamp 2000).

Mike Pearson trained as an archaeologist. He is currently Professor of Performance Studies in the Department of Theatre, Film and Television at the University of Wales Aberystwyth and a collaborator in the performance group Pearson/Brookes. With Michael Shanks, Professor of Classics at Stanford University, he is co-author of *Theatre/Archaeology*, which deals with points of convergence between the two disciplines and will be published by Routledge in December 2000.

Jennie Smith (designer) has worked as an educational TV director, medical illustrator and exhibition designer, among other things. She lives in Hackney with the painter Pete Smith and their black pug dog, Elmore.

Verity Leigh (editorial assistant) is the administrator of Forced Entertainment.

The Projects

The Millennium Collection Just before Christmas 1999, 1000 people were invited by targeted mail shot to propose a thing of their own that they considered to be 'not worth keeping' on or about New Year's Eve, and to suggest why this might be the case. From a large response approximately 100 'things' were chosen and collected to form a Millennium Collection: individual examples of what might best be forgotten, discarded or given away.
www.thingsnotworthkeeping.com

Flood This project focused on the individual submerged within the mass. Scanner sampled popular images of the Millennium celebration crowd scenes and focused in on random individuals, pulling them to the surface. Reproduced and then distributed on a series of free postcards, these exploded images were countered with imagined textual accounts of the featured characters on the rear side, exploring the tiny surface marks we all leave within the public stream.

The Disciples *Of the Days* is the final manifestation of Brian Catling's work for *Small Acts at the Millennium*. It is a video grown out of *The Disciples,* a series of shielded performances; interventions in the city streets, made in near seclusion in London and Cambridge. The video was also driven and conjured by the text of the same name which appears in this book.

Class of '76 In January 2000, Alex Kelly began tracking down the 34 classmates pictured in his 1976 Chuckery Infants School class photograph, to ask them what they had been doing for the last 24 years. In May 2000 Third Angel staged a unique performance on the spot where the original photograph was taken, based on the stories and memories of Alex's classmates.

Overhead Projection Graeme Miller asked people of diverse backgrounds in diverse locations to rename the stars in order to set these new constellations against their particular horizons. Throughout the Millennial year he produced a series of images depicting these skylines.

Conceiving Difference In this Millennium year, against a background of new developments in genetics and their alarming eugenic implications, Ann Whitehurst and Paul Darke celebrated the conception of all disabled people and examined how society and the media attribute significance to individuals. They posted not-invitations to an exclusive party to 'significant' people, using the post office as an index of celebrity by including only descriptions and no addresses on the envelopes.

In **The Second Kommen** the concept of religion and the role of the shepherd were reconstructed as Ronald Fraser-Munro, Peter Marsh, John Cornes, Chris Dorley-Brown and Nick Wells assumed the identity of the Reverend for a series of societal outings. In a special ceremony in the remote English countryside, Fraser-Munro appeared as the Black Pope and so-called

Anti-Christ. The works are live art based investigations into our acceptance of the visual exterior (the costume of the priest) and the political power of the religious device.

In **10.01.00 > > 30.01.00 > > > <** Daniel Gosling undertook a three week destinationless hitch hike with short presentations at the end of each week at motorway service stations. The work is now a half-realised, half-forgotten activity that can only be manifested through other, more definable works, such as this documentation.

A Clean Slate was a site-specific film installation at Annesley Bentinck Colliery, made in collaboration between the miners and artist Meloni Poole, whose father worked at the colliery. The project explored the notion of a 'clean slate' and asks what the future means to a community whose identity continues to be erased.

Unknowing was an anonymous birthday party in which Kira O'Reilly marked her making it to 2000. A small act for a few strangers in an unfamiliar city, ending with a simple ritualised act of mark making on her body.

Pull Yourself Together Strapped to the back of a truck, Bobby Baker toured the streets of London, shouting at the world through a megaphone to pull itself together. This day-long event formed Bobby's contribution to Mental Health Action Week in April 2000.

Staying In Instead of joining in the revelry on the night of 31st December 1999, Chris Dorley-Brown stayed at home and did not stray from his immediate surroundings. He made photographs, watched television, listened to the radio, "inhabited" internet chat rooms, transcribed programmes onto VHS tape and DAT, shot video footage and recorded the voices and sounds around him. His 13 minute audio CD *The Sound of Midnight* documents the audible sound from an upstairs window during the minutes before and after midnight. A signed limited edition of 500 has been produced to coincide with the publication of *Small Acts: Performance, the Millennium and the Marking of Time.* Free copies will be sent to the first 500 people to request them from:
> Chris Dorley-Brown
> 2 Southborough Road
> London E8 7EF.

Suspended Sentence was a series of strategic works by Robert Pacitti, based around the construction of lies and rumours. By employing a range of interventionist tactics to disseminate the pieces, the work attempted to disrupt passive modes of receiving information.

Snow Portraits On a dark night (New Year's Eve 1999) Hugo Glendinning placed his face in the snow and snapped the faint impression. The unexpected result was an image of shocking detail and intensity. The image recorded a living moment, a movement, a change of state – cooling and melting – a signature that would last minutes at most. In Stockholm in February 2000 he repeated this fragile gesture with friends and artists after a fresh snow fall.

Each impression was photographed and the identity, date and time noted in a series of portraits which spanned three days. These pictures, part death mask and part physical graffiti, remain as evidence of the fleeting nature of experience and actions while also stating "I was here".

The World from Memory Details from a larger drawing in pencil on paper, 250cm x 150cm, shown here actual size. *The World from Memory* relates to other pieces by Emma Kay which are made without any reference to the original text or source. Including *The Bible from Memory* (1999), *Shakespeare from Memory* (1998) and *Worldview* (1999), they are recollections of everything that Kay already knows, rather than attempts to memorise and reproduce an original.

Bubbling Tom On Easter Monday 2000 Mike Pearson revisited the landscape of his earliest childhood in Hibaldstow, North Lincolnshire. Guiding family, friends and guests to a series of locations – once intimately familiar, now infinitely strange – he recalled village characters and events from the mid-Fifties. In its mix of performed texts and informal chat, *Bubbling Tom* was a personal meditation on notions of place, memory, loss and identity and on the impact a particular location can have on our lives.

Colophon

Small Acts: Performance, the Millennium and the Marking of Time

Editor	Adrian Heathfield
Picture Editor	Hugo Glendinning
Graphic Design	Jennie Smith
Editorial Assistant	Verity Leigh

All photographs by the contributors except: *The Disciples* (pp. 34-44), *Unknowing* (pp. 113-123), *Pull Yourself Together* (pp. 127-135), *Bubbling Tom* (pp. 173 and 175) – all by Hugo Glendinning. *Overhead Projection* (p.58) image design: Mary Lemley. *Conceiving Difference* (p. 66) © The Telegraph Group Ltd 2000. *End Time Now* (pp. 108-111), images excerpted from *One Year Performance* 1980-81 © Tehching Hsieh. *Bubbling Tom* (pp.176-185), photographs of old Hibaldstow courtesy of Peter and Sheila Gilbert. Scanning and manipulation of original photographic images by Mike Brookes.

The performance series *Small Acts at the Millennium* was conceived by Tim Etchells and curated and produced by a consortium of Tim Etchells and Verity Leigh of Forced Entertainment, Lois Keidan, Adrian Heathfield and Hugo Glendinning. Public relations by Chris Lord.

The project was funded by the Millennium Commission and the Arts Council of England's Live Art Commissions Fund.

Acknowledgements:
Pete Smith, Helen Burgun, Ebba Matz, Live Art Development Agency, Forced Entertainment

Thank you to all of the other individuals and organisations who have supported *Small Acts at the Millennium* and contributed to the realisation of each project.

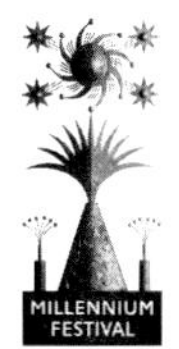

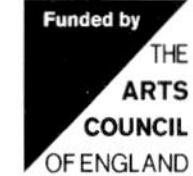

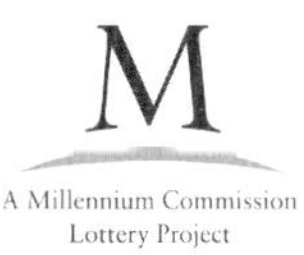

A catalogue record for this book is available from The British Library.

ISBN 1 901033 57 0

Printed in the European Union

British Library cataloguing-in-publication data:
Small Acts: Performance, the Millennium and the Marking of Time

Black Dog Publishing Limited
PO Box 3082
London NW1 UK

T: 020 7613 1922
F: 020 7613 1944
E: info@bdp.demon.co.uk

Architecture Art Design
Fashion History Photography
Theory and Things